D1447440

Pillars of Community

Four Rules
of Pre-Benedictine Monastic Life

Terrence G. Kardong, OSB

LITURGICAL PRESS
Collegeville, Minnesota

www.litpress.org

Cover design by David Manahan, OSB. Fresco from Agia Triada, Crete, Greece. Photo © Paul Cowan/istockphoto.com.

Scripture texts in this work are taken from the *New American Bible with Revised New Testament and Revised Psalms* © 1991, 1986, 1970 Confraternity of Christian Doctrine, Washington, DC, and are used by permission of the copyright owner. All Rights Reserved. No part of the *New American Bible* may be reproduced in any form without permission in writing from the copyright owner.

1   2   3   4   5   6   7   8

Library of Congress Cataloging-in-Publication Data

Kardong, Terrence G.
    Pillars of community : four rules of pre-Benedictine monastic life /
Terrence Kardong.
        p.   cm.
    Includes bibliographical references (p.   ) and index.
    ISBN 978-0-8146-3315-1 — ISBN 978-0-8146-3921-4 (e-book)
    1. Monasticism and religious orders—Rules—History.   I. Title.

BX2436.K37   2010
255.009'015—dc22   2009045713

Contents

Preface   vii

Introduction   xi

Chapter One: The Life of Basil   1

Chapter Two: The Rule of Basil: I (Long Rules Prologue and 1–7)   15

Chapter Three: The Rule of Basil: II
            (Themes from Long Rules 8–55)   45

Chapter Four: The Life of Pachomius   61

Chapter Five: The Rule of Pachomius: I (Precepts 1–57)   87

Chapter Six: The Rule of Pachomius: II (Precepts 58–97)   107

Chapter Seven: The Rule of Pachomius: III (Precepts 98–144)   125

Chapter Eight: Monastic Issues in *The Life of Augustine* by His
            Disciple Possidius   147

Chapter Nine: *Praeceptum*: The Rule of Augustine   167

Chapter Ten: The Rule of the Four Fathers   191

Chapter Eleven: The Second Rule of the Fathers   225

Select Bibliography   243

Index of Scripture References   249

Index of Rule of Benedict References   250

Index of Names and Terms   251

Preface

I might begin this book by answering the question of what prompted it. The main reason is highly personal: I like cenobitism. That is as it should be, since I myself am a cenobite. I professed vows as a Benedictine monk in 1957, so I have now been a member of my community (Assumption Abbey, Richardton, ND) for half a century. Therefore it is not unusual for me to write a book about the founders of the communal form of monastic life.

It might surprise some readers to note that St. Benedict is not among them. In fact, according to the genealogy established by Adalbert de Vogüé,[1] Benedict's Rule is actually in the *fifth* monastic generation! In his ordering of the Rules, Vogüé lists the Rules of Basil, Pachomius, and Augustine as the first generation, with the Rule of the Four Fathers situated in the second generation because it shows slight influences from the three Rules of the first generation.

Even though some of the texts I deal with in this volume have been well known throughout monastic history, for some reason the cenobitic legislators have not ranked among the favorite writers of most monastic readers. That pride of place seems to belong to the anchorites, or at least those who wrote (and write) about the solitary monastic life. Just mentioning a few of the primary anchoritic writers—Evagrius, John Cassian, Bernard of Clairvaux, and Thomas Merton—should prove this point. Even though the last three lived in community, it seems to me they wrote mostly about the monk alone with God.

Of course, it can also be said that they did not write monastic Rules, but treatises couched in literary genres that are generally more attractive

---

1. "Cenobitic Rules of the West," *Cistercian Studies* (1977): 175–83.

reading: essays, sermons, dialogues, and so forth. Granted, some of the monastic Rules are fairly readable, but some of them are dry as dust. In this volume I hope to inject some life into the rather jejune texts of Pachomius and the two French Rules by means of commentary. At any rate, I believe that these cenobitic writers deserve to be better known and this book is my way of bringing that about.

A second reason that moved me to publish such a book is more practical, namely, I woke up one morning and discovered that I had accumulated enough research on this subject to warrant a book. Though I had been working on these authors for about twenty-five years, this realization came to me only gradually. About half of the material in this volume has appeared in the form of articles in monastic periodicals. Some of the chapters were written as lectures, mainly for the Junior Institute held in American Benedictine abbeys of men every summer. None of that material has appeared in print before now. Finally, I wrote some of the material precisely for this book.

When I say that this book presents my own research from the past two decades I do not mean to imply that I did all the primary work. As a matter of fact, in most cases I made use of the excellent work of specialists that is now available to us. Indeed, we have witnessed a recent explosion of first-class scientific research on all the authors and Rules included in this book. Anyone who is interested in digging into these ancient writings can now rely on magnificent, detailed commentaries by a variety of patristics scholars. Although I used the work of dozens of scholars in my research, I would like to acknowledge at least the chief of them.

In studying Basil I was able to consult the monumental new translation and commentary on the *Great Asketikon* by the Australian historian Anna Silvas. Not only has she given us a comprehensive introduction to Basil's monastic life and thought, but she has also done a new translation of *both* the Long and Short Rules. Since the English of the Short Rules has been out of print since the 1920s, this translation was long overdue. I should also credit two other scholars whose commentaries on the Long Rules were of great help to me: Lisa Cremaschi of the Bose Community in Italy and Augustine Holmes, OSB, of Pluscarden Abbey, Scotland.

The Pachomian Rule (*Praecepta*) has been less known than that of Basil. The Cistercian scholar and abbot of Scourmont (Belgium), Armand Veilleux, put an end to that sad situation in 1980–1982 with the appearance of his *Pachomian Koinonia I–III*. Not only did he translate the Pachomian Rule in those three volumes, but he also gave us two versions of the *Life of Pachomius*, plus some of his sermons and other Pachomian materials. Since the *Lives* were written in Coptic and Greek, these translations have been very helpful to students in the West. In addition to Veilleux, I must credit Heinrich Bacht, SJ, whose meticulous commentary on the *Praecepta* I found of great use. Further, I got good help from Lisa Cremaschi in her notes on the Rule of Pachomius.

The Rule of Augustine (*Praeceptum*) was better known in the West than any monastic Rule except for that of Benedict, but as with the other Rules studied here, in-depth research on the little document has been fairly recent. Because so many Western religious Orders claim that Rule as their own, there probably has been more serious study than I am aware of. But I did have access to the magisterial commentary on this Rule by the Louvain Augustinian scholar Luc Verheijen, and I am satisfied that he is the gold standard in this field. In regard to the *Life of Augustine*, I found a good commentary to Possidius's *Vita* in the study by A. A. R. Bastiaensen.

Finally, I was able to study two of the little French Rules, namely, the Rule of the Four Fathers and the Second Rule of the Fathers, in a systematic manner due to the important study of the great Benedictine historian and exegete Adalbert de Vogüé. He provides not only a good modern translation (in French) but also a copious commentary in the manner of his epochal commentary on the Rule of St. Benedict. For these obscure and hard-to-locate texts we also have a serious commentary by the French monk Vincent Desprez, of which I have also made extensive use.

To repeat, then, I could not have written this book without relying on the primary research of all these scholars. I stand on their shoulders. I should also mention that I could not have found time for this work except for the generosity and confidence of my own community of Assumption Abbey. Not many American monks have had the time and the educational opportunities for monastic studies that I have been given.

Introduction

Perhaps a logical way to start here would be to discuss the appropriateness of the title of this book. Why are these four monastic authors and their Rules termed "Pillars of Community"? "Pillars" in this connection is not so much a value judgment as simply a claim to priority. While it can be argued whether these are the greatest of all cenobitic monastic Rules, they are indisputably the first. Chronologically speaking, Pachomius (ca. 346–370) comes first; Basil wrote in the 370s; Augustine wrote his *Praeceptum* about 395; and the two Rules from Lérins were probably written in the period 410–427.

Not only are these four cenobitic Rules primary in time, they are also quite original. In none of these cases can it be said that the author models his work on earlier Rules. Certainly Pachomius and his successors (Theodore and Horsiesi) had no previous monastic legislation to depend on. In fact, they even wrote prior to the famous *Life of Anthony*, which was the earliest anchoritic text and one that became world famous. Of course, Pachomius himself had an anchoritic novitiate, but he had no monastic literature upon which to base his Rule.

Those familiar with the traditional biographies of St. Basil might be a bit surprised when I label his Rule (*Asketikon*) original. According to the received legend Basil toured the Syrian and Egyptian deserts as a young man, studying the monastic life before he founded his own community. Nowadays, however, it is seriously questioned whether Basil actually met that many monks on his journey, which was primarily undertaken for the purpose of catching up with his mentor, Eustathius of Sebaste. Even if Basil did meet some of the monks of northern Egypt (Nitria, Skete, etc.), he surely did not make the long, arduous journey up the Nile to visit the Pachomian congregation. Basil may have been influenced by Syrian asceticism, but not by formal cenobitism of any kind.

When we come to the third Pillar we encounter a monastic founder who not only lived far from the Eastern cenobia but even tried to keep his distance from them! At least Augustine seems studiously to have avoided the use of the word "monk," probably in order to steer clear of some of the bad reputation adhering to local "cenobites" such as the Donatist monks of his home territory of North Africa. When Augustine finally crafted his brief Rule for the monks of Hippo and Tagaste he relied mainly on biblical models (Acts 2 and 4) as well as his own profound understanding of community and the human heart.

The fourth Pillar we will discuss in this study, namely, the two earliest Rules of Lérins (R4P and 2RP), are probably the latest of the group. Although there was already a monastery in Gaul, founded by St. Martin at Marmoutier near Tours, those monks left us no Rule. The founder of Lérins, Honoratus, is said by his biographer, Hilary of Arles, to have toured the Egyptian and Syrian communities before making his foundation on an island off the French Riviera. The Eastern influence is seen in the fact that both of these Rules claim to have been written by synods of monastic leaders in Egypt. But that is a literary conceit and not to be taken literally. In fact there are few, if any, direct literary reminiscences of the earlier Rules in these Little French Rules. They are quite original.

The Rules

When we compare these four Rules with one another, what do we find? It seems to me that they are remarkably distinct. That does not mean that when we use them we are dealing with apples and oranges. They all legislate for communal monasticism, and that in itself dictates much of what they say and take for granted. They all have the same fundamental understanding of what a Christian monk should be and what a Christian community should be. There may be specific elements in a given Rule that some of the other founders would not want to adopt. They all worked in different circumstances, which required distinctive legislation. For example, Augustine's monastery was in a city (Hippo) so he had to warn the monks how to behave on the streets. The Pachomian monks lived on a great river, so they needed rules for use of the boats. But in essential matters these Rules are homogeneous.

Nevertheless, there is a great deal of difference in the form and literary tone of these four Rules. First, they are not all the same length. Three of them are short, but one is very long. The *Asketikon* of Basil is a great, sprawling treatise that is much longer than the other three Rules combined. The Pachomian *Praecepta* are of some length, perhaps half the size of the Rule of Benedict. The Rule of Augustine and the Rules of Lérins are tiny productions, each of them covering only a few pages in a modern book.

But the greatest difference lies in the literary form of these pieces of monastic legislation. Here again, Basil's *Asketikon* stands apart from the other three. It is not a rule book in any normal sense of that word, but rather a collection of questions and answers concerning the monastic life. Apparently the *Asketikon* is a stenographic record of conversations Basil had with monastic communities in his role as their adviser. Later, as bishop, he also added some material, but it is mostly a long record of rather free-form dialogues on various monastic questions. Although the Rule of Basil contains extremely precious insights into the mentality of the first cenobites, it is a somewhat disorderly jumble of material that tends to digression and also obscurity. Many of the questions and answers of the *Asketikon* concern Scripture, and although the discussions are not always crystal clear they at least witness to the deeply biblical mentality of the Cappadocian monks.

As for the other three Rules, they are much more prescriptive than Basil's, but they also differ among themselves in tone. The Rule of Pachomius is extremely pragmatic and no-nonsense. It lays down rules for behavior from the beginning to the end. Since many of these rules pertain to social realities that are quite strange to us (how to hang out the wash in the burning Egyptian sun), they can be off-putting. This Rule tends to jump about from topic to topic without much visible structure. It does not develop its rules to any great extent, so it has not acquired a very good reputation down through the ages. But it should be remembered that for the Pachomians the Bible was the primary monastic Rule.

Probably the most influential of all the cenobitic Pillars is the *Praeceptum* of Augustine. In fact, this little Rule has been adopted by many of the Orders of friars since the Middle Ages. No doubt the reason why this was and is so is because Augustine always seems so contemporary with every age. He treats only a few aspects of the monastic/religious life, but he treats them well. He knows how to develop a theme to full effect. What is more, Augustine had the good sense to begin his Rule with a discussion of love and community, which corroborates his reputation as the premiere theologian of the Latin church. Finally, Augustine uses Scripture to maximum effect in his Rule, and that certainly recommends the document to every generation.

The Rules from Lérins are probably the least impressive of the set. In their form they resemble that of Augustine, but they lack his skill in developing a topic and also in the use of Scripture. It might be added that these little Rules have been virtually unnoticed throughout monastic history. They were included in the *Codex Regularum* of Benedict of Aniane, but there is little indication that any community other than Lérins ever followed them. Nor do we have any commentaries on them by later monastic scholars. So in a sense they have the least claim to being considered Pillars of Community. I consider these two little Rules to be virtually one, since most scholars think that the Second Rule of the Fathers was written as a sort of appendix to the Rule of the Four Fathers.

The Biographies

If it is true that the Rules of the four cenobitic Pillars are quite varied, the same is true of the lives of the founders. First, it should be said that three of the founders were memorialized by their admirers through biographies. The *Life of Pachomius* was written by an anonymous disciple, probably Theodore, shortly after his death in 346. Augustine's protégé, Possidius, Bishop of Calama, wrote a biography of his mentor shortly after the death of the latter in 430. The same dynamics were at work in the south of France (Gaul), where Bishop Hilary of Arles wrote the biography of his predecessor Honoratus after his death in 429/30. The only one of the founders who was not the subject of a biography was Basil of Caesarea. That is a bit surprising, since his brother Gregory of Nyssa and his friend Gregory of Nazianz were both great writers, but perhaps neither of them wished to take on the formidable task of presenting that great man to posterity.

Of the three biographies we have, I myself much prefer that of Pachomius. The reason I like it so much is because it seems so fresh and direct. Overall, Pachomius comes across as a truly original and spontaneous religious genius rather than a plaster saint. That does not mean that some parts of the *Life of Pachomius* are not strange. In fact, they may seem positively weird! But overall one gets the impression that a minimum amount of whitewash has been applied to the subject. Another factor that makes this *Life* attractive to the scholar is the existence of two different versions, plus a number of fragments from yet others. This enables us to construct a somewhat nuanced and rounded picture of the saint.

The same cannot be said of the other two biographies we study here, namely, those of Augustine and Honoratus. In both cases the biographer appears to be a dutiful admirer of the subject, which tends to give us a somewhat idealized version of the man. Since both of these saints were great churchmen they definitely deserve to be the subject of biography, but both seem to suffer from less than talented authors. Of course, nobody was quite like Augustine, so it is unfair to expect Possidius to be so. As for Hilary, he does not say too much about Honoratus as the abbot of Lérins, so I do not pay him much heed.

Differing Treatment of the Four Subjects

Since each of the four founders is distinctive, as are their Rules, it can be expected that a book such as this one will have to approach them somewhat differently. That is what I have done. For example, regarding Basil, we do not have a *Vita* of him by his contemporaries but we have a massive record of his monastic thinking in the *Asketikon*, including the Long and Short Rules. It would have been impractical to reprint a translation of the *Asketikon* here, so I have contented myself with describing it for the reader. Moreover, even a full description would be a book in itself, so I have limited my treatment to the first few chapters of the Long Rule. Still, these are major treatises and they contain much of Basil's essential monastic doctrine, so this is probably enough for a survey such as this.

In regard to Basil's life, even without a formal *Vita* from ancient times we still know enough to reconstruct this important early Christian life. Basil left us a voluminous correspondence that contains many helpful remarks concerning monasticism. Furthermore, to some extent it is possible to establish the chronology of these letters, so we can document the evolution of his monastic thought. As will be apparent in the life we have reconstructed, this development is very interesting and it is only now coming to be better understood by scholars. In this regard Philip Rousseau and Anna Silvas were very helpful to my work. Of course, it should be remembered that Basil was one of the most important bishops of the early church, so much of his thought and work had to be left aside in this volume.

Even though Pachomius is not nearly as important in the general history of the church as were Basil and Augustine, nonetheless we are remarkably well endowed with written material concerning both his life and his Rule. As with Basil, the Pachomian Rule is too extensive for me to provide a full translation in this volume. Therefore I have limited myself to a summary description of the material. But unlike my presentation of Basil's Rule, with Pachomius I have worked through the entire document in some detail.

As for the *Life of Pachomius*, it was not hard for me to present a summary of it with highlights. Unlike the life of Basil, it was not necessary to tease out the monastic elements from the larger life. With Pachomius, monasticism *was* his entire life. Indeed, the *Lives* of Pachomius deal with nothing else but his work as a monastic founder and abbot. These *Lives* are very interesting to work with, since they present somewhat different angles on their subject. Not surprisingly, they have generated a fair amount of scholarly heat and light, which will be duly reported in my treatment here. This is by all means one of the most fascinating biographies of any ancient monk.

Augustine, of course, was a truly monumental figure in the Latin church, as important for the West as Basil was for the East. Yet it must be admitted that his monastic experience and writing were limited to the first decade or so of his long career. For example, his Rule takes up but a few pages in the whole shelf of his writings found in the famous collection of J. P. Migne. Yet the Rule of Augustine is still a precious document, which has provided light and inspiration to centuries of religious Orders such as the Augustinians and the Dominicans. I did not reprint a translation of this Rule in this book since it is so easily available in the United States, nor did I produce a complete commentary on the document. The reason is simple: my major source of information and insight, namely, Luc Verheijen, only comments on certain select verses.

The *Life of Augustine* by Possidius certainly does not come up to the quality of the *Life of Pachomius*. Again, it deals with more than Augustine's monastic contribution. Still, there is enough interesting commentary in this *Life* to enable a modern scholar to distill a sketch of the topic. In addition, we have a considerable amount of other writing by Augustine commenting on the monastic life. Fortunately for us, the great bishop of Hippo never lost interest in the topic. He continued to live like a monk and think like a monk. He also continued to write like a monk.

Finally, the Rule of the Four Fathers and the Second Rule of the Fathers need to be treated somewhat differently. In this case alone have I printed a new translation, and I have also supplied a line-by-line commentary. I have done this because these Rules are still not well known in monastic circles. Not only that: we now have a major commentary on these Rules by one of the greatest monastic commentators of all time, namely, Adalbert de Vogüé. On the basis of his relatively new work I was able to put together a somewhat detailed commentary.

When it comes to a biography of the author or authors of the French Rules, the possibilities are much less favorable. The simple fact is that we do not know much about the subject. Indeed, before Vogüé identified Lérins as the point of provenance for these little Rules we had no real idea of their origin. Now we are beginning to piece together some idea of the earliest years of that famous monastery. It always helps to know the circumstances in which a document arose, and in this case at least the documents can help us reconstruct their genesis.

I hope that this study of materials on cenobitic monasticism will prove interesting and edifying for the modern reader. I am convinced that human community is essential to world peace and prosperity. I am also hopeful that the example of ancient cenobitism will be able to make some contribution to current understanding of community life. And since I think community is close to the very heart of Christianity, I hope and pray that the story of the ancient cenobites will build up community life within the church of Christ.

Chapter One

The Life of Basil

Saint Basil is one of the most prominent figures in the history of the church. In the Eastern church he is credited with many of the basic ideas and institutions that formed the community and sustain it to our time. For example, he was a brilliant theologian who laid the groundwork of the doctrine of the Holy Spirit that was decided by the First Council of Constantinople in 381. One of the main eucharistic prayers of the Eastern church is called the Liturgy of St. Basil. Finally, the Great Rule of Basil is the fundamental monastic rule for all Eastern monks.[1]

Because he was so important for the church it was only natural to imagine that Basil was a sort of genius who sprang full-formed from his mother's womb. The reality was quite different. Like most people, Basil needed time to develop into the person he eventually became. Basil was a brilliant man, and he was a very strong personality, but he went through a period of formation and, like the rest of us, he required help from other people in his life-project. In this chapter I will only discuss Basil's "monastic" mentors. I do not intend to discuss his theological influences.[2] As we will see, the history of Basilian biography has involved the progressive discovery of hidden factors.

---

1. This does not mean that the Eastern monks take the Rule of Basil as their actual, practical rule of life. For that each monastery has its own *typicon* or customary. Indeed, it is said that the Rule of Basil is not widespread in those monasteries and that most Eastern monks have never read it. Nevertheless, it stands as the ur-text and inspiration of all Eastern monasticism.

2. For this see Philip Rousseau, *Basil of Caesarea* (Berkeley: University of California Press, 1994), 101–2.

Family Background

Basil grew up in one of the most prominent Christian families of Pontus, an area of modern Turkey just south of the Black Sea. He was the second child of ten in the family of Basil Senior and Emmelia. Their home city was Neocaesarea, and not Caesarea as is often stated.[3] Neocaesarea was a smaller town, but still locally important and located on the main highway between Armenia and Constantinople. Neocaesarea was christianized by Gregory Thaumaturgus (d. 271), and Basil's grandparents were converts from paganism. They had to flee to the mountains during the persecution of Diocletian in the early fourth century. Basil himself was born in 327, shortly after the church emerged from persecution in the Edict of Milan (313) and held its first and decisive ecumenical council at Nicaea (325).

Basil's first teachers were his grandmother, Macrina the Elder, who taught him the Christian catechism, and his father, a prominent lawyer (*rhetor*), who taught the boy the elements of Greek grammar. Like most promising sons of the Greek aristocracy, Basil was given the best education money could buy. When his father died in 346 he was sent to school in Caesarea in Cappadocia. From there he matriculated at Constantinople and finally at the University of Athens, the pinnacle of Greek education, for law school. At Athens, Basil was a close companion of Gregory of Nazianz, who also hailed from central Anatolia. Yet, contrary to Gregory's later claim, their Athenian education was strictly secular,[4] nor was Basil a baptized Christian at that time.

All this was to change in 356 when Basil finally completed his graduate studies and returned to Pontus. At that point he did take the decisive step of going down into the baptismal font, but it seems that he needed a bit of a shove. According to an account by his brother, Gregory of Nyssa, Basil's older sister, Macrina Junior, confronted him with what she saw as his swollen ego, and probably convinced him to give himself over to Christ:

> The great Basil, brother of the girl we have been speaking about, came back from the school where he had been trained for a long time in the

---

3. This elementary point is made by Anna Silvas in her landmark study, *The Asketikon of Saint Basil the Great* (Oxford: Oxford University Press, 2005). See especially "The Geography behind the History," pp. 38–50.

4. Gregory of Nazianz, *Funeral Orationes*, trans. Leo P. McCauley, 15.24, in Fathers of the Church (FC) 22 (New York: Fathers of the Church, 1953), 39–49; Rousseau, *Basil of Caesarea*, 64–65.

discipline of rhetoric. Although when she took him in hand he was monstrously conceited about his skill in rhetoric, contemptuous of every high reputation and exalted beyond the leading lights of the province by his self-importance, so swiftly did she win him to the ideal of philosophy that he renounced worldly appearance, showed contempt for the admiration of rhetorical ability and went over of his own accord to this active life of manual labor, preparing for himself by means of his complete poverty a way of life which would tend without impediment towards virtue.[5]

Although we do not know the exact sequence of these events, it seems that upon his return from Athens, Basil took a temporary teaching post at Caesarea in Cappadocia. He also took a swing around the eastern Mediterranean, supposedly visiting monastic communities in Syria and Egypt. Actually he was looking for Eustathius, the bishop of Sebaste (Roman Armenia), who was making the same pilgrimage. This man was a prominent spiritual guru in Pontus and Armenia of whom we will have much more to say. At any rate, it seems that on his return Basil attached himself to Eustathius as an ascetic disciple.[6] More concretely, he moved to Annisa in Pontus to become a hermit.

Annisa, which was located about fifty miles west of Neocaesarea on the Pontine Highway, was the family property of Basil's family. After the death of his father, his mother Emmelia had moved the family to this rural estate, which was located in the picturesque hills of northern Pontus. This move also involved the transformation of the family into a kind of domestic monastery. The head of this community, however, was not Emmelia, but her eldest daughter, Macrina Junior. She assisted her mother in managing the extensive property, but in religious terms she was the clear leader of the family. Macrina had declared herself a Christian virgin at the age of twelve, and she never went back on that promise.[7] She had an important hand in raising her younger siblings in the Christian faith, and at some point she convinced her mother to free the family slaves and live with them in what we would now call cenobitic community. Eventually the youngest son, Peter, would become the superior of the male branch of this double monastery.[8]

5. Gregory of Nazianz, *Funeral Orationes* 43.19, FC 22, 69.

6. See Jean Gribomont, "Le Monachisme au IV s. in Asie Mineure: de Gangres au Messalianisme," *Studia Patristica* 2 (1957), 400–15.

7. Gregory of Nyssa, *Life of Saint Macrina* (VSM), trans. Kevin Corrigan (Toronto: Peregrina, 1997), 22–23.

8. See Silvas, *Asketikon*, 71–75.

First Monastic Experiment

As for Basil, he spent about five years at Annisa, but he did not live in the family monastery. Rather, he lived in a rustic retreat elsewhere on the property. In fact, it seems that he succeeded his brother, Naucratius, who had founded this retreat but had died tragically in a drowning accident in 356.[9] During this period Basil probably started by pursuing something like a Greek philosophical ideal of rustic contemplation.[10] This secular ideal was no doubt tempered by the Christian ascetical model taught by Eustathius, who often visited the family on his journeys back and forth on the Pontine highway. For example, one of Eustathius's emphases was service to the poor, which Naucratius and Basil both lived out in the form of a hostel for elderly family slaves. They fed them by hunting and fishing. What was missing in this first monastic experience of Basil was any form of structured community.

For a long time the standard hagiography of St. Basil claimed that during this rustic period he was joined by his friend St. Gregory Nazianz in a sort of holy seclusion.[11] It was also said that the two of them spent some of their time culling useful passages from the works of Origen, which collection became the famous *Philokalia*. Both of these ideas need correction. First, Gregory spent little, if any, time at Annisa. As we learn from Letter 2,[12] Basil tried hard to lure him to his wilderness retreat, but the delicate and urbane Gregory resisted. Second, although they probably did collaborate on the *Philokalia*, this did not require that

---

9. Gregory of Nyssa, VSM, 25–27.

10. Silvas, *Asketikon*, 86–89, traces the "revolution of Basil's ascetic discourse."

11. Already in ancient times Jerome and Rufinus claimed that Gregory of Nazianz was a major influence on Basil's monastic vocation. Jerome, in his *Chronicle* for 379, indicates that Gregory was the true "mystic," while Basil was a proud autocrat. Rufinus, in his extension of Eusebius's *Historia Ecclesiastica* (PL 21.461–540) says that Gregory persuaded Basil to give up a career as a lawyer and to embrace monasticism. In his article "L'Influenza de Basilio sul Monachesimo Occidentale," in *Basilio tra Oriente e Occidente: Convegno Internazionale "Basilio il Grande e il monachesimo orientale," Cappadocia, 5–7 ottobre 1999* (Magnano [Biella]: Edizioni Qiqajon, Comunità di Bose, 2001), Adalbert de Vogüé suggests that neither of these writers knew the actual facts of the case. Each of them had ideological reasons for favoring Gregory over Basil.

12. Basil, *Letters*, trans. A. Clare Way, FC 13 (1951), Letter 2, pp. 5–11.

they live together. Furthermore, not all scholars are that impressed with the editorial work on this collection.[13]

It might be added that Gregory and Basil had a long and troubled friendship. Gregory was a shy, retiring poet who often found himself pushed into things by people and circumstances he could not withstand. Thus he was pressured into priestly ordination by his bishop-father about 362. Eventually he was more or less forced by Basil into becoming a rural bishop.[14] Just how distressed Gregory was with Basil's pressure is evident in the following passage: "As for you, play the man, be tough, drag everything into the service of your own glory, just as rivers in winter draw into themselves the smaller streams. Why honor friendship, that shared appreciation of goodness and piety? Why worry what sort of person you seem to be, behaving in this way? Content yourself with the solitude of your own spirit. As for me, I have gained one thing from your friendship: I shall not trust friends."[15]

Eventually, on the basis of a few sermons he gave in the capitol Gregory of Nazianz was made Patriarch of Constantinople by Emperor Theodosius I in 381. This was a role that so terrified him that he resigned after one year.[16] He was prominent at the Council of Constantinople, but soon retired to his estate at Nazianz, where he spent the rest of his life writing spiritual and theological poetry. Like Basil, he was one of the chief theological architects of the trinitarian theology laid down by the church. But he was not a monastic cooperator with Basil.

Since we have suggested that Basil was a kind of Eustathian monk during this first period at Annisa we should add some comments on the obscure figure of Eustathius. Although he was virtually unknown before the middle of the last century when Jean Gribomont pointed out his importance, Eustathius was in fact one of the most significant and influential spiritual masters of the Anatolian region in the

---

13. This is the view of Rousseau, *Basil of Caesarea*, 82–84.

14. This complicated story is told by Rousseau, ibid., 233–39.

15. *Letters* (PG 37), Letter 48, p. 9; Rousseau's translation of the Greek, *Basil of Caesarea*, 236.

16. In fact, Gregory was in a very weak position in Constantinople since the Nicene community was a tiny minority. Rousseau, however (*Basil of Caesarea*, 235–36), has no sympathy for Gregory: "We are perfectly entitled to ask why he let himself be consecrated in the first place: there is a limit to what can be included under the heading of compulsion."

fourth century.[17] The reason why he remained under a cloud for so many centuries was that as a young ascetical leader he was feared and hated by many bishops. Indeed, we have the proceedings of the Synod of Gangra (ca. 345) in which the bishops of Paphlagonia list the erroneous teachings of a group of ascetics they are trying to rein in.[18]

Among the teachings of these radical Christians that worried the bishops, probably the chief one was encratism: these people downgraded marriage. But they also questioned the value of work, and they promoted ideals of fasting that call into question the goodness of normal food. Although some of these teachings are indeed worrisome, it should be noted that in the larger view of early Christian history this was a conflict between the "old church" and the "new church." The old church was a continuation of the pre-Constantinian church of the martyrs, a form of Christian life that was battle-hardened by persecution and lack of respect from society. The "new church," represented by the bishops at Gangra, was popular and respectable.[19] These bishops felt that the church must conform to the mores of Greco-Roman society. The old radical asceticism would no longer work in a world where the Catholic Church was the official state religion.

Although Eustathius was not named by Gangra, he seems to have taken this weighty admonition to heart. He must have, because he was himself named bishop of Sebaste in 356, the same year that Basil moved to Annisa. From what we can tell, as bishop he strove to moderate some of the extreme tendencies of his followers, who lived in conventicles spread around Roman Armenia and Pontus.[20] Sometimes he succeeded

17. Gribomont, "Le Monachisme" (n. 5 above). This was virtually the first study that was appreciative of the contribution of Eustathius. In his note to Basil's Letter 1 (FC 13), Roy J. Deferrari said that Eustathius was a peripatetic pagan philosopher. Adrian Fortesque, in his article on "Eustathius of Sebaste" in the *Catholic Encyclopedia* of 1914, knows more about his subject, but he has nothing good to say about him. But Gribomont (p. 402) cites Sozomen, an important Greek historian of the fifth century, who calls Eustathius "the father of monasticism in Asia Minor."

18. Silvas, *Asketikon*, 486–94, gives both the Greek text of the Gangra decrees and an English translation.

19. Gribomont, "Le Monachisme," calls the bishops at Gangra "court bishops," meaning that they were in close league with the emperor at Constantinople.

20. According to the *Atlas of the Early Christian World*, ed. Frederik van der Meer and Christine Mohrmann (London and New York: Nelson, 1958), inside cover, Sebaste was in the Roman province of Armenia Prima. This is to

and sometimes he did not. For example, when he set up a hospice for the sick and the poor at Sebaste some of his radical disciples accused him of bending to the culture, and so they separated themselves from him.[21] And sad to say, Eustathius ended as a definite heretic on doctrinal matters. In their last few years Basil broke completely from his old mentor.[22]

If we ask the question whether Basil and his family were part of the "old" or the "new" church, a simple answer will not do. We know that his parents were extremely loyal to the official church, so they were not about to go to schismatic extremes. If Eustathius became a friend of the family, as he did at both Neocaesarea and Annisa, then he must have transcended the extremes condemned by Gangra. But there also can be little doubt that Basil's family was uncomfortable with the new conformity to Greco-Roman culture. In their deepest feelings they were still part of the old martyr church. Certainly Macrina was a radical ascetic,[23] and even as a bishop Basil was not afraid to make extreme demands of his flock in matters of sharing with the poor in times of need.[24]

During his first sojourn at Annisa, Basil also compiled a curious document now called *Moralia*.[25] This work consists of nothing but excerpts from the New Testament that Basil deemed to be "commandments" of Christ. Since he has a broad definition of commandment, the collection includes no fewer than 1,500 items. From what we can

---

be distinguished from Regnum Armeniae, which would correspond to modern Armenia in the Caucasus.

21. According to Epiphanius, *Panarion* 75, (PG 42, 504–508), Eustathius appointed a certain Aerius as head of the hospice he founded in Sebaste. But Aerius thought that Eustathius was betraying the radical principles of the ascetics by this charitable work, so he led a group of disciples out from Sebaste. In his turn Basil asked Eustathius for advisers in setting up his own hospital at Caesarea. But by that time the relationship of Basil and Eustathius had soured, to the point that Basil (*Letters* 223.3) accused Eustathius of sending the helpers as spies! See Gribomont, "Eustathe," in *Dictionnaire de Spiritualité*, col. 1709.

22. This sad story is told in great detail by Rousseau, *Basil of Caesarea*, 233–69.

23. Rousseau refers to Basil's "fanatical sister." In his account of Macrina's influence on Basil (*Basil of Caesarea*, 9–11), Rousseau indicates that he finds Macrina overbearing.

24. *Sermons* 322, 325, and 336 (PG 29–32) are analyzed by Rousseau in *Basil of Caesarea*, 137–39.

25. The *Moralia* is printed with the Long Rules in *St. Basil, Ascetical Works*, trans. Monica Wagner, FC 9 (New York: Fathers of the Church, 1950).

tell, Basil's motivation for this project stemmed from an experience he had at Constantinople. It seems he accompanied Bishop Eustathius to the capital to attend a synod of bishops discussing the Christology of the Council of Nicaea. Although that council had declared Jesus Christ divine, there was wide and lasting doubt about what that really meant. At Constantinople, Basil was rather shocked by the rancor he witnessed in the synod. He concluded that the church was in danger of destroying itself through controversy.[26]

When he returned to his retreat in Pontus, Basil brooded on this problem and finally came to a conclusion. The only way out of this morass of *odium theologicum* (theological hatred) was through obedience. If everyone would just follow the commandments of Jesus as found in the New Testament there could be no serious conflict in the church. Therefore one had to let people know what these commandments were. Of course, we know that the problem was not solved by this means. In fact, there are also some indications that Basil himself was not too sure about the correct interpretation of the Nicaean formula (the Father and the Son are *homoousion* = same in substance) for some years. At any rate, this strong tendency toward law and order, even rigorism, would stay with Basil throughout his life as a churchman and as a monastic legislator.[27]

Second Monastic Experiment

In 362 or thereabouts Basil was ordained a priest by Eusebius, bishop of Caesarea. In those days before seminaries, all that was necessary for ordination was for the person to be a baptized male. Of course, it was obvious to everyone that Basil was a capable man. Nevertheless, things did not work out at Caesarea, and he was soon back at Annisa.[28] This

---

26. Silvas, *Asketikon*, 90–91. Basil also wrote *De Judicio* at the same time. It is printed along with the *Moralia* in FC 9.

27. This judgment was strongly argued by Emmanuel Amand de Mendieta, *L'Ascèse monastique de saint Basile: Essai historique* (Liège: Éditions de Maredsous, 1949). In his article entitled "A propos du rigorisme de saint Basile: gravité du péché, libération du pécheur," *Studia Anselmiana* 70 (1977): 139–73, Etienne Baudry tried to refute Amand. But thirty years later he admitted he had not succeeded very well. So he tried again in "Il 'Radicalismo Evangelico' e la Questione del 'Rigorismo' de Basilio il Grande," in *Basilio tra Oriente e Occidente*, 67–91.

28. Rousseau discusses this in *Basil of Caesarea*, 87–89.

time, however, he did not live alone but in the family monastery, and according to Anna Silvas it was during this second sojourn in Pontus that he learned what cenobitic (communal) monasticism was all about.[29] It should be remembered that his sister, Macrina, was the head of this double monastery. Basil was by no means the superior. Indeed, he was not even superior of the men's department of the monastery. That office was filled by his youngest brother, Peter.

Still, Basil soon began to play a role of monastic leadership in the region of Pontus. Apparently he served as a roving consultant to the ascetic communities of the area, no doubt representing Bishop Eustathius.[30] According to Silvas, Letter 22 is a historical marker of this period for Basil.[31] More important, she thinks that the *Small Asketikon* is basically a record of the conversations Basil had with those communities.[32] If so, we can say that Basil was learning the lessons of community living very quickly and very well. At this point in his life, when he had no ecclesiastical authority over these Eustathian communities, he still endeavored to help them learn the fundamentals of cenobitic

29. Silvas, *Asketikon*, 86–98.

30. I have not seen any reference that proves that Basil was acting as a consultant to the communities of Bishop Eustathius in Pontus. Still, we know that he was circulating among these communities at this time, so the conclusion seems obvious. Eustathius was not bishop of Pontus, which was in the diocese of Amaseia. But he still had great moral influence over his disciples wherever they were settled.

31. Letter 22, trans. A. Clare Way, FC 13. The letter is analyzed by Silvas in *Asketikon*, 88.

32. *Small Asketikon* refers to the first draft of Basil's Rule, as opposed to the *Great Asketikon*, which is the final version. We do not have the Greek original of the *Small Asketikon,* but we have a Latin translation made by Rufinus of Aquileia in the year 400. The critical edition of this text can be found in CSEL 86, edited by Klaus Zelzer (Vienna: Hoedler, Pichler, Tempsky, 1986). It is the strong opinion of Anna Silvas that these Eustathian communities were real monasteries (*Asketikon*, 28–29). Against Jean Gribomont ("The Commentaries of Adalbert De Vogüé and the Great Monastic Tradition," *American Benedictine Review* 36 [1985]: 255), she says: "The picture of Basil's ascetic teaching and of community structure that emerges from the above analysis does not confirm any image of a Basil benignly offering 'advice' to an *ad hoc* party of lay enthusiasts who might be considered free to come and go and do as they please, the 'spontaneous groups of Basilian ascetics' that some scholars persuade themselves constitute the *Sitz-im-Leben* of the *Small Asketikon*. No, the earliest version of the *Asketikon* condones no such sarabaitic lifestyle. Rather, it sets out to correct it."

monasticism. No doubt he had the lesson of Gangra in the back of his mind as well, but there is no sign in the *Small Asketikon* that he distrusted or feared their radical ascetical ideals. Furthermore, we can probably assume that Bishop Eustathius agreed with the direction Basil was giving to his followers.

If Silvas's new theory is correct, that Basil was learning the cenobitic ropes at Annisa at the same time he was teaching the communities of Pontus, then we have the curious situation of a novice functioning as a novice-master! Anyone who knows the history of Basil's subsequent life as a bishop might wonder how he would take to being a novice. For if there was one thing that almost everyone who knew Basil agreed on, it was that he was a formidable man and a natural leader. For example, we have the record of Bishop Basil's interview with Modestus, Praetorian Prefect of the East, in the days when the government was trying to force him into an anti-Nicene position: the mere personality of Basil entirely cowed the most powerful politician next to the emperor himself.[33] We have seen how much Gregory of Nazianz himself resented the force of Basil's will in his own life, but later Gregory admitted it was for the good of the church.[34]

So then, is it plausible that Basil would have put himself back to school at the feet of his sister at Annisa, in the years 362–365? I think it is, especially if we take into account that Macrina was probably at least as powerful a personality as her brother.[35] And in fact we have some evidence on just this point from their younger brother, Gregory of Nyssa. In 380, as Macrina lay dying at Annisa, Gregory rushed to the monastery to be at her side in her last hours. He had not seen her for many years, and he seems to have felt some guilt about that. Sure enough, on her deathbed the matriarch found the strength to tell her little brother the following:

> Our father was very well thought of in his day for his education, but his reputation only extended to the law-courts of his own land. Later on, although he was a long way ahead of everybody else in his mastery of rhetoric, his fame did not reach outside Pontus, but he was glad to be

33. Gregory of Nazianz, *Funeral Orationes* (43) 50 (Sources Chrétiennes [SC] 384; FC 22, 69). The crucial passage is: "Modestus: 'I have never been talked to like that before!' Basil: 'Perhaps you have never met a bishop before.'"

34. Rousseau, *Basil of Caesarea*, 37.

35. This is the thesis of Anna Silvas in *Macrina the Younger, Philosopher of God* (Turnhout: Brepols 2007).

widely recognized in his own country. But you are known in the cities, the townships and the provinces. Churches send you forth and call upon you as ally and reformer, and you do not see the grace in this? Do you not even realize the true cause of such great blessings, that our parents' prayers are lifting you on high, for you have little or no native capacity for this?[36]

In order to savor the full force of this rebuke we should note that Gregory of Nyssa himself was a bishop at this time. Not only that: after the death of Basil he had emerged from the shadows as a famous theologian in his own right. But Macrina is telling him that he should remember that in comparison to his great father he is still not much. And apart from his parents' prayers he is nothing at all.

A good and humble person like Gregory might be ready to listen to almost any piece of wisdom from his regal sister on her deathbed. Still, we might wonder why he would be so willing to advertise his own humiliation? Scholars have suggested that Gregory had some ulterior motives in writing the *Life of Macrina*. According to Philip Rousseau it is not unthinkable that Gregory wanted to show the world that Basil was not the only genius in the family. Indeed, he may have wanted to demonstrate that Macrina was greater.[37] Of course, she left us no writings, but in person she was at least the equal of the bishop of Caesarea.

Actually, Gregory tells us more about Macrina than what he includes in her *Life*. He has also left us a discourse called *On the Soul and Resurrection*, which he claims she delivered on her deathbed.[38] One does not have to be entirely skeptical to doubt whether anyone, even Macrina, could have come up with a philosophical meditation this long and this

36. Gregory of Nyssa, *Life of Macrina* (n. 7 above), 38. In his commentary on this passage (*Life of Macrina*, 11), Kevin Corrigan remarks: "This is part of the great charm of the VSM, that it reveals to us, however unconsciously, the gentle, saintly character of the famous, beleaguered bishop who acknowledges with a faint smile the justice of his elder sister's reproach. In the VSM the people of the fourth century come alive, passionate and with humor even at the most sacred moments."

37. Rousseau, *Basil of Caesarea*, 9. He also points out that Gregory never mentions Eustathius at all. No doubt he knew that the bishop of Sebaste was a mentor of Basil, but he also knew that the old man had connived at having him (Nyssa) exiled from his diocese by the emperor.

38. *De anima et resurrectione cum sorore sua Macrina dialogus: grecae et latine*, ed. Johann Georg Krabinger (Leipzig: Wuttigius, 1837). A new translation of this work is given by Silvas in *Macrina the Younger*.

intricate on her deathbed. Furthermore, the Neoplatonism of this treatise is much more characteristic of Gregory himself than of Macrina.[39] He tells us that she never went to school, but was educated entirely on the Bible at home. Yet it is also hard to believe that Gregory would have put these words in her mouth if she was just a simple woman with no sophistication, and it is not at all difficult to imagine that Basil spent long hours at Annisa conversing with Macrina about the meaning of the monastic life and of Christianity itself. He may not have sat at her feet, but they were at least spiritual equals.

Bishop of Caesarea and Founder of the Basiliade

After about three years in Pontus, Basil returned to Caesarea to assist Bishop Eusebius. He was urged to do this by Gregory of Nazianz, who worried that the aged bishop could no longer defend the church from its enemies.[40] The particular threat at this time was the attempt of Emperor Valens to make all the bishops conform to a compromise position on Christology. Instead of considering Christ one in substance with the Father (*homoousios*), as required by Nicaea, the government wanted the bishops to assent to a more moderate adjective, namely, "like" the Father (*homoiousios:* note the extra "i"). By the late 360s, Basil had come to see that the latter formula was inadequate, and he was ready to do battle to defeat it.[41]

This in itself was sure to win him some enemies among the clergy of Caesarea. But it is also likely that Basil's strong personality and his moral rigorism caused him to be feared and even hated by those who did not see Christianity as a radical break with ordinary mores. At any rate, when Bishop Eusebius finally died in 370 the election for his successor was a bitter one. Basil finally prevailed, but only with difficulty. This does not mean that he *contended* for the position. But there was no doubt that a vote for Basil was a vote for strong, decisive leadership.[42]

This is not the place to talk about Basil's embattled reign as bishop. Much of his struggle was on a theological plane, where he came to be recognized as one of the main architects of the "neo-Nicene" synthesis of

---

39. Silvas, *Macrina the Younger*, Introduction.

40. Rousseau, *Basil of Caesarea*, 135–37.

41. Basil's theological development is described in great detail by Rousseau in *Basil of Caesarea*, chap. 4 on Eunomius, 93–133.

42. Rousseau, *Basil of Caesarea*, chap. 5 on City and Church, 133–90.

Catholic faith.[43] Here our topic is Basil's monastic thinking and activity. It would have been easy enough, and even natural, for him to put aside his earlier monastic experience and thought when he was faced with the broader task of guiding the diocese of Caesarea. Yet, far from forgetting the monastic enterprise, he seems to have pursued it to the end of his life, which ended somewhat prematurely in 379. While he was bishop, Basil's monastic activity took practical, concrete form and also involved continued development of his monastic Rule.

On the practical level, Bishop Basil set about the development of an extensive hospital and shelter for the needy on the outskirts of Caesarea. This institution, which was probably modeled on a similar one founded by Bishop Eustathius at Sebaste,[44] was staffed by men and women religious. The bishop had been greatly moved by the plight of the poor of Pontus in the plague of 369, when the nuns and monks of Annisa took in orphans, so as bishop he decided to create some kind of institutional bulwark at Caesarea against such recurring disasters. This hospital, aptly called the *Basiliade*, is considered the model for many similar institutions in the early church. Moreover, the work of the religious community he founded to staff the *Basiliade* is reflected in some of the later questions found in his Rule.

This last reference suggests that Basil continued to develop the monastic Rule he had begun in Pontus. This ongoing work resulted in what is now called the *Great Asketikon*. It came to include about twice as much material as was found in the *Small Asketikon*. Unlike the earlier version, the *Great Asketikon* is divided into two main sections, usually called by the confusing labels of Long Rules and Short Rules. In fact, the section called the Short Rules is somewhat longer than the Long Rules, but the chapters (questions) in the Long Rules are more highly developed.[45]

---

43. On a more political level, in the 370s the emperor divided the civil diocese of Cappadocia into two parts, leaving Basil with the less populous eastern half. Although it was not necessarily meant to harm Basil, this political change impacted the church as well, for it necessitated a new ecclesiastical archbishopric at Tyana. Basil fought back vigorously by creating new suffragan bishops in western Cappadocia (e.g., the two Gregorys). Rousseau, *Basil of Caesarea*, 169–70, says that Basil's purpose was basically ecclesiastical, not political.

44. Rousseau, *Basil of Caesarea*, 139–42.

45. The Latin title for the Long Rules is *Regulae fusius tractatae* = the more highly developed Rules. Both of these collections are translated in Silvas, *Asketikon*.

When we examine the relationship between these two versions of Basil's Rule we find that some questions are broached in the *Great Asketikon* that are not taken up in the earlier version. But even though Basil apparently reworked all of the material, it does not look as if he changed his fundamental thinking on cenobitism from the time he studied it in the family monastery at Annisa.[46] In the analysis that follows we will limit our study to the *Great Asketikon*, for the simple reason that the *Small Asketikon* has not been translated into English; the average reader (and the author!) would not find easy access to the original.[47] Furthermore, we will not be able to study every question, since the *Great Asketikon* is very long.[48] In fact, we will consider only the first questions of the Long Rules. This means that we will not confront every issue Basil discusses, but at least we will find most of his monastic philosophy in this material.

46. Silvas, *Asketikon*, 36.

47. One of the puzzles that remain to me is simply this: Why didn't Rufinus translate the *Great Asketikon* instead of the *Small Asketikon*? It is possible that he did not have access to the former document, but it may have been too long for his purposes.

48. As far as I know, the only longer monastic Rule from ancient times was the Rule of the Master. In comparison, the Rule of Benedict is one-third as long as the Rule of the Master, and less than half as long as the *Great Asketikon*. It is also considerably shorter than the *Small Asketikon*, which was the only Rule of Basil that Benedict knew.

Chapter
 Two

The Rule of Basil: I
(Long Rules Prologue and 1–7)

Long Rules Prologue

The message of the Long Rules of Basil's *Great Asketikon* is very simple: keep all the commandments! This theme may seem somewhat surprising, coming as it does at the beginning of a Rule for monks. Is monasticism primarily a moralistic approach to Christian life? Should monks, who have "left everything and followed" Christ,[1] need to be told to keep the commandments? Finally, why this emphasis on *all* the commandments?

In the previous chapter we saw that Basil was extremely sensitive to the rancor and disorder in the church of his day.[2] It was for this reason that he compiled the *Moralia*,[3] which was indeed an anthology of every single commandment he could find in the New Testament. At one point in his life he felt the church could regain its peace and unity if everyone just kept the commandments.

At the time Basil compiled the *Moralia* he was a recent graduate of law school in Athens, so he was still quite wedded to Greek philosophy, and especially Stoicism. One of the basic ethical ideas of Stoicism was this same

---

1. Mark 10:28.

2. See especially pp. 7–8 above.

3. In fact, the *Moralia* is printed just before the Long Rules in the standard English translation in FC 9 (New York: Fathers of the Church, 1950).

notion that the moral life is an integral skein of precepts. If one of these precepts is knowingly broken, then, like a woven garment, the whole fabric begins to unravel. In fact, this kind of thinking is not entirely absent from the Bible. In James 2:10 we read: "whoever keeps the whole law (*holon ton nomon*) but fails in one point has become accountable for all of it."[4]

But why should Basil feel he must emphasize this stringent teaching when addressing himself to a group of radical Christian ascetics? It could be that he meant to bind them closer to the main church body. Although the Eustathian ascetics kept many of the church's laws in the strictest possible manner, they were tempted to pick and choose which ones they would emphasize. For Basil this is a sure formula for dissension and disunity in the church. In order to be united to the whole church, one must obey every single commandment, even the ones that are distasteful—indeed, *especially* the ones that are distasteful.[5]

But it is also possible that Basil's Prologue was not addressed exclusively to the ascetic communities. In the opinion of Anna Silvas, Basil has added a *protreptic* sermon to the original Prologue (*Small Asketikon*) that puts things in a somewhat different light.[6] A *protreptic* was a special kind of exhortation aimed at catechumens who were putting off the decisive step of baptism, even till their deathbed.[7] Moreover, throughout his ministry Basil was a resolute opponent of "two-track Christianity." To his mind there was no basis whatsoever in the New Testament for a system in which a few chosen souls would keep the whole law while the unwashed masses would keep the minimum of a few commandments.

4. According to Marjorie O'Rourke Boyle, "The Stoic Paradox of James 2:10," *NTS* 31 (1985): 611–17, the keeping of every moral law reflects the Stoic tradition.

5. The bishops at Gangra complained that the Eustathian ascetics tended to disparage ordinary work, marriage, and even the sacraments of the church (see Silvas, *Asketikon*, 490–93).

6. Silvas thinks that Basil added this material when he was a bishop. She also points (*Asketikon*, 154 n. 2) to a couple of passages in the Prologue that speak of the Holy Spirit as divine and equal to the Father and the Son. These no doubt originated in the 370s when Basil was focused on the divinity of the third person of the Trinity.

7. Silvas, *Asketikon*, 153 n. 1. She says that one *protreptic* of Basil survives in its entirety: *Holy Baptism*, PG 31.423–44, trans. T. P. Halton in Adalbert-G. Hamman, ed., *Baptism: Ancient Liturgies and Patristic Texts* (Staten Island, NY: Alba House, 1967), 76–87.

Apparently, when Basil was revising his Rule in his later years as a bishop, he thought it appropriate to include this kind of moral wake-up call even to holy ascetics.[8] Certainly this Prologue does not mince words. It does not hesitate to use rather tough language on the hearers: "But here we are, thinking that we have fulfilled perhaps one of the commandments—I would not say that we really had fulfilled it, but according to the sound meaning of the word the commandments are so interdependent that if one is broken, the others are of necessity broken too—and we do not expect any wrath for those we have transgressed, but go so far as to look for honors for keeping one!" (LR Prol 2).

Basil makes it quite clear in his Prologue that he *is* addressing ascetics. In fact, he makes some references to the concrete circumstances in which the questions and answers of the *Great Asketikon* arose. For example, the second paragraph begins thus: "The present time is indeed most suitable for us and the place provides tranquility and complete freedom from outside disturbances." Toward the end of the same Prologue he says: "So then, in whatever way each of you thinks he is lacking (in knowledge), let him bring it forward for common examination, for if something appears difficult or obscure, it is more easily uncovered by the labor of several looking into the matter together."[9]

From these two passages we can glean a general picture of the way the *Asketikon* developed. Apparently it arose in discussions between Basil and the ascetical communities he visited. The first quotation indicates that these discussions took place at a quiet time when maximum concentration was possible. Indeed, the Prologue of the Short Rules shows that the colloquies were held at night and may have lasted till dawn.[10]

---

8. In fact, St. Benedict seems to have thought the same way. His Prologue to the Holy Rule is largely a baptismal homily he has copied from the Rule of the Master. Germain Morin claims that the RB Prologue bears close resemblance to a baptismal homily from the 6th–7th centuries: "Étude sur une série de discourses d'un évêque [de Naples?] du Vie s.," *RBén* 11 (1894): 384–402.

9. Silvas, *Asketikon*, 159. Unless otherwise noted, all translations of the *Great Asketikon* given here are from Anna Silvas, *The Asketikon of St. Basil the Great* (Oxford: Oxford University Press, 2007).

10. Silvas, *Asketikon*, 273 n. 15, fills out the picture: "Basil has attended, if not presided at, a vigil in common with other Christians, for the Sunday liturgy maybe, or for one of the synods or local festivals, or for a gathering of superiors of communities that Basil advises" (LR 54). In Letter 223 he indicates to Eustathius that there was a stenographer present to take notes. No doubt that was how these discussions became the *Asketikon*.

Even more interesting is Basil's remark that people should feel free to bring their questions to the group so that *everybody* can search for solutions. If we are to take this literally, and I do not see why we should not, this means that the *Asketikon* of St. Basil is more the product of communal thinking in the early church than it is the legislation of a single leader.

Yet even after we have explored some of the possible background that could explain Basil's stress on *all* the commandments, it is likely that it still leaves a fairly unpleasant taste in our mouths. The Catholic Church has recently emerged from a period of its history, at least in the United States, characterized by a Jansenistic stress on sin. For many older Catholics who feel liberated by Vatican II, it could seem that Basil's stress on commandments and sin is an unwelcome regression to a church they are glad to have left behind.[11]

An interesting suggestion that could explain Basil's moral rigorism comes from Etienne Baudry,[12] who points to a somewhat puzzling passage in the Prologue: "In that case, someone will say, is it no use that the great number of Christians who do not keep all the commandments, keep some of them? In this connection it is well to remember the blessed Peter, he of so many good deeds and such great blessings, yet who for a single fault heard: *If I do not wash you, you can have no part with me* (John 13:8). And I need hardly say that the occasion itself showed no sign of indifference or contempt, but was rather an expression of honor and piety" (LR Prol 3).

What is Basil's point in this passage? We should notice that he is responding to a question we too may be tempted to ask: Do you mean to say that someone who keeps *some* of the commandments will not get credit for that? Not only does Basil not capitulate to this objection from common sense, he refutes it with an even more radical example. He brings forth the example of Peter, who was warned by Jesus even though he had committed *no* sin at all.

Remember the context of this rather mysterious passage. When Jesus seeks to wash the feet of the disciples at the Last Supper, Peter refuses to accept his service. Instead of commending him for his humility, Jesus lashes out at him: "Unless I wash you, you have no share with

---

11. Among the major scholars who find Basil excessively moralistic is Emmanuel Amand de Mendieta, *L'Ascèse monastique de saint Basile: Essai historique* (Liège: Éditions de Maredsous, 1949).

12. Etienne Baudry, "A propos du rigorisme de saint Basile: gravité du péché, libération du pécheur," *Studia Anselmiana* 70 (1977): 139–73.

me" (John 13:8). What is Peter's "sin" in this passage? According to Basil it was resisting God's will to save him. And that will was manifest in Jesus' desire to wash him. So underneath the somewhat abstract discussion of keeping all the commandments lies the question of my *personal* commandment. Once I learn what God wants of me, I must conform or forfeit all.

In a more recent article[13] Baudry confesses that he is no longer completely convinced by his own argument from thirty years ago. But he has not therefore decided that Basil really is a moral rigorist. For one thing, Baudry notes that Basil stresses the gravity of sin so as to accent God's mercy. On the psychological and spiritual level there is no therapy without disclosure. To cover over our sin is to preclude its healing.

What is more, Basil is well aware of the various grades and types of sin. Even though he sometimes insists that there is no minor sin,[14] that does not mean he is unaware of moral nuances.[15] He knows there is a big difference between the slip of a fervent person and that of a lax person whom sin has mastered (SR 81). Most tellingly, Basil is aware of himself as a real sinner:

> Whenever I call these things to mind—if I may speak openly of my own experience—I am struck with a kind of shuddering and cold terror in case it happens that through carelessness of mind or preoccupation with vanities I fall from the love of God and become a reproach against Christ. (See Ps 68:6-10; Rom 15:3). For the one who now deceives us and eagerly employs every device to induce us to forget our Benefactor through worldly enticement, who leaps on us and tramples us down to the destruction of our souls, will one day fling our contempt as a reproach against the Lord and will boast of our disobedience and apostasy. He neither created us nor died for us, yet he will have won us as his followers in disobedience and neglect of God's commandment.

We can see here Basil's own experience and horror of sin, and the way he connected it to the cosmic drama of good and evil. Satan is seen as the master manipulator who tempts us to sin and then flings our

13. "Il 'Radicalismo Evangelico' et la Questione del 'Rigorismo' di Basilio il Grande," in *Basilio tra Oriente e Occidente: Convegno Internazionale "Basilio il Grande e il monachesimo orientale," Cappadocia, 5–7 ottobre 1999* (Magnano [Biella]: Edizioni Qiqajon, Comunità di Bose, 2001), 67–91.

14. Thus in *De Judicio Dei* and SR 4, 233, 293.

15. Baudry, "Radicalismo," 73, cites Short Rules 46 to show that Basil knows there is venial sin, involuntary sin, and so on.

disobedience in the face of Christ, who died for our sins. It is hard to imagine a starker vision of the Christian drama. This text is a window on Basil's soul, making it clear that he is not a mere moral crank but someone with a profound understanding of the true depth of sin.

Long Rule 1: On the Order and Sequence of the Lord's Commandments[16]

"Good order" (*eutaxia*) is one of Basil's key ideas. This is evident from the fact that he starts both LR 1 and LR 24 with this concept, and these are the opening chapters of the two major units of the Long Rules.[17] We have seen in the previous chapter the existential background for Basil's passion for order, which arose as a reaction against the theological turmoil in the fourth-century church over Christology. This explains the rather unusual discussion in LR 1 about why it is necessary to start with the correct order of the commandments. The reason is that Jesus himself made love the first commandment.

This is a reference to Mark 12:28-31, where a scribe asks Jesus which is the most important commandment. In answer, Jesus does not hesitate to tell him that love of God is the greatest, and he adds that love of neighbor comes a close second. Mark says that this answer pleased the scribe very much, and that Jesus returned the compliment by telling him: "You are not far from the kingdom of God" (v. 31).[18] It is worth noting here the simple fact that Basil bases the order of his discussion of the commandments on the New Testament itself. A glance at the whole extent of the *Great Asketikon* shows that it is saturated with Scripture. Indeed, many of the questions are simply exegetical: How should we interpret such and such a passage?

Yet the question for LR 1 is not one of those biblical questions. It merely asks where to start, since one could start anywhere in discussing

16. This is Silvas's translation of the first phrase of LR 1, which functions as its title. Many of the chapters of the Long Rules are supplied with a title, but not all of them. By contrast, none of the Short Rules has a title.

17. At least according to the analysis of Adalbert de Vogüé in "The Great Rules of St. Basil: A Survey," *Word and Spirit* 1 (1979). We will take up his structural suggestions further on.

18. To close the episode, Mark adds the puzzling comment: "After that, no one dared to ask him any question." I suspect that this remark pertains more to the whole second part of Mark than to the irenic dialogue in 12:28-31. But this is not the place to delve into that question.

the monastic life. Probably we can say that this is not an actual question from the discussions that lay behind the *Great Asketikon*.[19] It is rather an artificial question concocted by Basil himself in order to start the Long Rules where he wishes to start. Some of the other Long Rules have the same kind of question, that is, basically a lead-in to issues Basil wishes to discuss.

The very genre of the dialogue, consisting of questions and answers, is a good one to produce lively discourse, but it is not something Basil himself invented. In fact, the literary form of the dialogue is commonplace in ancient literature. The most famous dialogues, of course, are those of Plato, where Socrates discusses all sorts of philosophical questions with his friends. And at least two famous early monastic texts are in dialogue form: the *Dialogues* of Sulpicius Severus (405 AD) and those of Pope Gregory (593 AD).

But Basil's decision to begin his Rule with the topic of love deserves more examination. As we said, it is very biblical, since Jesus himself taught it. And theologically it has to be insisted that love is the bedrock reality of Christian theology. After all, the First Letter of John is not afraid to declare that "God is love" (1 John 4:8). So this should be an ideal place to begin a monastic Rule. But in fact not all monastic Rules begin this way. The Rule of Augustine does, as we shall see in a later chapter.[20] The Rule of Benedict, however, does not, based as it is on earlier monastic texts that do not stress love as much as ascesis.[21]

We have mentioned that Adalbert de Vogüé has surveyed the contents of the Long Rules.[22] In doing so he notices that Basil actually seems to follow the distinction of Jesus in his structuring of the whole document. Just as Jesus divided love into love for God and love for neighbor, Basil also has chapters on both topics in this collection. Not only that:

19. See above, n. 10.

20. "The first purpose of your coming together is to live harmoniously in house intent on God with one heart and soul." My own translation of *Praeceptum* 1.2. This is based on Acts 4:32, which is a description of the first Christian community in Jerusalem immediately after the resurrection of Jesus.

21. Specifically, the beginning of the Rule of Benedict is based on the Rule of the Master. The latter is heavily influenced by the monastic theology of John Cassian, who was in turn formed by Evagrius Ponticus. For better or worse, Evagrius starts with Neoplatonic theory, not Scripture. That does not mean he is unbiblical. It just means that Evagrius (and Cassian) sometimes writes for pages without mentioning Jesus Christ.

22. See n. 17 above.

Vogüé claims that Basil interprets these two commands in very distinctive ways, especially in what they require of us. For Basil, love for God primarily demands separation from the enemies of God. And love for neighbor is the corollary to that: love for neighbor means forming community with like-minded Christians. It is easy to see that this particular slant on love is aimed primarily at communities of Christian ascetics. Nevertheless, it should be added that at times Basil seems to want *all* Christians to live separately from non-Christians.

By dividing the Long Rules into vertical and horizontal love Vogüé is able to account for two large units: Love of God: LR 8–23; Love of Neighbor: LR 24–55. This leaves the first part, which is our focus here, somewhat mixed. Vogüé thinks LR 2, 5, and 6 concern love of God, while LR 3 and 7 are aimed at love of neighbor. Actually these divisions are not airtight, since one topic naturally calls forth the other. Still, this outline is useful for ordering our own reading of the Long Rules.

Long Rule 2: Concerning Love for God

Since Basil has announced that love for God is the first commandment, the first question that follows it, that is, LR 2, deals with a very poignant issue. "We have heard that it is necessary to love; what we want to learn is how this is to be accomplished" (LR 2.1). While this may seem to be an obtuse question, in fact it is very penetrating. Love is usually taken for granted, but Basil is quite willing to provide his interlocutors with an extensive and fascinating answer. In doing this he lays a solid theoretical foundation for the practical monastic rules that follow.

First, let us summarize his argument. We can love because a generative word (*logos spermatikos*) has been implanted in us. This word creates in us a yearning for God (*tou theou pothos*). This virtue includes the ability to keep all the commandments. At the first, natural level we experience this divine yearning as a love for beauty, kin, and friends. By gazing on the natural beauties of our life we are purified and can rise to longing for the divine beauty. As proof of this we only need look to nature. There we see that even wild offspring love their parents. Moreover, everyone loves a benefactor, therefore all the more so a divine Benefactor.

To translate this general, philosophical theory into a specifically biblical one based on salvation history, we can say with the book of Genesis that God made us in his own image and likeness (Gen 1:26). This is a superior equivalent to the *logos spermatikos* of Greek philosophy. Nevertheless, we have obscured and tarnished this image in ourselves by our sin. Rather than banish us from his concern, God then provided us with the Law and Prophets of the Hebrew Bible. And when even that did not convince us to reform, he gave us his only son, Jesus Christ.

To provide some depth to this almost breathtaking theory, let us look at the idea of the *logos spermatikos*, the generative word. It has to be said that this was not a Christian concept, but one derived from the philosophy of the Stoics. One of their basic ethical ideas was that the universe makes sense because all of us are equipped with a bit of the universal word or spirit: we personally participate in the fundamental structure of the universe. Therefore we have access to truth and we can do what is right.

We saw in the last chapter that Basil was well instructed in philosophy in preparation for the life of a lawyer (which he never took up). Even though some of the church fathers like Jerome claimed to rue the secular education they had received, Basil never did. In fact, says Silvas,[23] the text of LR 2 shows that he thought in Stoic terms throughout his life. This is clear because he *added* Stoic arguments to *Small Asketikon* 2, apparently after he moved to Caesarea as a priest and bishop.

At any rate, the use of Greek philosophy by our author is worth pondering. It was often said (by Adolf von Harnack, for example) that the primitive Christian message was corrupted by its contact with Greek philosophy in the first centuries of church history. But it should also be noted that much of Greek philosophy was extremely high-minded and provided an excellent theoretical basis for sophisticated Christian theology. As Anna Silvas comments, "(Stoicism) laid the groundwork of the Christian ascetic life in a religious anthropology based on reason and giving full accord to natural mysticism."[24]

Furthermore, this same doctrine of the *logos spermatikos* was taken up by many of the Greek fathers such as Origen, who was clearly one of Basil's theological guideposts. Like the other Greek fathers, Origen made sure to christianize this Stoic idea. Thus, commenting on 1 Corinthians 15, he teaches that all the baptized have a *logos spermatikos* that eventually grows into a resurrected body.[25] When he is commenting on the Canticle of Canticles, Origen remarks that the love that is the

---

23. *Asketikon*, 162 n. 38.

24. *Asketikon*, 169 n. 80.

25. Cited in Henri Crouzel, *Origen* (Edinburgh: T & T Clark, 1999), 254. I got this reference from Augustine Holmes, *A Life Pleasing to God* (Kalamazoo, MI: Cistercian Publications, 2000), 72–73.

subject of this Wisdom book is none other than the *logos spermatikos* of the philosophers.[26]

Yet all this talk of Greek anthropology makes some people nervous because, after all, the Stoics were not Christians. They were not even theists. But it must be remembered that church fathers see the *logos spermatikos* as a gift from God. What is more, they see it as a kind of circular system in which God's gift propels us—toward God. Silvas says that the essential thrust is a divine gift, but ascesis, that is, our efforts, aim it Godward.

Some readers may find Basil's anthropology excessively optimistic. That is probably due to the fact that we in the Latin church have been shaped and formed by the anthropology of St. Augustine, who is less optimistic. There is no question that most of the Greek fathers are more sanguine than the Latin fathers about the basic human situation. The thing to be remembered is that the Greeks simply assumed divine grace, while the Latins put more emphasis on it.[27] What is more, as a consequence of his anthropology Basil, along with the rest of the Greek church, expects a lot from us. "From everyone to whom much has been given, much will be required" (Luke 12:48).

When we move on to examine a second distinctive idea in LR 2 we find Basil using an unusual term for the desire for God spurred by the *logos spermatikos*. His favored word for desire is *pothos*, an unusual term that appears in LR 2.20-24:

> Yet such beauty is not visible to fleshly eyes; it is comprehended only by the soul and the mind. Whenever it illumined any of the saints it left embedded in them an intolerable sting of yearning, (till at length, as if languishing in the fires of such love) they, chafing at this present life, said, *Alas for me, that my sojourning is prolonged!* (Ps 119:5), *when shall I enter and appear before the face of God?* (Ps 41:3) and this: *To depart and be with Christ would be far better* (Phil 1:23) and again: (such a one, burning in the flames of his ardour would say) *My soul has thirsted for God, the strong one, the living* (Ps 26:4) and *Now O Lord, let your servant depart* (Luke 2:29). Oppressed by this life as in a prison, they found it

26. Holmes, *A Life*, 87 n. 8, says this statement is found in Origen's *Commentary on the Song of Songs*, Prologue 2. He adds: "This text only survives in Rufinus' Latin translation and in this text he uses the words *caritas* and *amor*, which presumably translate *agape* and *eros*."

27. In the *Great Asketikon* Basil does not discuss grace a lot. But he does mention it in SR 224 and SR 271.

hard to contain the impulses which the divine yearning had kindled in their souls. Insatiable (in their desire) of the vision of the divine beauty, they prayed that their vision of the sweetness of the Lord might extend into eternal life (cf. Pss 15:11; 26:4).

First, we should note that *pothos* is not a common word in the Long Rules, but Basil uses it often enough in the Short Rules.[28] The translation "sting of intolerable desire" suggests that this is not bland discourse. Silvas acknowledges this when she says, "Erotic register, so evident in the Greek, is somewhat tempered in the Latin."[29] Yet we may wonder why Basil did not use the ordinary Greek term for passionate desire, namely, *eros*. He may have thought that *eros* was so loaded with erotic overtones that it was best to avoid it. But we must admit that this is hardly a moralistic way of thinking.

Indeed, it could be called an aesthetic way of thinking, for it is based on the idea of divine beauty. To make it even more poignant, Origen speaks of being wounded by the beauty of creation, and Basil, by the beauty of God.[30] Of course, Basil has spoken earlier in this chapter about rising to God from creation, and we know that he is not insensitive to the splendors of the creation.[31] Furthermore, we can be quite sure that Basil was not speaking merely speculatively about these matters. In a passage just before the one we quoted, he says: "Wholly ineffable and indescribable, as I at any rate experience it, are the lightning flashes of the divine beauty."[32]

At this point we might return to the issue of Greek philosophy and early Christian discourse. The fact is that this remarkable notion of "the sting of intolerable desire" for the transcendent was also something from the Greeks. According to Augustine Holmes, both Plato and Plotinus

28. Holmes, *A Life*, 75–76. I owe most of my thinking about *pothos* to this excellent book.

29. *Asketikon*, 165 n. 58.

30. Holmes, *A Life*, 176. Origen is commenting on Canticles where it says, "I am wounded by love." Holmes comments: ". . . while Origen speaks of being wounded by the dart that is the Word of God himself, he associates it with the beauty of the creation rather than the Creator. Basil's prose soars towards mystical poetry in this section."

31. See Letter 2, on the beauties of the countryside near his retreat at Annisa.

32. Actually the personal note "as I at any rate experience it" occurs only in the *Small Asketikon*, translated by Rufinus. For some reason it has been dropped from the *Great Asketikon*. Perhaps Basil felt it was too deeply personal and revealing.

spoke quite frankly of this kind of powerful attraction for the Good and the Beautiful.[33] Here again Basil has added this language to the *Small Asketikon* in his later years. Apparently he grew *more* comfortable with Greek philosophy as he grew older!

In case anyone is still nervous about this kind of enthusiastic take-over of pagan thinking by a Christian writer, Silvas points out that parts of LR 2 are saturated with Christian language. She analyzes LR 2.43-47 and shows that the language is very close indeed to the language of the Liturgy of St. Basil, one of the main eucharistic prayers of the Greek church. Here are the words they have in common: *"God made man in his image . . . delight in the inconceivable beauties of paradise . . . beguiled by the serpent . . . he did not turn away . . . gave him the Law for a help, set angels over him . . . sent prophets . . . he did not deem equality with God as something to be grasped, rather he divested himself, accepting the form of a slave"* (Phil 2:6-7).[34]

Long Rule 3: Love of Neighbor

In LR 3, Basil continues the discussion of LR 2, namely, that God has implanted in us the "law of love." Since this law impels and urges us to love God (LR 2), the question in LR 3 is whether the same law draws us toward our neighbor. Basil's answer is a resounding yes, as is shown by the following remarkable passage: "Now who does not know that man is a domesticated and sociable animal, not a solitary and wild one? Nothing is more characteristic of our nature than that we have fellowship with one another, need one another and love our own kind. Since the Lord himself gave us the seeds of these things in anticipation, he therefore seeks fruit from them, and as the testimony of our love for him, he accepts our love for our neighbors, saying: "I give you a new commandment, that you love one another" (John 13:34; LR 3.61-63).

If there is any lingering doubt about Basil's humanism and his strong attraction toward human community, this quotation should dispel it. Of course, since we are claiming in this book that Basil is one of the pillars of communal monasticism it is no surprise to see him expressing such sentiments. But it seems to me that this quotation is so heartfelt and passionate about human fellowship that it simply cannot come from anything but a deep conviction on this matter. Sometimes legislators

33. Holmes, *A Life*, 76.
34. Silvas, *Asketikon*, 169 n. 82.

mouth nostrums about the need for community that seem rather perfunctory. Not Basil: he really believes this, and it also sets him at radical variance from the pessimistic saying: "Man is a wolf unto man."

It is curious, however, that in making his case Basil uses the Greek term *monastikon* in a pejorative sense, for this is the original term that lies behind "solitary"! Jean Gribomont points out that this negative use of a word that became the basic root of the later term "monastic" appears to stem from the Greek *monios*, which is used in the Bible to describe the "wild" boar of the forest in Psalm 79:13.[35] What is more, Basil uses the same word to describe a fierce lion in *Hexameron* 9. The point here is not that Basil was against what we today call "monastic life." Far from it! But he may have been wary of those extreme ascetics of his time who were using the name. If they were disdainful of human community, then he wanted nothing to do with them.

Of course, it is not enough simply to say that we have been endowed by God with the milk of human kindness. We know that we sometimes find other people very hard to be kind to, much less love. That is why Basil makes sure to include in this little chapter exhortations to mutual love. In fact, his use of John 13:34 in the quotation above is something he added later to the *Small Asketikon*. Probably his experience as a bishop convinced him all the more that communal love is the heart of Christianity.

In order to show that he wants to be taken utterly seriously on this point, Basil does not hesitate to add a couple of biblical passages that enunciate an extreme attitude toward love of neighbor. In Deuteronomy 32:32 and Romans 9:3, Moses and Paul both state that they are quite willing to lose their own lives (souls) for the salvation of their respective flocks. What could be more altruistic than that? But Basil does add the moderating remark that these great spiritual leaders knew that God would not fail to reward them for their selfless attitude.

Where did Basil learn his profound commitment to community? As we have seen, his early philosophical training was primarily Stoic. Now this school of thinkers often speaks of *oikeiosis*, the natural attractiveness of beings of the same class to one another.[36] But this leaves ambiguous

35. This interesting point is found in Jean Gribomont, *Saint Basile, Évangile et Église, Mélanges*, 2 vols. (Bégrolles-en-Mauges [Maine-&-Loire]: Abbaye de Bellefontaine, 1984), 375 n. 1. I owe this reference to Holmes, *A Life*, 93.

36. See Anthony Meredith, *The Cappadocians* (London: Geoffrey Chapman, 1995), 29. Jean Gribomont corroborates this, remarking in regard to LR 2 and 3 that "there is clearly here a use of Stoic insights" (*Saint Basile*, 171 n. 35). Both of these references are found in Holmes, *A Life*, 105.

the matter of the extent of one's human attraction. Is it just to one's family or tribe, or perhaps one's race? As a matter of fact, even the New Testament presents a somewhat mixed testimony on this point.

No doubt the most universalistic passage in the New Testament is found in the Sermon on the Mount, which exhorts us to "love your enemies and pray for those who persecute you" (Matt 5:44). But other passages do not seem to have the same breadth. For example, in Matthew 25, the great scene of the Last Judgment, Jesus instructs his disciples, "Truly I tell you, just as you did it to one of the least of these who are members of my family, you did it to me." Even though there is a strong temptation to take this command in the widest sense, many scholars today believe it really applies to fellow Christians.[37]

As for Basil, it is not perfectly clear how widely his vision extended. As we have seen in our comments on the overall plan of the Long Rules, one of Basil's main themes is the need for the Christians of his time and place to band together with fellow believers into tight social units (whether monastic or parochial). There are also other clues to Basil's practical attitude in these matters. In Short Rule 155 someone asks him about a patient in the hospital (*Basiliade*) run by the monks at Caesarea. If such a person is not a believer and in fact behaves like an unbeliever, what is one to do? Basil's answer is to ask the person to leave. Yet it should be remembered that the Rules are mostly ad hoc answers to questions of the moment, and not necessarily considered theological opinions. In another context a different answer might have been given.[38]

In closing our commentary on LR 3, it would seem appropriate to contrast Basil's huge enthusiasm for human community with the social situation we find in our own time. The sharpest social critics agree that the besetting sin of our society is *individualism*.[39] For whatever reasons, and surely this is a very complex matter, the citizens of our postmodern,

---

37. Thus the note for Matt 25:40 in the Revised New American Bible (1986) suggests that "little ones" or "the least of these" refers to the persecuted preachers of the early church. Matthew 25:35-40 is quoted in LR 3, but in a general way that makes it unclear who is included.

38. And in fact a different answer *is* given in Short Rule 186, where someone asks how far we should go in "laying down one's life for one's friends" (John 15:13). Basil answers that "we are taught to show love even unto death on behalf of both righteous and sinners without distinction."

39. See Robert Bellah et al., *Habits of the Heart* (Berkeley: University of California Press, 1996).

postindustrial society are finding it harder and harder to live with each other in mutual love and forbearance. Since the candidates to our monasteries come to us from this kind of world, it is quite to be expected that they will find monastic socialization difficult. This is especially so since even some veteran monks now seem to find common life a hard cross to bear. A periodic reading of texts such as Basil's Long Rule 3 might be a helpful tonic in this situation.

Long Rule 4

LR 4 is a short and somewhat abstract unit that will not need too much analysis. The main idea is that this book, namely, the *Great Asketikon*, is not for everybody; it is aimed at mature Christians only. Today the document is considered a *monastic* Rule, but we have to recall that Basil was writing at a time when monasticism as we know it was in a very inchoative state. What is more, as a bishop Basil was never afraid to make heavy demands on his whole flock. But in this little treatise he acknowledges that some Christians are not yet ready for the full ascetical program he is setting out here. To make his point Basil employs the initiatory categories of the early church: "For those, therefore, just being introduced to piety, an elementary introduction through fear is more useful. . . . But for you who have passed through your *infancy in Christ* (see 1 Cor 3:1-2) and no longer have need of milk but are able to *be perfected in the inner man* (Eph 3:16; 4:13) through the *solid food* (Heb 5:12) of teachings, there is need of the more specific commandments through which the whole truth of the love which is in Christ is accomplished" (LR 4).

In this passage Basil uses the technical vocabulary of the church: *eisagomenoi* (those just being introduced = catechumens) and *teleioi* (able to be perfected). He does not ask the newcomers to the church to follow his *Asketikon*, just those who are more advanced. As is clear from the quotation, this discussion is saturated with New Testament vocabulary and concepts. Probably the most memorable image is the contrast between milk and solid food from Hebrews 5:12 and Paul's letters.

Actually, the stated subject of LR 4 is "the fear of God." This theme is used to make the same point: for those who are just beginning, fear is a useful means of progress. But for those who have grown beyond the initial stages of their Christian formation, love is the predominant motivation. Nevertheless, Basil is careful to warn mature souls (that is, the intended audience of the *Asketikon*) that they must not become presumptuous in the graces received, lest a "heavier judgment" fall on them.

The reason why Basil brings up "fear" at this point in his collection is the text he quotes from Proverbs 1:7: "The fear of the Lord is the beginning of knowledge." This, of course, is quite appropriate for beginning or casual Christians. But Basil also knows that there are other kinds of fear that pertain to more advanced spiritual practitioners. This is seen in a passage from the Prologue to the Long Rules: "In all, I observe three different dispositions which lead inevitably to obedience: either we turn aside from evil from the fear of punishment and so are in a servile disposition; or, seeking the profits of a wage, we fulfill what is enjoined for the sake of our own profit and are therefore mercenaries; or else we do so for the good itself and for love of him who gave us the law, rejoicing to be thought worthy of serving so glorious and good a God, in which case we are surely in the disposition of sons."

From this passage it is obvious that Basil is aware that there are kinds of fear that are by no means merely rudimentary. Although he does not explicitly speak of the fear of mercenaries and the fear of sons, these are higher stages that he fully appreciates. But in LR 4 he limits himself to the use of the first stage of fear.[40]

Long Rule 5: On Keeping the Mind from Wandering

The title of this Long Rule indicates that we have moved from the first, fundamental discussion, namely, on the love of God and neighbor, to something a bit more internal and subtle. The question of mental and spiritual concentration is treated by Basil as the means to the end. If the focus of the Christian and the monk must be on God, then the question is how to maintain such a focus. The context, of course, is the world in which we live. It is a world that does not know God because it is crippled by sin (see John 15:19; 17:25; 14:17). To live in such a world has the effect of distracting us from our goal of union with God. Therefore we need to separate ourselves from this world, and when we do we also need to remain mindful of God at all times.

On the first point, that is, separation from the world, it could be asked whether Basil is requiring every serious Christian to physically abandon the world in the fashion, say, of the Egyptian monks. Although

40. For a full discussion of the theme of fear in Basil's work, as well as in John Cassian, see Holmes, *A Life*, 99–105. My own contribution to this topic can be seen in "The Biblical Roots of Benedict's Teaching on the Fear of the Lord," *Tjurunga* 43 (1992): 25–50.

his community at Caesarea certainly *did* practice physical separation, LR 5 does not seem to require just that. Rather, it seems to be a discussion of what might be called the "withdrawal of the heart," as this text will show: "Therefore, unless we estrange ourselves from both kinship of the flesh and the worldly life and migrate as it were to another world by our habit of mind, as the Apostle said—'but our citizenship is in heaven' (Phil 3:20)—it is impossible that we should succeed in the aim of being well-pleasing to God, for the Lord laid down definitely: 'So therefore, none of you can become my disciples if you do not give up all your possessions' (Luke 14:33)."

For Basil it is not enough for the Christian to mentally withdraw from the distracting world. Rather, he requires that we acquire a special spiritual disposition that he terms *diathesis*, which could be translated "undistracted disposition" for want of a single appropriate English equivalent. This Greek term occurs no less than sixty times in the *Great Asketikon*. Indeed, Augustine Holmes says that *diathesis* is the connecting theme of Short Rules 157–186.[41] According to John Eudes Bamberger, who is himself a psychiatrist, *diathesis* is not a passing disposition but a "deep and stable emotional attitude."[42]

As for the origins of this concept, Bamberger tells us that it was a technical medical term among the Greeks. As such, Basil could have picked it up in his graduate studies in Athens. But *diathesis* was also a term employed by the early ascetics and contemplatives. According to Jean Gribomont, Basil probably came across it in the well-known treatise on the Therapeutae by Philo of Alexandria. The following passage is an example of the kind of concept presented by Philo: "The (Therapeutae) always retain an imperishable memory of God, so that not even in their dreams is any other object ever presented to their eyes except the beauty of the divine virtues and of the divine powers."[43]

The mention of memory in this passage leads us to another concept that is almost equivalent to *diathesis* and is perhaps easier for us to grasp. As can be seen from the following passage, *diathesis* and memory are almost synonymous for Basil: "Question. In what disposition (*diathesis*) should one serve God and generally what is this disposition? Response. I consider it a good disposition (or cast of mind) if we have within us a

41. Holmes, *A Life*, 115.

42. "ΜΝΗΜΗ-ΔΙΑΘΕΣΙΣ: The Psychic Dynamisms in the Ascetical Theology of St. Basil," *Orientalia Christiana Periodica* 34 (1968): 233–51, at 241.

43. Quoted in Holmes, *A Life*, 116. Gribomont connects the Therapeutae and Basil in his essay "La Prière selon Saint Basile," in *Saint Basile*, 426–42.

desire to be well-pleasing to God that is eager, unquenchable, fixed firm and unchanging. Such a disposition is attained through conscientious and unremitting contemplation of the majesty of the glories of God, by (devout and pure) thankful thoughts and unceasing remembrance of the benefits that have been bestowed on us by God" (SR 157). As can be seen here, memory for Basil was not some kind of Platonic recall of one's previous existence, nor was it a mere storehouse of information. Rather, memory, along with contemplation and thanksgiving, is our primary psychological connection with God.

Another way of looking at memory as Basil sees it is to contrast his kind of remembering with the usual understanding of the phenomenon. For him it is not a passive function, but rather a spiritual strategy whereby we actively keep God in mind as much as possible. In this way Basil's remembering is akin to what goes on in the Catholic Mass, where one crucial aspect of the Eucharistic Prayer is *anamnesis*. This is a special kind of commemoration in which we *make present* the passion and the parousia (second coming) of Christ by publicly and liturgically mentioning them.

It is also true that God is present and active everywhere on his own and does not depend on our memory. Nevertheless, according to Basil it is vitally important for us to hold in mind the active presence of God by means of memory. This idea can be clearly seen in an excerpt from a very early letter of Basil to his friend Gregory of Nazianz: "Prayer is to be commended, for it engenders in the soul a distinct conception of God. And the indwelling of God is this—to have God set firm within oneself through the process of memory. We thus become a temple of God whenever earthly cares cease to interrupt the continuity of our memory of him."[44]

It should be noted that this letter dates from Basil's earliest monastic days as a hermit in Pontus, a time when his full cenobitic philosophy was not yet formed. Still, it is evident that this basic spiritual idea of remembering, which was to endure throughout his whole career as a spiritual master, was present from the beginning. But LR 5 develops the concept of memory even further. Another aspect of memory for Basil is the way it holds us to our basic goal. He notes that any competent craftsman, when working on a commission, needs to keep in mind what the client wants and not forget it: "A smith, for example, when making, say, an axe (or a scythe), is constantly mindful of him who gave him the

---

44. Letter 2, quoted by Holmes, *A Life*, 120.

charge and keeps him in mind as he plans the shape and size and kind and directs the task according to the intention of him who ordered it . . . for if he forgets, he will no doubt make something else or of a different quality to that which was proposed to him. So also the Christian ought to direct every effort whether small or great to God's intention."

This very concrete and practical image for remembering the presence of God has the advantage of showing that Basil's notion of spiritual remembrance was not primarily intellectual. If it were, it would seem to preclude ordinary work and, indeed, ordinary life. We know that we cannot do many kinds of work without concentrating our mind on the thing at hand. Modern-day cell phone accidents are making this all too clear. Certainly Basil does not agree with the Messalians of his day, who thought that the biblical command for constant prayer (1 Thess 5:17) forbade them to work. For Basil, the remembrance of the presence of God is fully compatible with ordinary life on this earth.

At this point it is hard for a commentator on the Rule of Benedict like the present author to pass by the clear influence of this Basilian theme in the RB. A quote from RB 7.10-11 makes this plain enough: "Thus the first step of humility is to utterly flee forgetfulness by keeping the fear of God always before one's eyes. We must constantly recall the commandments of God, continually mulling over how hell burns the sinners who despise God, and eternal life is prepared for those who fear God." If this quotation from RB seems more austere than what we have seen of Basil's thought, it might be noted that many of the same themes from this part of RB 7 are found in the rest of Basil's Rule: (1) divine gaze and presence; (2) God's examining of hearts and minds; (3) avoiding all sins; (4) perpetual vigilance.[45]

In his fine study of this material in *A Life Pleasing to God*, Augustine Holmes titles his commentary on LR 5 "The Heart of Basilian Spirituality: *Diathesis* and the Undistracted Memory of God." Although he does not seem to explain this title in what he says in his penetrating analysis of LR 5, I think he must mean that *diathesis* and memory are the *distinctive* element of Basil's ascetical thought. After all, the New

---

45. Here are the Basilian references supplied by Vogüé, *La règle de Saint Benoît*, introduction, translation, and notes by Adalbert de Vogüé, text by Jean Neufville, 7 vols. (Paris, Cerf, 1971–77), 4:307: Divine Presence and gaze, *Reg.* 46; 66; 79; God examines hearts and minds, *Reg.* 34; 79; 108; Avoid all sins, *Reg.* 34; 46; 60; 66; 79; Perpetual vigilance, *Reg.* 2; 55; 57; 58. Readers should note that these are all references to Rufinus's Latin version and not to the Greek *Great Asketikon*.

Testament insists that love is the heart of Jesus' Gospel, and Basil deals with love abundantly in LR 1 and 2. But his treatment of monastic life as a culture of mindfulness of God really sets him apart from most other patristic writers.[46]

Long Rule 6

LR 6 is part of a set of three responses to Basil's basic conviction that we must love God and love our neighbor (LR 1). In LR 5 and 6 the author tells us what love of God entails. LR 5 dealt with the interior means of fostering love for God, namely, *diathesis* or the memory of God. LR 6 has to do with the exterior necessity of separating ourselves from ungodly people if we are to grow in love for God. To complete the series, LR 7 will discuss how we are to promote love for our neighbor.[47]

Basil's general argument is that it is very harmful for a Christian to live among those who despise God's commandments. The reason for this is not hard to understand, for we are social creatures who tend to harmonize with our social environment. Since Basil shares the general Christian view of the world as seriously corrupt, he assumes that the ordinary person will share in the world's vices. If we are to break with this condition—that is, if we are to take up Christ's cross, we need to break with the sinful world.

Perhaps the first question we might ask is how literally Basil actually meant this? No doubt the answer depends somewhat on the further question as to the audience of this Rule. As we have pointed out, it looks as if the origins of the questions and answers lay in the ascetical communities of Pontus where Basil once served as an adviser. From what we know, those communities were indeed communes where fervent Christians had created a life cut off from ordinary society. So these were people who needed no urging to go apart from the corrupt world.

---

46. In my article "Benedictine Spirituality" in *The New Dictionary of Catholic Spirituality* (Collegeville, MN: Liturgical Press, 1983), 84–91, I take this idea one step further, suggesting that this same cluster of concepts (God present and watchful, memory, fear of God, etc.) are also the heart of *Benedict's* Rule. I do so because in fact the same cluster of ideas occurs no less than four times in RB: 4.46-49; 7.10-13; 7.26-30; 19.1. Notice too that this would indicate that Basil is the primary influence on Benedict, if not in quantity, at least in quality. These ideas of Basil were mostly transmitted to Benedict through the Rule of the Master.

47. This taxonomy is that given by Holmes, *A Life*, 110ff.

But it is also pretty certain that Basil was urging some form of separation for *all* Christians, and particularly for his flock in Caesarea. It must be remembered that this Rule was written at a time when the majority of the population in the Hellenistic world was still pagan. Although the Christians were strong and growing stronger, they still formed a minority. Far from being a situation of "Christendom," where ordinary life was somewhat penetrated by Christian ideals and customs, life in fourth-century Caesarea was much as it had always been. In that sense the first-century admonitions of Paul to the Corinthians still applied: "Do not be mismatched with unbelievers. For what partnership is there between righteousness and lawlessness? Or what fellowship is there between light and darkness? What agreement does Christ have with Beliar? Or what does a believer share with an unbeliever? What agreement has the temple of God with idols? For we are the temple of the living God; as God said: 'I will live in them, and walk among them, and I will be their God, and they shall be my people. Therefore come out from them, and be separate says the Lord" (2 Cor 6:14-17; cf. Rev 21).[48]

Certainly Basil could not have expected *all* the Christians of his province to separate themselves from the general population, at least not in a physical sense. In fact, he admits that this is not strictly necessary when he says: "to emend and correct oneself while continuing in the same habits and former way of life is very difficult, if I do not say entirely impossible."[49]

At any rate, the question here is not simply one of where to live. Rather, it has to do with the state of one's soul. In other words, no matter where you live, you take yourself with you. So the question is primarily one of spiritual health and maintenance: how to promote a lively awareness of God's presence and activity no matter where one lives. In Letter 2, written to Gregory of Nazianz from his hermitage at Annisa, Basil waxes eloquent on *hesychia* or quiet as the proper atmosphere for contemplation and claims that in order to achieve that condition one needs separation from the hubbub of ordinary life. But he is honest enough to admit that although he has gone apart, he has *not* in fact

48. Paul here quotes a pastiche of Old Testament passages, but probably the most relevant parallel for our theme is Rev 18:4: "Come out of her, my people, so that you do not take part in her sins."

49. Silvas, *Asketikon*, 179 n. 136, suggests that Basil has in fact modified the text of Rufinus (that is, his own first edition) at this point. Whereas Rufinus spoke about one's *own* formerly indifferent moral life, now Basil speaks, as bishop, of being surrounded by moral indifference.

achieved the interior peace he sought. "Since we carry around with us our innate passions, we are everywhere subject to the same disturbances. Therefore, we have not profited much from this solitude. This is what we should do and it would have enabled us to follow more closely in the footsteps of Him who showed the way to salvation."

This same note of healthy realism comes through in the first sentence of LR 6: "Retirement to a secluded and separate dwelling is of great assistance in keeping the soul from distraction." Note that withdrawal only *helps* promote recollection. True spiritual maturity is a far more difficult thing than merely separating oneself physically.

Still, problematic surroundings can be, and almost always *are*, a significant obstacle to Christian holiness. Basil is not willing to merely assert this; he offers two ways in which it is so. First, a mediocre moral environment encourages us to lower our own standards. Basil shrewdly remarks that it is very easy in such circumstances to look around and say: "Well, I guess I am not so bad!" This is particularly easy in the modern world, where sociology presents us with endless polls and surveys of how other people live. When we read such studies it is very easy to conclude that our own adherence to difficult Christian standards is no longer necessary.

Second, Basil returns to his master theme of the previous question, namely, the memory of God. Probably his deepest reason for urging Christian separation is the preservation of this continual awareness of God and his commandments. He says that it is very easy in the midst of the tumult of daily life to forget God and his judgments. The result of such forgetting, he says, will be a "loss of gladness and joy in God and delight in the Lord." But even worse, loss of the memory of God can eventually result in "disdain . . . of the judgments and . . . habitual contempt, and a greater or more ruinous misfortune than this it is not possible to suffer" (LR 6).

In discussing the same question of withdrawal as a means of maintaining our love for God, Basil also broaches another theme of great importance in the history of subsequent cenobitism. This is the matter of "self-will." Actually, this is another aspect of the same issue we talked about above, namely, that it is not merely a question of moving our bodies. Spiritual progress has to do with dealing with our own internal issues. Basil's statement is this: "But to deny oneself is to forget everything to do with one's former way of life and to withdraw from one's own will."

In this pregnant statement Basil actually deals with two rather different matters. Of course, separation from the world will necessarily involve the memory, for the world perdures in our memory. At least to some extent, to take on Christian values means to remove unchristian values from our hearts and minds That is a good kind of forgetting that must take place in all genuine conversion.

But the problem is more serious than that, for Basil also urges us to "withdraw from one's own will." On the surface of it this is a rather disturbing demand, for the abandonment of the will is precisely the sacrifice that all true cults ask of their members. In the literal sense someone who has put aside her will is no longer a moral agent, for the exercise of the will is of the essence of the moral and spiritual life. So we have to say that Basil cannot mean this in a totalitarian way.

To understand this theme in his writing, and it is widespread therein, we need to start with the Christian approach to the question. In fact, the gospels inform us that Christ himself came "not to do my own will, but the will of him who sent me."[50] This is, of course, a very solid basis for Christian behavior, but we have to remember that Jesus was not troubled with the selfishness the rest of us suffer due to the primal sin. Moreover, he did not have to discern whom to obey, or what to obey, for he knew his Father's will by intuition, as it were. So Jesus did not have to abandon self-will.

We might also note that self-will for the early monastic writers is very close to the primitive drives that are part of human life. For example, St. Benedict, who uses exactly the same language as Basil on this question (*propria voluntas* = self-will)[51] also speaks of "desires" (*voluptas*) in the same breath.[52] Granted, our desires and our will are often all mixed together. But there is still a big difference between the faculty called "the will" and our lower and unconscious drives. Christian life can hardly involve the abandonment of the will, since a strong will is necessary to pursue a moral and holy life in a hostile world. But "self-will," which many people no longer understand as a common English term, generally indicates *willfulness* or the need to jealously guard our autonomy

---

50. John 6:38, quoted in SR 1. The same point is made in LR 41.1. In SR 28, Basil says that the true fast is to abandon self-will, and in LR 28 he insists that to cling to self-will is to undermine our monastic life. My source for Basil's treatment of self-will is Lisa Cremaschi, *Basilio di Cesarea, Le Regole* ([Magnano] Qiqajon: Community of Bose, 1993), 97 n. 155.

51. E.g., RB Prol. 3 and 5.7.

52. RB 7.19: "Turn aside from your desires." The quotation is from Sirach 18:30, where it clearly refers to gross passions. For *voluptas* see RB 5.12.

at all costs. That frame of mind is quite incompatible with monastic obedience and humility.

Long Rule 7

When Basil comes to discuss the concrete aspects of love of neighbor he launches into a long treatise on the advantages of the common life. This passage is introduced by a very precise question: "whether it is better for one who has withdrawn from such society to live privately by himself or to live with brothers of the same mind, that is, who have chosen the same goal of piety." In his answer Basil makes it abundantly clear that he much prefers life together, and also that he fears and distrusts life apart from other people.

Basil makes this case with many arguments, some of which are better than others. First, we need each other for physical necessities. Second, the Gospel of Jesus is very clear in its demand that we care for others. Third, there can be no possibility of mutual correction without others who love us enough to tell us when we are straying from the right path. Fourth, if we are all members of the one body of Christ, how can we live scattered? Fifth, since each one receives a different gift of the Spirit, we need to live together to profit from all the gifts. Finally, in what is a different (and rather strange) form of number five, no one can fulfill all the commandments at once.

Even in its skeletal summary form this is obviously a massive argument for human and Christian community. Indeed, one of the Basilian experts from a century ago, W. Lowther Clarke, said of this chapter in the Long Rules: "This very remarkable passage shows that in Basil's view the community as a whole could alone fulfill the Christian ideal. Cenobitism rests in the last resort on this and on no economic or even spiritual advantages accruing to the individual from the presence of companions."[53] Because this question is so central to Basil's cenobitic enterprise, we need to explore it here at some depth. Since there is little question that this is indeed one of the most controversial and remarkable treatises ever written on the common life, we do well here to examine it closely.

---

53. W. Lowther Clarke, *St. Basil the Great, a Study in Monasticism* (Cambridge: Cambridge University Press, 1913), 164; quoted in Silvas, *Asketikon*, 183 n. 160.

Even if the treatise does seem a bit overwrought and perhaps even fanatical, there can be little doubt that Basil loved community. He also was convinced that it is at the heart of Christianity, and so it has to be a central monastic value. We recall that already in LR 2, Basil introduced an interesting element from Stoic anthropology, namely, the *logos spermatikos*. The claim there was that each of us has a divine seed within, drawing us toward God and also toward our neighbor. In other words, we are programmed, as it were, for community. But when he comes to discuss community as such, Basil is able to draw on some of the most important passages in the whole New Testament. Probably the keystone of his argument rests on a famous text from 1 Corinthians:

> Furthermore, no one is sufficient of himself to receive all the spiritual charisms (of the Holy Spirit). Instead, the supply of the Spirit is given *according to the proportion of each one's faith* (Rom 12:6), such that, in the communion of life the individual charism becomes the common possession of *fellow citizens. For to one is given the word of wisdom, to another the word of knowledge, to another faith, to another prophecy, to another the gift of healings* (1 Cor 12:8) and so on. Each of these the recipient has from the Holy Spirit not so much for himself as for others. Therefore in community life the activity of the Holy Spirit of God in one passes over to all alike (is brought forth in common). Thus one who lives by himself (and separated) may perhaps have one charism, yet this very charism he renders useless by his idleness, having buried it in himself. (LR 7.13-17)

The argument here is one that is hard to gainsay. Any experience of life teaches us that there are all kinds of people, and most of them are not like us. In theological terms, we all have special gifts. These gifts are not just natural endowments but instead are gifts of the Holy Spirit. Since Basil is widely recognized as one of the intellectual and theological architects of the doctrine of the divinity of the Holy Spirit, which was first proclaimed at the Council of Constantinople in 381 (shortly after his death), we do well to take seriously his arguments for community based on this teaching.

This approach to community life seems to be a very good way to keep the question in a positive light. Those of us who live in monastic community, cheek by jowl with other people day after day, sometimes find it a discouraging experience. The very differences that Basil here extols can sometimes seem almost impossible to cope with. As Jean Paul Sartre famously said, "Hell? That's other people!" But as someone else said, in regard to his wife, "Vive la différence!" In other words, he did not know *what* she was going to do next, and that is what made her so interesting. This same point of view can help us to maintain a healthy sense of humor in the midst of communal foibles. Rather than seeing the differences of other people as constant irritations, we can, with the grace of God, see them as delightful quirks.

But these remarks should not detract from the serious nature of this point of Christian theology. The Bible claims that the Holy Spirit, in whom are contained all the riches of wisdom and creativity and burgeoning life, has been given to each of us—but only partially. We have received the whole Spirit as the essential life of God for salvation, but we have still only received a few facets of the whole Spirit. Therefore, each of us is partial and limited. In order to be complete, we need other people. That is, we need the fullness of the Spirit as embodied in that very different person, our neighbor. LR 7 is laced (four times) with references to the Holy Spirit by the greatest theologian of the Holy Spirit.

Another key to this question lies in the theme of mutual correction. This is not an entirely pleasant discussion because no one likes to be corrected. But Basil recognizes that it is absolutely essential to Christian growth and also to healthy community life: "The individual does not easily recognize his own faults and vices in his withdrawal, for he has no one to reprove him and set him right with gentleness and compassion. Although rebuke even from an enemy often induces in the well-disposed a desire to be cured, nevertheless, the cure of sin is carried out adeptly by one who has sincerely loved, for *he who loves*, it says, *is diligent in discipline* (Prov 13:24)."

This rather remarkable passage calls to mind the remark of a modern monastic commentator on St. Benedict's chapters on correction (RB 23–30; 43–46). He noted that we do not correct each other enough because we do not love each other enough.[54] He went on to explain that the correction of another person demands a considerable commitment. For one thing, we lay ourselves open to rejection. But even when our criticism is well received, it often entails further involvement and that can disturb our privacy. Of course, correction is never easy to take, so Basil insists that it be "gentle and compassionate." Too often correction is given in a fit of pique or rage. Needless to say, this kind of correction is almost impossible to stomach. At any rate, where people do not

---

54. Fr. Ambrose Wathen, OSB, speaking at a symposium on monastic penalties held at Benet Lake, Wisconsin, in the 1970s.

know how to give or take correction, there really can be no effective community life.

As with many of Basil's answers to questions in the *Great Asketikon*, this one is studded with biblical citations. It is not hard for Basil to find good scriptural corroboration for the importance of community, since this is one of the main emphases of the Bible, and especially the New Testament. Indeed, he would have had a much harder time finding good biblical warrants for the solitary life, for that is not something envisaged by Jesus or the biblical writers. Of course, some of the texts he adduces are more important than others. Probably the most influential passages for subsequent Christian community life occur at the very end of the treatise. "This is the dwelling together of brothers in unity among themselves (Ps 132:1). Its goal is the glory of God . . . and it preserves the character (and example) of what was reported of the saints in the Acts of the Apostles, of whom it is written: *All the believers were of one mind and held all things in common* (Acts 2:44) and again: *And the multitude of believers were of one heart and soul; and not one of them said that anything he possessed was his own; but they held all things in common* (Acts 4:32)."

This is one of the best-known texts of the Bible, and it makes an important claim. According to Luke, in response to the Lord's resurrection from the dead the first Christians spontaneously banded together in an intensely communal life. Although this probably did not involve communal property,[55] it certainly meant some kind of shared existence. Above all, the animating spirit of the first Christians was fraternal love, and this is an ideal that has haunted the church ever since. Certainly the early monastic founders and Rules and texts consider these passages as precious heirlooms to be treasured. They also thought of themselves as the continuators of the first Jerusalem community.[56]

After dwelling on the positive aspects of this issue, we might ask some other questions. Doesn't this passage call into question Basil's

---

55. See the comments of Richard Dillon on Acts 4:32-35 in the *New Jerome Biblical Commentary* (Englewood Cliffs, NJ: Prentiss Hall, 1990).

56. Here is the note on RB Prol 50 in *Rule of St. Benedict 1980*, ed. Timothy Fry (Collegeville, MN: Liturgical Press, 1981), 167: "References to these texts from Acts describing the life of the Jerusalem community abound in early monastic literature, for monastic authors saw in the practices of the Jerusalem community a justification for the practices of cenobitic monasticism." See Adalbert de Vogüé, "Monasticism and the Church in the Writings of Cassian," *Monastic Studies* 3 (1965): 19–51.

own experience? After all, his first monastic experience was precisely the solitary existence he so roundly criticizes here. After his university education he first visited the monks of Syria and Egypt and then spent several years in the hermitage of his deceased brother Naucratius in the wilds of the family estate in Pontus. Is Basil repudiating this experience in this question? Although he does not refer to himself, it is hard to avoid the probability that he does not look back on that time as a very helpful one for him.[57] It can also be pointed out that other cenobitic founders felt the same way. Both Pachomius and Augustine began their monastic careers as solitaries, but they turned to community as a better way for them.[58]

On the other hand, some cenobitic founders thought of the eremitic life as a kind of flowering of the common life. Thus Benedict remarks in RB 1.4-5: "Community support has taught them how to battle the devil, and this excellent training in the fraternal battle-line enables them to venture out to the single combat of the desert." Here Benedict seems to present cenobitic life as a preliminary training ground for the hermit. Since Benedict himself started out as a hermit, but moved to the common life, this could also be an attempt to correct his own past.[59] In fact, Basil makes a similar comment in LR 7: "(A correcting brother) is difficult to find in solitude, unless one was already united to him in one's earlier way of life." But this is a very slender concession to anchoritism in a chapter that has little else good to say about it.

But we still have to make the strongest criticism of the chapter, namely, that it flies in the face of the history of the Eastern church. A cursory reading of that history shows that many of the first monks were hermits, and that this type of monastic life was always very highly valued by the whole Eastern church. For various reasons the solitary monastic

57. Although LR 7, written when Basil was a bishop, adds quite a bit to RBas 3 (Rufinus's text, written about 365), it is substantially the same thesis. This means that Basil was already convinced of the necessity of monastic (and Christian) community soon after his first, abortive experience in the hermitage.

58. Holmes, *A Life*, 144, gives the following references: Pachomius extols the common life and warns of the dangers of solitude in *Bohairic Life* 35 and 105 (see *Pachomian Koinonia I*, trans. Armand Veilleux [Kalamazoo: Cistercian Publications, 1982]). As for Augustine, a top commentator says of him, "He was rarely alone" (George Lawless, *Augustine of Hippo and his Monastic Rule* [Oxford: Oxford University Press, 1990], 30).

59. See the early chapters of Gregory the Great's *Dialogue II*, or *The Life of St. Benedict*.

life was not easy to maintain in many periods, but it has perdured down to the present. Therefore it does seem that Basil is fundamentally out of the mainstream on this point. What could have caused this?

One scholar who has ventured an answer was Jean Gribomont, who suggested that Basil's criticism of anchoritism was really not aimed at the hermits of Syria and Egypt but at someone else.[60] He did not believe that Basil ever visited those heroic monks, even on his alleged *Wanderjahr* before he himself took up the solitary life.[61] Gribomont thinks that LR 7 is really addressed to the ascetics of Pontus—in other words, the same people in the background of the rest of the *Great Asketikon*. Basil's great concern was to keep those radical ascetics from separating themselves from the mainstream of the church. In his view such folk would only exaggerate their schismatic tendencies if they lived alone. What they needed was the regular support and criticism of Christian community.

Finally, not all of Basil's readers have taken him literally on this point. For example, his (sometimes) close collaborator, Gregory of Nazianz, claims that Basil actually was able to integrate the best elements of both monastic traditions into his own Rule and practice. From the solitaries he learned *hesychia* (contemplation), but avoided pride; from the communards he learned service, but avoided turbulence.[62] That may be so, but we can also note that Gregory himself was a natural solitary who did not find the rough and tumble of community life very appealing. Basil was the opposite. Hence Gregory would downplay this aspect of Basil's teaching.

Nonetheless, even though it is necessary to tone down some of the excessive exuberance of LR 7, it still stands as one of my favorite monastic texts. Where else can we find this kind of enthusiasm for the communal life? When one has read a good range of what has been written about Christian monasticism over the ages one becomes aware that the anchorites have had most of the best writers. Who can match

60. See his article, "Basilio," in *Dizionario degli Istituti di Perfezione,* 1.1107 (no. 17, "cenobitismo").

61. For example, in Letter 2, written to Gregory Nazianz shortly after his return from his supposed study tour of Eastern monasticism, Basil has little or nothing specific to say about the hermits of the East and of Egypt. The solitude he extols in this early letter is simply a mental construct based on Greek ideals of philosophical leisure.

62. Gregory, Funeral Oration for Basil, *Funeral Orationes* (FC 22), 62. See the good discussion in Holmes, *A Life,* 156–58.

what Evagrius and Cassian have to say about the solitary life? And what was Thomas Merton if not an apologist for anchoritism? It could be that hermits just have more time for the hard, solitary task of writing. Whatever the case, Basil's Long Rule 7 goes far to offset the imbalance in monastic reporting.

Chapter
Three

The Rule of Basil: II
(Themes from Long Rules 8–55)

In this chapter we will change our approach to Basil's Long Rules. In order to meet the requirements of this study and also to avoid repetition, we will not follow the consecutive method we used with LR 1–7. Now we will lift up certain characteristic and important themes for examination. This will mean that we cover more ground less thoroughly, but it is not possible here to comment on all the Rules.

Renunciation and Self-Control: LR 8–23

The Scope of Renunciation (*Apotaxia*)

After seven chapters that discuss love of God and neighbor under the aspects of withdrawal and community, we now come to a whole block of chapters dealing rather exclusively with the first theme, namely, the renunciation necessary to purify and consolidate our love for God. Before discussing any of the specifics of renunciation, Basil makes a blanket statement showing how he understands ascesis:

> Since our Lord Jesus Christ, after much demonstration, confirmed by many deeds, says to all: *If anyone comes to me, let him deny himself and take up his cross and follow me* (Matt 16:24), and again, *Whoever does not renounce all that he possesses, cannot be my disciple* (Luke 14:33), we consider that this summons involves a necessary estrangement from many things. For indeed, before all else we renounce the devil and the cravings of the flesh—we who have rejected the hidden

45

things of shame—and bodily relationships and human friendships and any manner of life at war with the strict way of the Gospel of salvation. And, what is still more necessary, one who has *put off the old man with his works* (Col 3:9) *which is being corrupted by illusory desires* (Eph 4:22), renounces his own self. And he also renounces all those *cares of the world* (1 Cor 7:33) that can hinder the goal of piety. (LR 8)[1]

From this long, rather prolix and confusing quotation we can at least see that Basil does not have a simplistic or materialistic notion of Christian renunciation. He sees that the physical act of withdrawal from ordinary life is not an automatic solution to spiritual problems. The reason is that the difficulties we flee are multiple and complex.

Of course, there is the obvious enemy one wants to put behind, namely, Satan with all his pomps and works. And then there are those disordered human desires that can run unchecked in regular society, and especially a licentious society such as the one in which Basil lived (and we live!). Presumably life in a disciplined Christian commune will offer considerable help to anyone wishing to overcome this kind of problem.

But Basil is far too sophisticated to think it is adequate to avoid blatant evil and dissipation. He knows that the effects of sin in us take far subtler forms that need to be rooted out by long years of devotion and discipline. Some of these obstacles are quite legitimate in themselves, but they still form a barrier to spiritual advancement. Thus family or riches could stand between some people and the kingdom of God. Basil includes them under the phrase "all worldly affections."[2]

But there is a level of renunciation that is still beyond all this. After one has repudiated crass evil and immorality, and when one has even relativized the things the world holds dear, such as wealth, power, and family, it is still by no means certain that one has dealt with the most difficult obstacle that prevents God from working fully in our hearts. That last barrier is simply self. We have already discussed this problem under the title "self-will." Here it is enough to note that Basil is always

---

1. Translations of biblical texts within quotations from the original sources are the author's.

2. The Greek term is *prospatheia*, which was Stoic language for inordinate attachments that fuel passion (*pathai*). Basil uses this term for attachment to relatives (LR 34; SR 190), riches (SR), and even life itself (LR 6.1; SR 234). See Lisa Cremaschi, *Basilio di Cesarea: Le Regole* ([Magnano] Qiqajon: Community of Bose, 1993), 108 n. 208.

aware that its eradication is the ultimate object of all Christian asceticism. This seems to be an obvious point, but too many monks and nuns have been deluded into thinking that their formal asceticism is a sure sign of spiritual success. In fact, monstrous pride can rage beneath the humblest exterior.

A Key Text: Matthew 16:24

In the text of LR 8 that we are studying, we note that Basil uses Matthew 16:24 to make his point: *If anyone wishes to come to me, let him deny himself, take up his cross and follow me.* With this passage of the Gospel, Basil links renunciation directly with the following of Christ. Jean Gribomont notes that this is one of Basil's fundamental texts. A glance at the biblical concordance of the *Asketikon* shows that he employs the passage no fewer than seven times, always to make the same point.[3]

We might wonder, though, how appropriate Matthew 16:24 is for the renunciation Basil is talking about. Surely Matthew is addressing every Christian. Is Basil asking *all* Christians to withdraw from society into protective sectarian enclaves? Probably not, but he certainly does think that these radical gospel texts apply to all Christians. We have seen that Basil's own background was in the ascetical communes. We have also noted that one of his concerns was to help these radical groups to remain firmly rooted in the church. But the other side of the coin is that Basil is also intent to apply the radical Christian ideals, based on texts such as Matthew 16:24, to the church. In a sense, then, he wants to make the whole church into a monastery.

Flight from the World

In discussing Basil's teaching on renunciation it is customary to resort to the shorthand that one must renounce the "world" in order to please God. Thus we read: *"all those cares of the world* (1 Cor 7:33) that can hinder the goal of piety." But what does "world" mean here? Another term that functions similarly is "those outside" (*exothen*). This is the term he uses when he talks about "profane" jeering as the reason to withdraw from the "world." In fact, Basil uses these terms somewhat

---

3. LR 8.1; SR 2; 234; 237, etc. See Gribomont, "Suivre le Christ dans les Écrits ascétiques de Saint Basile," in idem, *Saint Basile, Évangile et Église, Mélanges*, 2 vols. (Bégrolles-en-Mauges [Maine-&-Loire]: Abbaye de Bellefontaine, 1984), 413–25.

loosely and his use of them evolves over time. At first he sometimes contrasts the world with the church. Later, though, he at times contrasts the world with the monastery, or at least the sectarian commune.[4]

But Basil does not use the term *kosmos* (world) too often in a negative sense, and that for at least two reasons: First, he is not primarily a pessimistic thinker. Any writer who uses "world" in a negative sense, such as the author of the Gospel of John, has to be classified as a pessimistic thinker or at least one with no tendencies toward humanism. The second reason, though, goes right back to our regular benchmark regarding Basil: What did the Eustathians need to hear? They were the primary audience of the *Great Asketikon*. Presumably the great need was not so much to get them to withdraw from the world as to keep them from going right on into a kind of Manichean disdain for the world. And that was not something Basil could abide.

The Evolution of Vocabulary

A word like *anachoresis* (withdrawal, LR 5), which later became a technical term to refer to all monasticism, is still used by Basil in the common Greek sense of any retreat. We have to remember that with Basil we are dealing with the earliest beginnings of monasticism, at least in Anatolia (Turkey). The fact that terms are still quite vague in his writing shows that the monastic institution is yet in its infancy.

Another word he does not use in a technical sense is *monachos*. It is astonishing that he never uses the word in his vast *Great Asketikon* at all! He uses the ordinary Greek word *monastikon* to mean "alone," but without any technical intent. When he wants to refer to the members of the ascetical communes he calls them Christians, brothers, or ascetics. The point is that they *had* no technical title at that point.[5] We will return to this matter in later discussions.

We might also mention that the evolution of vocabulary likewise goes on *within* the writings of Basil. Thus a certain word will start out with a general meaning, but as time goes on and the institution crystallizes, so does the term. In order to get a clear idea of these matters it is necessary to know when Basil wrote such and such a document, or such and such a question. Even within the *Asketikon* it is quite certain

---

4. See Gribomont, "Le renoncement au monde dans l'idéal ascétique de Saint Basile," ibid., 275.

5. Cremaschi, *Basilio di Cesarea*, 85 n. 101. See also Gribomont, "Obéissance et évangile selon Saint Basile le Grand," *Saint Basile, Évangile et Église*, 2, 275.

that some parts of the material are very early and some much later—
perhaps twenty years later.

Self-Control (*Engkrateia*): LR 16

After discussing various external aspects of "leaving the world," Basil
concentrates on the internal dimension. Hard as it may be to forsake
ordinary society, it is a fairly simple operation compared to escaping from
those internal forces that cause us to try to turn everything to our own
advantage. Of course, we need to appropriate certain elements such as
food in order to live, and we need to have a sexual partner if we are to
continue the species. But the problem is that these natural desires, plus
others, are hard to control. In LR 16, Basil puts the matter thus:

> In summary, then: abstinence from all that those who live according to
> passion crave to enjoy, this is the abstinence necessary for those training
> themselves to piety. Consequently, training in continency[6] is accom-
> plished not only with regard to the pleasure of food, but also extends to
> abstinence from everything that harms us, by which we may be gratified
> but also wounded in soul. Accordingly, one who is truly self-controlled
> will not both master his stomach and be worsted by human ambition;
> he will not overcome the craving for what is shameful, and at the same
> time not also of wealth or of any other unworthy disposition, whether
> it be anger or despondency or any of the things by which undisciplined
> souls are apt to be enslaved.

When we read this passage closely we might be surprised that Basil
evidently uses "continency" to mean a careful avoidance of gluttony,
whereas we normally refer it to sexuality. But Basil's interest in asceticism is much broader than that. In fact, this whole question and answer
is about *engkrateia*, an extremely touchy subject in early Christianity. In
some sections of the church such as Syria, *engkrateia* certainly referred
to an avoidance of all sexual activity, even in marriage. Indeed, some
scholars think that at one period those who came forward for baptism
in Syria had to give up marriage.[7] It is not hard to imagine the repercus-
sions of such a theology for the church and for all of society.

---

6. In Anna Silvas's translation, which we are following, the word used is "self-
control," but for our discussion here we use the translation "continency."

7. See Gabriele Winkler, "The Origins and Idiosyncrasies of the Earliest Form
of Asceticism," in *The Continuing Quest for God*, ed. William Skudlarek, 9–43
(Collegeville, MN: Liturgical Press, 1982).

Obviously, such thinking could pose a great threat to ordinary society. In fact, after the Peace of Constantine (313 AD) there were bishops who were determined to eliminate radical encratite thinking and behavior from the church. At all costs, the government must be reassured that this kind of subversive thinking was not part of respectable Christianity. And so at the Council of Gangres, the bishops of Paphlagonia condemned the Eustathians for abandoning their marriages and procreation.[8]

But apart from political considerations, there was an even more serious theological one. It was one thing for early ascetics to advocate *engkrateia* as a way to keep the physical passions under control. But sometimes this fear of the physical slipped over the line into hatred of the material world. Then we have full-blown metaphysical dualism, which was typical of early Gnosticism and was the most serious problem faced by the church up to the time of Basil.[9]

Confronted with danger from both sides, what did Basil do? He adopted the Stoic view of *engkrateia*, which emphasizes that *all* the senses need to be controlled, and not just the libido. This balanced approach enables Basil to avoid discussing chastity throughout most of the *Asketikon*, apparently because his Eustathian audience was all too prone to undervalue marriage.

Marriage

Nevertheless, it would not be accurate to conclude that Basil agreed with the bishops of Gangres in their fear and loathing of ascetic celibacy. By no means! In fact, he clearly did *not* agree with their attitude that marriage and family were to be preserved at all costs. For Basil it was quite all right for spouses to put aside marriage to enter ascetic communities. Thus LR 12 explicitly agrees to accept married persons who wish to join the commune. If the other spouse does not agree to the separation it will have to be delayed, but one should pray and fast until the other is convinced.

All this sounds like St. Paul and the famous Pauline Privilege, and indeed that is its obvious source.[10] It should also be added that in

---

8. See Gribomont, *Saint Basile, Évangile et Église*, I:26–41; see also idem, "Le monachisme au sein de l'église en Syria et en Cappadoce," ibid., I:3–20.

9. Of course, Arianism ran a close second, but it was primarily a controversy among bishops and theologians. Encratism was a behavioral problem and more widespread among the most fervent and devout elements of the early church.

10. 1 Corinthians 7:15-16. The term "Pauline Privilege" is not biblical, but rather used by Catholic canonists to refer to the right of converts to Catholicism to separate from a spouse who refuses to turn Catholic.

Cappadocia it was not unusual for whole families to enter religious conventicles. The *Great Asketikon* assumes this in many places. But if Basil is not in agreement with the political bishops, neither is he unaware of the dangers of the other extreme. There is a reference to that in LR 18:

> Q. 18: Should we taste everything set before us?
>
> A. Nevertheless, it needs to be laid down clearly from the outset that, if there is to be that *rigorous treatment* of the body (see 1 Cor 9:27), continency is indispensable for all contestants for piety, *for every contestant is self-controlled in all things* (1 Cor 9:25). But in order to avoid falling in with the enemies of God who *are seared in their conscience* and thereby refrain from foods *which God created to be partaken of by the faithful with thanksgiving* (1 Tim 4:2-3), we should taste each food as the occasion presents itself, to show observers that *to the pure all things are pure* (Titus 1:15) and that *everything created by God is good and nothing is to be rejected if it is received with thanksgiving; for it is hallowed by the word of God and prayer.* (1 Tim 4:4)

Here again the subject is food, not sex, but the stakes are still quite high. The apparently trivial question of whether we should eat everything set before us suddenly turns into a highly charged discussion of the goodness of all things. The "enemies of God" in the middle of the quotation are almost certainly those who claim that certain aspects of the material world are evil.[11]

The modern reader might be bewildered that Basil could turn such a banal question into a metaphysical declaration that "every creature of God is good." But that was indeed the issue: Is the material world good or is it not? The dualist mentality tends to call the spiritual "good" and the physical "bad." At its worst, encratism condemned marriage simply because it would increase the number of physical bodies in the world. Even though Basil did come down firmly on the side of the goodness of creation, I suspect that he did not find it easy to do so. Though he was philosophically and theologically committed to the orthodox position, there is a streak of asceticism in him that verges on the radical. Like many of the early saints, he is reputed to have ruined his health with unwise fasting. He died at the age of 49.

---

11. See Cremaschi, *Basilio di Cesarea*, 137 n. 349. In Letter 199, Basil calls such people the "offspring of the Marcionites."

Community Life: LR 24–55

Good Order (*Eutaxia*): LR 24–36

In his outline of the Long Rules, Adalbert de Vogüé classifies questions 24–55 under the rubric of "good order."[12] To illustrate this topic I would like to quote an earlier passage from LR 21, which is really on the same subject:

> Q. 21: How ought one conduct oneself with regard to sitting and reclining at the midday meal or at supper?
>
> A. Since we have a command from the Lord who in every place accustoms us to humility (by which he declares) that when we recline at dinner, we should seek *the lowest place* (and not take the higher place) (Luke 14:8-10), whoever strives to do all according to the commandment must not overlook this command. . . . (We should realize that), when those who all have the same (purpose and) goal have come together, especially among the many or the great, in order to give proof of their own humility each ought to choose the lower place, in accordance with the command of the Lord. On the other hand, to jostle each other aside contentiously for this (even though from a lower place), is unacceptable as destructive of good order and a cause of turbulence (and disquiet). Indeed, to be unwilling to yield to one another and (to be stirred) to fight over it, makes us as bad as those fighting over the first seats. Therefore if we carefully consider in this matter what is fitting (for each of us) we ought assuredly leave it to him who has the responsibility for arranging the order of reclining. (And we should also keep order and comply with him in other matters as well as seating at meals), as the Lord instructed when he said that the ordering of these matters belongs to the *master of the house* (Luke 14:10).

Though this is not our main interest in the passage, we should note that it is important not to allow its pious verbiage to blind us to its intrinsic silliness. The ascetics are perplexed: how can each one take the last place? This causes fights, battles over who will be the most humble. With a completely straight face, Basil warns them that this will not do; the only solution is to take the place assigned by the community—even if it is the first place.

At any rate, here as in many passages Basil is concerned about *eutaxia*, that is, good order. Over and over he will invoke this concept when

---

12. "The Great Rules of St. Basil: A Survey," *Word and Spirit* 1 (1979): 49–85.

dealing with the fervent ascetic communities he is addressing. Probably we can say that common sense and good order were not among their strengths. As a matter of fact, the subject of "order" is also not particularly prominent in the gospels. Since when is cutting your right hand off or gouging out your eye "good order" (Matt 5:29-30)?

But we can also appreciate Basil's position. As an aristocrat he would have a natural sense for the good order of society. After all, the aristocracy did think they had a responsibility for maintaining the common good. And as a bishop, Basil certainly had to look out for the reputation of the church. He knew that it would not be for the good of the church if the practices of the ascetic communities caused public scandal.

Yet we should also note that a concern for good order can sometimes be a mere cover for injustice. In this regard we find Basil more or less condoning slavery in LR 11. By and large he does not want runaway slaves received into the monastic communities except when the master has been unusually cruel. Of course, St. Paul says essentially the same thing, but with an aristocrat like Basil it makes one suspicious. In those times and places slaves were an integral part of the power of the rich.[13]

The Superior: Eye of the Community

In the previous section we saw that Basil solved social problems in the communities by invoking authority: the members should not take the last place, but the place assigned to them "by the one who has the responsibility." This is in fact a rather offhanded and casual way of referring to the superior. Of course, the question of authority must be dealt with in any human community, and that includes religious communities. Here is a famous quotation from LR 24, where Basil discusses the matter at some length:

> Since the Apostle says: *Let all things be done decently and in order* (1 Cor 14:40), we consider that when believers are joined together there will be a decent and well-ordered way of life in which the principle of the

13. According to Cremaschi, *Basilio di Cesarea*, 120 n. 270, Cappadocia was notorious slave country. Basil did criticize the bishops of Gangra, who also forbade slaves to flee to religious communities (see Gribomont, *Saint Basile, Évangile et Église*, 1, 23). But his own record was not completely clean, since he sent slaves back to his friend Philagrius Arcenus (Letter 323). His brother, Gregory of Nyssa, condemned slavery in his *Commentary on Ecclesiastes* IV (PG 44.664B–666A).

members of the body is observed (see 1 Cor 12:27). Thus, the one who has the function of the eye, so to speak, is entrusted with the common supervision, both in approving what has been done and in providing for and keeping an eye on what is yet to be done; while another has the function of the ear or hand in hearing or giving effect to what is necessary—and so on for each member.

It is interesting to see that Basil does not use traditional vocabulary for the religious superior; he does not call him abbot or prior or hegumen. Yet we should recall that in his time there was *no* tradition, for he was breaking new ground. His term for the superior, the "eye of the community," did not become the term used by subsequent generations. Still, it is a noble image and one worth examining. Certainly the notion is eminently biblical. No doubt Basil is basing his thought on 1 Corinthians 12:14-26, where Paul talks about the church in terms of a living body, an animal organism. Though Basil does not emphasize it here, we should remember that Paul's point was that *all* parts have a vital function, not just the eye.[14] For Basil, the eye has a special function; it must guide the rest of the body, for it sees the way forward. Clearly, vision is of capital importance for the body that needs to move about, and that includes a community. "Where vision is lacking, the people perish" (Prov 29:18).[15] Notice, too, that the eye is primarily focused outward, not inward. Its role is to discern what is out there and to transmit this necessary information to the rest of the body.

When we translate this physical metaphor into Basilian terms for the religious community, we should recall that what the body needs to see above all is the will of God. It is incumbent on all the members to seek that will, but it is the special role of the superior to be the one with the sharpest eye for what God wants. For Basil this means a deep knowledge of Scripture, which we will discuss below.

When we have said all this, we still might wonder how Basil wants authority to be exercised in his community. Overall, it has to be said that his superior keeps a rather low profile. The very term "eye" suggests this.

14. The term "eye" was a regular metaphor for church leaders in early Christianity. Thus Origen: "You who preside in the church are the eye, and if you have this function, it is because you see all around you, you examine all and foresee all that could happen." See Cremaschi, *Basilio di Cesarea*, 152 n. 427.

15. The meaning of the original text is not quite the same as the one we are discussing here. For the author of Proverbs, vision was synonymous with revelation and authority; at least that is the way some of the translations have it.

Basil uses other equally unpretentious terms for the superior, terms that are sometimes so unassuming that we all but miss them. For example, the first time definite personal authority appears in the *Great Asketikon* occurs in LR 15. Here the superior is simply called "he/she who presides." The Greek term is *proestos*, which is a mere participle. And this is typical of Basil: most of his references to the superior are rather offhanded.[16]

Yet these low profile references may not even represent the earliest Basilian form of authority. In some of the questions, seekers for the will of God are not referred to the superior at all, but directly to the Bible for guidance (SR 1). Elsewhere they are bidden to obey the authority of everyone who is in accordance with the Bible (SR 114). These texts seem to come from a time when the communities did not yet have superiors. They worked things out for themselves by searching Scripture and by listening to each other. But there came a time when it became necessary to rely on those with a clearer eye, that is, on those with a gift for leadership. Finally, we can say that Basil's superior never arrives at the high profile held by Benedict's abbot.[17]

Superior as Shepherd and Doctor

Under this heading we will discuss some of the duties of the superior. There is no doubt that Basil sees the superior primarily as a spiritual guide for the individual members of the community. For example, LR 26 exhorts the members to reveal the secrets of their hearts to the superior, a procedure that should be understood in a pastoral sense and not in a legalistic way. Indeed, the members must accept the pastoral ministration of the superior (LR 31.46). Otherwise, how can they expect to be cared for? But the superior has another role as well:

> Q 28: What should be our approach towards a disobedient member?
>
> A. To one showing reluctance in obeying the commandments of the Lord, we first of all show sympathy as to a diseased member of the body, while the one who presides should endeavor to cure his ailment through private admonitions. But if he persists in disobedience and will not accept

---

16. Other Basilian terms for the superior are *pepisteumenos* (SR 87; 132; 141; 173); *pisteutheis* (SR 148; 153); *epitetagmenos* (SR 100; 135; 142; 145); *encheinzomenos* (SR 152). See Cremaschi, *Basilio di Cesarea*, 152 n. 428.

17. The abbot is discussed in Benedict's Rule, chap. 2. This is based on the same early positioning in the Rule of the Master (chap. 2). But Benedict also adds another chapter (64) on the abbot, which balances off the sternness of RB 2 with a gentler, more pastoral picture.

correction, then he must rebuke him sharply before all the community and apply remedies to him with every manner of appeal. But if after much warning he remains unmoved and takes no measures to remedy his conduct, he is *like one who destroys his own self*, as the saying puts it (see Prov 18:9). Then, with many tears and lamentations, but resolutely nonetheless, we must cut him away from the body as a corrupted and wholly useless member, following the example of doctors . . .

In this passage we see how quickly Basil moves from the responsibility of all the members to that of the superior. As soon as things become really difficult he turns toward the superior and demands special measures be taken. It is simply a fact of experience that a community as a whole, or even a committee, is not well placed to deal with disciplinary problems, or at least to deal with them in a pastoral manner.

Following the procedures required by Matthew 18:15-18, the superior should begin with private admonition. If this does not succeed in producing amendment, the person should be brought before the entire community. If even this is not sufficient, the final step of expulsion should be used.[18] This is probably the most distasteful task a superior could undertake, but the hard facts of life dictate that a community in that situation needs protection. Long Rules 25 warns the superior that failure to correct will result in the dreadful judgment of God.

On the other hand, Basil is aware that superiors themselves are not perfect. For one thing, they must be very careful how they correct others; obviously, harsh or vindictive corrections are counterproductive and not at all pastoral (LR 50). Further, Basil is realistic enough to see that superiors themselves sometimes need correction. When that happens, he wants this done by "eminent brethren."[19] Yet he knows that some persons are prone to criticize superiors, and he will not tolerate that either. Long Rules 48 warns people to use the right channels and to give the superior the benefit of the doubt.[20]

---

18. In fact, Matt 18:15-18 is used by Basil in many texts of the *Great Asketikon* (LR 36; SR 3; 47; 232; 293). SR adds internal excommunication (*aponismos*). Basil speaks of expulsion more than once: LR 47; SR 44; 57; 102; 281. See Cremaschi, *Basilio di Cesarea*, 158 n. 449.

19. A council of advisers is mentioned many times in the *Great Asketikon*: LR 27; 35.2; 45; 49; SR 104; 119. See Cremaschi, *Basilio di Cesarea*, 201 n. 650.

20. For a general study of authority and obedience in the *Great Asketikon* of Basil, see Joel Rippinger, "The Concept of Obedience in the Monastic Writings of Basil and Cassian," *Studia Monastica* 19 (1977): 7–18.

Work and Prayer: LR 37

In the last chapters of the Long Rules, work assumes a central place. This is not surprising, since work, or its lack, was one of the points of contention in the church of Cappadocia. More specifically, fervent ascetic communities sometimes interpreted the biblical command "pray always" (1 Thess 5:17) in literal fashion. For them this ruled out all work since one cannot do both at once. Basil, however, realized that this kind of thinking is not only simplistic but also potentially very harmful to society. So he devotes the whole of a long question (37) to this topic:

> Q. 37: Should we neglect work on a pretext of the prayers and the psalmody; and what times are suitable for prayer—but first, is it necessary to work?

> A. Our Lord Jesus Christ says: *Worthy of his food is* not just any and every one, but the *laborer* (Matt 10:10) and the Apostle commands us to *labor and do honorable work with our hands that we may have something to give to those in need* (Eph 4:28). So it is clear from this that one must work, and work diligently. For we must not reckon the goal of piety an excuse for idleness or a means of avoiding toil, but as a prospect of training, of even greater toils and of patience in tribulations. . . . For this way of life is good for us not only because of the rigorous treatment of the body, but also because of love for our neighbor, so that through us God may provide sufficiently for the weak among the brothers.

Of course, Basil's answer is already foreseen in the question, which implies that prayer does not rule out work. "Pretext for neglecting our work" is loaded language, and we can imagine that it was not really a question addressed to Basil, but one concocted by himself. It is simply a lead-in to a lecture to his audience that they probably did not want to hear.

We see in the answer that Basil thinks work is important for at least two reasons: it produces results, whether income or other products, that enable us to care for the needy. We should mention here that Basil's hostel in Caesarea was run by religious, who were certainly working for the poor in this way. In other questions Basil always implies that religious should work for a living, not beg. But these considerations may not have touched some of his audience, since it seems that at least some of the Eustathians were wealthy people who did not really have to work at all. That certainly was the case with Basil's own family, who lived in pious seclusion on the family estate on the River Iris in Pontus.

So he needs another reason why monks should work. The second reason why he thinks work essential for everyone is that it provides the "rigorous treatment of the body." Here the result of work is not its external products, but its benefit for the worker. Furthermore, he thinks work can focus the mind so as to promote recollection and make prayer easier.[21] Yet even if Basil is optimistic about mixing work and prayer, we should add immediately that he knows that not all work is conducive to prayer. Long Rule 38 discusses the question of what kind of work is suitable to monastic profession. This question is not exclusively devoted to prayer, but once again recollection (*ameteoriston*) turns up as a criterion: our work should be of such a kind as to allow us to focus on God.[22]

At this point we may refer to a theme we discussed earlier in these pages, namely, "remembrance of God."[23] We saw that Basil emphasizes this approach to prayer, rather than brooding introspection or any system of interior prayer that rules out other activity. In fact, Basil never discusses what we might call contemplative prayer at all in the *Asketikon*. Actually, Basil's whole approach to prayer seems rather simplistic. Is the world a distraction? Then leave it! Live with others and pray together with them. If our own minds are full of distractions, then simple work can focus them. After all, we can still be thankful to God at all times, and that is the essence of Christian obedience and prayer.[24]

Moreover, Basil seems more interested in public, communal prayer than in private prayer. In LR 37, which is, after all, about "constant prayer," we might expect that he would speak of interior meditation and contemplation. Instead, he discusses the hours of the Divine Office throughout the day. It is as if he wants to emphasize the objective rather than the subjective aspect of prayer. But we should not conclude from this that Basil himself was spiritually shallow. The whole range of his writings shows that he had profound knowledge of the spiritual life. He may not have been particularly mystical himself, but he certainly knew all about interior states and problems with spiritual growth.

21. See Gribomont, "La preghiera secondo S. Basilio," *Saint Basile, Évangile et Église*, 2, 427.

22. Basil also discusses incessant prayer in Letter 2 and *Homilia ad Julittam*. In suggesting that such prayer is possible during simple work by means of pious aspirations and prayer-mantras, Basil is in complete harmony with much of Eastern monasticism. For example, the Rule of Pachomius contains many references to this practice, e.g. Prec. 3; 28; 59. See Cremaschi, *Basilio di Cesarea*, 179 n. 537. The Eastern monks also brought handwork to the Night Office, a practice St. Benedict seems to reject in RB 52.

23. See the remarks on Long Rule 5 in chap. 2 above.

24. Gribomont, "La preghiera," 434ff.

Here again we should remember that he was not writing in a vacuum. He was addressing the Eustathians, by and large, who knew all about the interior life. In fact, they knew so much about it that they were tempted to abandon the outer life. And that is just what he will not allow them to do. No, they must learn how to achieve a healthy balance of prayer and work. On the same note, even though Basil devotes five chapters (37–42) of the Long Rules to work, that does not mean he thought it was an especially important "monastic" topic. He probably just saw it as a good way to keep the spiritual life anchored in the real world, and it also helps to keep religious women and men in solidarity with the rest of the human race.

Basil's Biblicism

As our final topic we will take up Basil's relationship to the Bible. Even a cursory glance at the Long Rules indicates that they are shot through with biblical references. Every page is sprinkled with passages Basil adduces to make his points. We might sometimes wonder how appropriate some of these texts are for that purpose, but we have to admit that the author is deeply rooted in the text of Sacred Scripture. We can also corroborate this from the rest of his work. We have already seen that he composed the *Moral Rules* entirely from biblical passages he took to be commandments. We also have numerous sermons and theological treatises from his pen, all of them studded with biblical quotes and allusions. The man was personally immersed in the Bible. Not only that. He saw the monastic life as itself deeply devoted to the study of Scripture. If the religious wants to know God's will for him or her, then this is imperative. This is what he says in Short Rules 1:

> Q. 1: Is it permissible or fitting for a person to allow himself to do or say (from his own feeling) whatever he thinks good, without the testimonies of the God-inspired Scriptures?
>
> A. For one thing, our Lord Jesus Christ says of the Holy Spirit: he shall not speak from himself, but will speak whatever he hears (John 16:13) and for another, he says of himself: *the Son can do nothing of himself* (John 5:19). . . . Who then can have attained such a pitch of madness as to dare to conceive of himself so much as a thought when he needs rather the Holy and *good Spirit as guide for the journey* (see Ps 142:10) that he might be *directed into the way of truth* (John 16:13) in thought and words and deeds. For he is blind and dwells in darkness (see John 12:35) who is without the *sun of Righteousness* (see Mal 4:2) that is

our Lord Jesus Christ, who illumines us with his commandments as
with rays.

Since the whole point of this section is to emphasize the biblicism
of Basil, I really should not have omitted any of the quotations from
Scripture in this passage, but they go on and on. They have the effect
of making this answer seem rather bloated and wordy, but that may
be because we ourselves are not as devoted to Scripture as we might
be. Nonetheless, we should pay close attention to the atmosphere in
which this question exists. People wonder if there is anything they can
do without biblical backing. Basil admits that many things are not even
discussed in Holy Scripture; in these cases we must consult the good
of our neighbor before our own desires. But the essential point is that
these people took the Bible utterly seriously.

In fact, many of the questions, especially in the Short Rules, are
directly based on biblical passages. The typical formula is: We read
such and such in Scripture; how shall we live up to this injunction?
What we have here are people who are attempting to live out the biblical word in concrete form. Usually these questions and answers are
somewhat abstract and vague in form, so fundamentalism is avoided,
but not always.

What is crucial here is the fact that Basil and his followers took the
Bible as their guide to Christian life. It was expected that each individual
was conversant with the Bible and continually consulting it for guidance. Moreover, when there were conflicts of authority, the Bible was
supposed to have the last word. In SR 114, for example, Basil is asked
whether they have to obey any and all orders from the monastic seniors.
His answer is that such orders have to be checked against the Scriptures.
Only those that are based on the Bible have any authority.

Over and over again he emphasizes that authority in the community
is mainly a matter of discernment of the will of God mediated through
the biblical word of God. The superior must study the Bible (SR 235);
he must break open the word of God for the brothers (LR 25). He must
fear to teach anything that is contrary to the will of God as revealed in
the Bible (SR 98).[25]

---

25. Cremaschi, *Basilio di Cesarea*, 152 n. 428. For a good general statement
of Basil's biblicism, see Enzo Bianchi, "Presentation," *Saint Basile, Évangile et
Église*, lix–lxi.

Chapter
Four

The Life of Pachomius

Introduction

The Pachomian literature is one of the treasures of early monasticism, but it was virtually unknown in the English-speaking world to all but specialists until about twenty-five years ago. At that time Armand Veilleux published the three volumes of his *Pachomian Koinonia*, containing not only the *Life of Pachomius* and the Rules, but various catecheses and sermons.[1] Yet Pachomius was not completely unknown down through the ages. At the beginning of the fifth century St. Jerome translated the Rules from Greek into Latin, and that material was well

---

1. *Pachomian Koinonia (PK)*, 3 vols. (Kalamazoo: Cistercian Publications, 1980–82). Another modern English translation of *The First Greek Life (G1)* is Apostolos N. Athanassakis, *The Life of Pachomius*, SBLTT 7 (Missoula, MT: Scholars Press, 1975). Veilleux stands on the shoulders of earlier scholars. For the Coptic material, L. Théophile Lefort spent a whole career (1915–1945) producing critical editions and French translations. His main publications were: *S. Pachomii vitae Bohairice scripta*, CSCO 89 (Paris: E Typographeo Reipublicae, 1925; repr. Louvain: Secrétariat du CorpusSCO, 1964–1965); *S. Pachomii vitae Sahidice scripta*, CSCO 99–100 (Paris: E Typographeo Reipublicae, 1933–1934; repr. 1952). François Halkin's *Sancti Pachomii vitae graecae* (Brussels, Société des Bollandistes, 1932) is the standard edition of *G1*. For the Latin text of all the Pachomian material, see Amand Boon, *Pachomiana Latina. Règle et Épîtres de St. Pachôme, Épître de s. Théodore et "Liber" de s. Orsiesius* (Louvain: Bureaux de la Revue, 1930).

known in the Latin church.[2] These Rules were quite influential in the Gallic church,[3] and they were also known by St. Benedict.[4]

Unfortunately, the Rules in themselves create a rather misleading picture of Pachomius and his movement. Since they are extremely dry and legalistic, he got a reputation as a hard-nosed, militaristic legislator who ran something akin to a boot camp or an industrial system.[5] What was not understood was that the Rules were never meant to be self-sufficient, but merely a supplement to Scripture itself.[6]

Another element that tends to lead people astray is the sheer size of the Pachomian congregation. Jerome (Preface 7) tells us that 50,000 monks used to gather at the annual chapter meeting at Phbow. That number seems preposterous, but we do know there were seven or eight monasteries, and they were not small. There may have been two thousand or more monks involved. That being the case, people assume that the Pachomian congregation was a vast mob of monks organized into a complicated, authoritarian structure that necessitated harsh rules and left no room for spiritual freedom.

It is true that it was a highly organized system. In fact, each monastery was a sort of village compound with many small houses of monks inside its walls—not unlike what we find today in warm places such as Africa. And there was a fairly complex hierarchy of officers. But it was certainly not a mob, for this structure contained human-size units. It is also true that the *koinonia* was a successful economic system, at least

2. See Boon, *Pachomiana Latina*.

3. See Introduction to *Early Monastic Rules*, ed. and trans. Carmela Vircillo Franklin, Ivan Havener, and J. Alcuin Francis (Collegeville, MN: Liturgical Press, 1981), 9–14.

4. Most of the Pachomian influence on RB is deduced from allusions to the Rules. There is one quotation from the *Life* in RB 58.6: "A senior chosen for his skill in winning souls should be appointed to look after them with careful attention." See *Rule of St. Benedict 1980*, ed. Timothy Fry (Collegeville, MN: Liturgical Press, 1981), 599–600.

5. An example of this is Emmanuel Amand de Mendieta, "Le système cénobitique basilien comparé au système cénobitique pachômien," *Revue de l'histoire des religions* 152 (1957): 31–80.

6. For an excellent detailed commentary on the Pachomian Rule see Heinrich Bacht, *Das Vermächtnis des Ursprungs: Studien zum frühen Mönchtum. 2: Pachomius. Der Mann und Sein Werk*. Studien zur Theologie des geistlichen Lebens 8 (Würzburg: Echter, 1983). For the relationship between Scripture and the Pachomian Rule see Placide Deseille, *L'esprit du monachisme pachômien* (Bégrolles-en-Mauges, Abbaye de Bellefontaine, 1968), xxxviii ff.

as far as we know its history (ca. 330–550 CE). This seems to have been due to the fact that it filled a social vacuum in the Nile Valley at that time. There are also signs that economic prosperity undermined the spiritual ideals of the system.[7]

But the element Veilleux's publication brings to light for the first time is the figure of the founder himself, Pachomius.[8] To judge from the *Life*, he was one of the most remarkable Christian and monastic leaders of all time, and he seems to have had a successor in Theodore, who was also an outstanding abbot. Once we read the *Life of Pachomius* in one of the two major versions translated by Veilleux (Coptic and Greek), it immediately becomes apparent that the saint himself supplied the spiritual and human element in the system. When we have encountered this spiritual master in person, or as close as we can get through literature, we can see that the Rules are not a clear window on the greatness of the man and his achievement.

Anyone who is familiar with the traditional lives of the saints might wonder how this one could live up to the claims I am making for it. We are well aware that traditional hagiography tends to create plaster saints and stereotypical holy persons who often do not strike us as very interesting. But the *Life of Pachomius* is different, so different that I wonder if it should be called hagiography. Certainly it is replete with visions, miracles, and amazing ascetical feats—all the things that make us wonder if we are dealing with a real person. But these are intermixed with stories and sayings that are so far from conventional that they could hardly have been made up. We come away convinced that Pachomius was a real spiritual master and one of the greatest of the early monastic fathers.

In this chapter we will concentrate only on the person of Pachomius and not on his system. We will also pay attention to the secondary figure of Theodore, since he was intimately associated with Pachomius from an early time. There are many other aspects of this cenobitic system that would be worth studying, but there is not space to do it here.

7. A good, short, and accessible summary of the Pachomian system can be found in Derwas J. Chitty, *The Desert a City: An Introduction to the Study of Egyptian and Palestinian Monasticism under the Christian Empire* (Oxford: Blackwell, 1966), 20–45.

8. In his Foreword to *PK* 1 (vii–xxii) (n. 1 above), Adalbert de Vogüé stresses the importance of the spiritual paternity of Pachomius.

The Call of Pachomius

Like many of the saints, Pachomius had an extraordinary sense of a special calling from God. He grew up as a pagan in the southern Egyptian town of Sne, but already as a child he was uncomfortable with the local pagan cult. His conversion experience was to come a bit later. In the year 312–313 he was conscripted into the Roman army for war on the Persian frontier. The experience of conscription was not a pleasant one. The new recruits were essentially prisoners, and were treated as such. On the long boat trip down the Nile they were kept in stockades overnight.

One night when they were in Thebes, the local Christians visited them and assisted them with food and drink. When Pachomius inquired why they did this gratuitously he was told that it was the very nature of their religion that impelled them to do so. Right then and there Pachomius's faith in Jesus Christ was born: "My Lord Jesus Christ, God of all the saints, may your goodness quickly come upon me, deliver me from this affliction and I will serve humankind all the days of my life" (*Coptic Life [Sbo]* 7). Notice here that Pachomius considers army life "an affliction" from which he wants deliverance. As a matter of fact, the war was quickly over and he was never in battle. But he had seen enough of the army to know he did not like it. Therefore those critics who claim he militarized monasticism are barking up the wrong tree. The huge numbers of his future community required strict order, but Pachomius was no lover of discipline for its own sake.[9]

At any rate, Pachomius made good on his vow to Jesus. When he was demobilized he returned to southern Egypt, where he sought Christian baptism. More than that, he began "serving humankind" in the pattern he had learned from the Christians of Thebes. He, too, ministered to the poor and the sick by cultivating a garden in the region of Seneset in the great east-west bend of the Nile. During this period of what we might call social work Pachomius's vocation was corroborated by a remarkable vision: "After he had spent some days there, he was brought to the church and baptized that he might be made worthy of the holy mysteries, that is to say, of the body and blood of Christ. On the night he was baptized he had a dream. He saw the dew of heaven descend on

---

9. Jean Gribomont, art. "Pacomio," in *Dizionario degli Istituti di Perfezione*, eds. Guerrino Pelliccia and Giancarlo Rocca, 9 vols. (Turin and Rome: Paoline, 1974–97), 6:1067–73, thinks the elaborate and tight organization of the *koinonia* was necessitated by the mentality of Egyptian peasants (*fellahin*) more than by Pacomius's military experience.

his head, then condense in his right hand and turn into a honey comb; and while he was considering it, it dropped onto the earth and spread out all over the face of the earth" (*Sbo* 8). This is a charming story, and it has a ring of authenticity to it, for the early Christians were given a taste of milk and honey at their baptism. No doubt this triggered his dream, but in fact Pachomius did not find social work to be all milk and honey. After a while he was worn out by the demands of people and he sought solitude. He became an apprentice monk to a local hermit named Palamon.

Before we proceed further with his story we should note that the manuscripts do not agree about certain details. For example, the very important *First Greek Life* (*G1*) completely omits the period of Pachomius's social work. In that version he proceeds directly from baptism to the eremitic life. Along the same line, *G1* does not have the honey spread out on the earth. The *Second Greek Life* (*G2*) has the honey remain in Pachomius's hand, so we can see a certain shrinkage operating here.[10]

Although *G1* is just as historically and literarily important as the Coptic text (*Sbo*) we have been following, it does seem that the Coptic version is more plausible.[11] For one thing, it meshes perfectly with Pachomius's original experience of Christianity and also accounts better for his subsequent activity. *G1* must have found social work to be a distraction to the monastic ideal it is promoting. Actually, *Sbo* itself shows some signs of the same doubts. Somewhat illogically, it has Pachomius cry out: "This service of the sick in the villages is no work for a monk. It is only for clergy and the faithful old men. From this day on, I will no longer undertake it, lest another should put his hand to this task and should be carried away by the scandal of my example" (*Sbo* 9).

10. This is the interpretation of Fidelis Ruppert, *Das pachomianische Mönchtum und die Anfänge klösterlichen Gehorsams* (Münsterschwarzach: Vier-Türme, 1971), 30. I will follow Ruppert in my exegesis of the *Life* for two reasons: (a) he goes through the text from front to back, and (b) I share his emphasis on community.

11. Armand Veilleux, *PK* 1, 1–21, describes and evaluates the various manuscripts of the *Life*. This is a highly technical question and can be ignored by the general reader, but one should remain aware that the manuscripts came from different periods and locales, and consequently have different views of monastic issues. It is well to remember that *none* of the manuscripts is from Pachomius's own lifetime. What is more, scholars are divided over the priority of *Sbo* (Lefort, Amelineau, Grützmacher) or *G1* (Ledeuze, Heussi, Chitty). Veilleux assumes an earlier *Life* on which both are based.

In fact, Pachomius was not a monk at this time, so the remark makes no sense, yet it must reflect a certain kind of monastic thinking. At any rate, Pachomius takes on the eremitical life under Palamon. Although the old man doubts whether Pachomius can cope with the strict asceticism of his way of life, Pachomius tells him he has been living this way for years already, and he quickly proves he is a great ascetic. After some years of mastering the monastic lifestyle and also the art of meditation and contemplation, Pachomius has another vision. Throughout his life he will be driven by visions. In fact, visions were very widespread and highly appreciated throughout the early Egyptian church. Still, this particular vision was somewhat painful for the hermit:

> One day he and his brother were reaping the harvest on an island. They were close to the deserted village of Tabennesi to which they had withdrawn. During that night, after they had finished praying according to their custom, he went off a short distance from his brother and sat down alone. He was downcast and brokenhearted, desiring to know God's will. While it was still dark, a luminous man appeared and stood before him. He said: "Why are you downcast and brokenhearted?" He replied, "I seek God's will." The luminous man said to him, "You really desire to know God's will?" [Pachomius answered] "Yes." He said to him, "God's will is to serve mankind and reconcile it to him." He replied almost indignantly, "I seek God's will, and you say to serve mankind?" The luminous man repeated three times, "God's will is to serve men in order to call them to him."

After this vision Pachomius recalls that he had promised to "serve humankind" at his conversion. Apparently his intense hermit training had caused him to turn away from that philosophy, but we should also notice that even before this vision he is portrayed as being "downcast and broken-hearted." Apparently he is vaguely aware that all is not right. He is not called to be a hermit like Palamon. *His call is to extend the communal dimension of monasticism.*

Nonetheless, this does not mean that Pachomius's time as a hermit was wasted. Far from it! Certainly the training in ascetical practices would serve him well as a communal founder, though he never asked others to rise to the ascetical heights he himself had attained. But from the beginning Palamon makes it clear that the purpose of this discipline is to get "to know yourself" (*Sbo* 10). Pachomius will become renowned for his discernment of spirits, but first he has to arrive at self-knowledge.

Moreover, the vision of Pachomius after his novitiate does not merely ask him to "serve humankind," as was the case in the original vision.

Now the mandate is also to reconcile them with God. This means that Pachomius's monastic training has deepened his theological vision so that he now understands the inner meaning of Christian service. It is not just imitation of the healings of Jesus the Servant, but also of his death and rising to take away the sins of the world.

It is interesting to study the different approaches of the commentators on the Pachomian beginnings. Some scholars, such as Veilleux and Ruppert, put a lot of emphasis on the horizontal, social aspects.[12] They see Pachomius as primarily a communal man who was momentarily sidetracked into eremitical life but regained his original orientation to community. Vogüé, on the other hand, considers the hermit background of Pachomius to be crucial to his whole enterprise. He will simply extend the eremitical values to large groups of people. So in his many studies of the Pachomian movement Vogüé always stresses the continuity he sees between his eremitical roots and his subsequent behavior.

No doubt there was a good deal of common ground between Egyptian anchoritism and the communal life designed by Pachomius. All monks have certain basic values: asceticism, contemplation, and so on.[13] But Vogüé seems to underestimate the breakthrough Pachomius made in regard to the older monastic models. It is to this that we must now turn.[14]

The First Experiment

Apparently it took a long time for Pachomius to implement his general call from God to "reconcile humankind with God." For one thing, his master Palamon was skeptical of the enterprise. But finally Pachomius got more explicit instructions from God:

12. Veilleux's work on Pachomius always stresses community. See his four lectures in *The Continuing Quest for God*, ed. William Skudlarek (Collegeville, MN: Liturgical Press, 1982), 40–79. For Ruppert see n. 10 above.

13. See Vogüé's Foreword to *PK* 1 (n. 8 above). In his long career of research Vogüé has not wavered in his emphasis on Pachomius's anchoritic roots. See *De saint Pachôme à Jean Cassien: études littéraires et doctrinales sur le monachisme égyptien à ses débuts*, Studia Anselmiana 120 (Rome: Pontificio ateneo S. Anselmo, 1996), 17–270.

14. In his classic article, "Antonius und Pachomius: von der Anachorese zum Cönobitentum," in *Askese und Mönchtum in der alten Kirche*, ed. K. Suso Frank, WdF 409 (Darmstadt: Wissenschaftliche Buchgesellschaft, 1975), 183–229, Heinrich Bacht discusses the relation of early cenobitism to anchoritism.

> Young Pachomius strove to imitate [Palamon] in every work that he put on himself. One day he set out, according to his custom, across that desert to the large acacia forest. Led by the spirit, he covered a distance of some ten miles and came to a deserted village on the river's shore called Tabennesi. Then he felt inspired to go in and pray there a little and he followed the one who gave him that inspiration. He came into that place, stretched out his hands and prayed to the Lord Jesus Christ that he might teach him His will. And as he lengthened his prayer, a voice came to him from heaven, "Pachomius, Pachomius, struggle, dwell in this place and build a monastery; for many will come to you to become monks with you, and they will profit their souls." Then at once he returned to his father the old man Apa Palamon and told him about what he had heard. (*Sbo* 17)

Once again he has a divine revelation at Tabennesi, but this time he is told to build a monastery there and that others will join him. We should reflect a minute on the geography involved here. Unlike earlier places associated with Egyptian monasticism, Tabennesi is not located in the desert but right on the bank of the Nile. Yet Tabennesi is described as a "deserted village." To anyone who knows Egypt this is a puzzling statement, for the Nile Valley is virtually the *only* habitable part of the country. It is basically a fertile strip about five miles wide running through the barren desert of Egypt. How could it be uninhabited? We don't know for sure, but it does seem that socioeconomic circumstances in the early fourth century had created this strange situation. Imperial taxes had become so burdensome that whole districts were abandoned by the owners and workers. Pachomius would move into this vacuum and virtually reconstruct agriculture and society in this part of southern Egypt. In this sense his movement is a parallel to that of the monks in early medieval Europe.[15]

First, though, he faced immediate opposition to his new project. Seeing that he was building a walled compound far larger than their own needs, his brother John, who was now his fellow hermit, tore it down in anger, accusing Pachomius of pride. Pachomius lashed back at him, but then was repentant, for he realized that he had not yet learned patience

---

15. Philip Rousseau, *Pachomius: The Making of a Community in Fourth-Century Egypt* (Berkeley: University of California Press, 1985), 1–10, discusses the socioeconomic situation of fourth-century Egypt. He does not think whole districts were abandoned, but if they were not, the monks must have acquired land very cheaply and quickly. There is no sign they acquired serfs as in medieval Europe.

and humility. How would he lead others? (*Sbo* 19). Nevertheless, he did welcome neophytes and began to form a monastic community. Unlike traditional training programs, as for example those employed by the army, Pachomius did not require the newcomers to serve him; instead he served them. This service had at least two purposes: first, it fulfilled his vow, and second, it was meant to teach the neophytes to serve in their turn.

According to the standard account found in both the Coptic (*Sbo* 23) and *First Greek* (*G1* 25) lives, Pachomius's first experiment worked like a charm: the new men were so edified and even shocked by Pachomius's humble service that they asked him what he was up to. He admitted that he was giving them an example to follow, so they took the hint and began serving each other. However, there are a few indications that things actually did not go so smoothly: "Still fifty others, who lived upriver in a place called Thbakat and had likewise heard of him, came to him. He accepted them likewise, but discovering they had a carnal mind, he expelled them from his dwelling" (*Sbo* 24).

Lest we suspect that a "carnal mind" means they were hopeless moral degenerates, we should know that this was a general term for everything that did not conform to the Gospel or the monastic ideal. Indeed, Pachomius accused himself of being "carnal minded" after his blowup with John (*Sbo* 19). At any rate, this short remark turns out to be but the tip of a much larger iceberg that can be seen in a fragment called the *First Sahidic Life*. It tells quite a different story than does the standard version:

> When he saw the brothers gathering around him, he established for them the following rule. Each should be self-supporting and manage his own affairs, but they would provide their share of all their material needs either for food or to provide hospitality to the strangers who came to them, for they all ate together. . . . He proceeded this way because he could see that they were not yet ready to bind themselves together in a perfect Koinonia like that of the believers which Acts describes. . . . Seeing his humility and obligingness, they treated him with contempt and great irreverence because of the lack of integrity of their hearts toward God. If he told them once to take care of some need they had, they would contradict him openly and insult him, saying, "We will not obey you." He did not punish them, however, but on the contrary, he bore with them with great patience. . . . During harvest time they all went out together to hire themselves out as reapers. At mealtime Pachomius harnessed a donkey and went to fetch them something to eat. When he arrived, he set the table and they ate. When evening came, they stopped

working. After work, some of them climbed on the donkey for fun, while others chased the donkey and laughed, saying, "Pachomius, our servant, pack the utensils and return them to the monastery." . . . He endured afflictions of this kind and pranks from them for a long time—not only for a year or two, but for four or five years. . . . (*S1* 11–15)

Rather than continue this long quotation, let me sum up the result. After a long prayer Pachomius decides enough is enough. He tells them that now he will have to require real obedience; if they wish to obey, he will be their leader; if not, they are free to leave. They merely laugh at him, but he grabs a stick and drives them out of the compound one by one (*S1* 16–18).

I think this is one of the most disturbing stories from early monastic history. We can understand why the main versions have omitted it, if they ever knew it.[16] But now that Veilleux has published a translation of it we have to take it into serious account and try to make sense of it. Someone of a pessimistic cast of mind might say that Pachomius got what he deserved. How could he have expected people to act any differently? Didn't he know about original sin? People do not respond to example, even saintly example, as much as they do to power and force. Pachomius was incredibly naïve to think that he could translate the Gospel into these terms: authority cannot be pure service. It must also be disciplinary.[17]

There is no doubt that Pachomius had misjudged the human heart to some extent. In his subsequent history, rules would be necessary, and especially when large numbers of people would flock to him. In fact, we have the original monastic Rule of the community and it does seem rather harsh and rigorous.[18] But we should remember that the Pachomians never considered their monastic Rule to be sufficient in

16. Veilleux, *PK* 1, 8–9, notes that with *S1*, a manuscript of the sixth century, we come closest to the original Pachomian tradition. Ruppert, *Das pachomianische Mönchtum*, 146, also thinks *S1* and *S3* have the true story of the founding.

17. Marie-Magdeleine van Molle, "Confrontation entre les règles et la littérature pachômienne postérieure," *La Vie Spirituelle. Supplément* 86 (1968): 394–424, thought the story in *S1* 11–18 was really a polemic against "servant authority." Ruppert, *Das pachomianische Mönchtum*, 53, disagrees.

18. Whether all of the Rules go back to the founder himself is not agreed by the scholars, but Vogüé thinks at least some of them do. See "Les pièces latines du dossier pachômien," in *De saint Pachôme à Jean Cassien*, 47ff.

itself. It was always considered a supplement and concrete application of Scripture itself, which they considered to be their real rule of life. Pachomius's ideals continued to be drawn from the Bible and not merely pragmatic discipline.

While it may be true that he had first adopted a naïve form of structure with the leader taking the lowest place, he never abandoned his ideal of servant leadership. We will see this in the next section, but here it is important to insist that these early, admittedly painful experiments were not simply failures. All through his life he would rely on example more than force in leading people.[19]

This episode may also shed some light on the anchorite/cenobite question we touched on earlier. It does look here as if Pachomius tried to establish a semi-eremitical system in which people retained their private property but contributed to a common fund. Perhaps these were already hermits whom he meant to serve and organize in this way. At any rate, the text indicates that he did not ask everything of them because of their weakness. A legitimate interpretation of this episode could be that such halfway measures do not work. True community, the kind Pachomius thought he saw in the Acts of the Apostles, must be based on more than a partial commitment. Primary community, such as marriage and the classic cenobitic life, needs to be grounded on the total self-gift of each one of the members.

Pachomius, the Spiritual Father

For the rest of his life Pachomius functioned as the spiritual father of a large monastic congregation composed of hundreds of monks living in about eight monasteries strung out over a hundred-mile stretch of the Nile. Even though the organization of this congregation is interesting, it is not our subject here. We will concentrate on Pachomius as a spiritual leader.

As we have seen, Pachomius's ideal was that of servanthood. Sometimes he took this ideology rather literally. Once, when his prior Theodore washed Pachomius's hands, Pachomius in turn washed Theodore's feet: "All this I did so that I might not be condemned for being served by you, when it is I who must be the servant of all" (*Sbo* 61). On a few occasions his servanthood took the form of a humble acceptance of

19. Ruppert, *Das pachomianische Mönchtum*, 166–200, has an extended study of Pachomius's views and practice of Christian leadership.

correction from one of the brothers. Even though he is the great *Apa*
(= father), he does not consider himself above criticism: "One day [Pa-
chomius] was weaving a mat in Tabennesi. A boy who was doing the
weekly service came by, and seeing him weaving, said, 'Not so, father. Do
not turn the thread this way, for Abba Theodore has taught us another
way of weaving.' He got up at once and said, 'Yes, teach me the way.'
After the boy had taught him, he sat down to work with joy, having
forestalled the spirit of pride in this, too. For if he happened to have a
carnal thought, he did not pay attention to it. And he did [not] rebuke
the boy for speaking unduly" (*G1* 86).

Along with a willingness to be corrected by subordinates was Pachomius's insistence that he himself must remain under obedience.
Even though he was the overall superior, he lived in one of the houses
with the brothers and placed himself under the authority of the master
of that house. Of course, he himself remained in overall charge, but he
did not take personal items without asking permission (*G1* 110). He
wanted no "perks." A related aspect of Pachomius's servanthood was
his refusal to accept personal privilege. It certainly would have been his
due as the great *Apa* of the congregation, and the brothers often tried
to extend it to him, but he persisted in rejecting it. Once when he was
gravely ill, this is what happened: "After they had prayed and withdrawn,
Pachomius said to a brother, 'Do me a charity, bring me a good blanket;
this one is heavy and my body does not bear it. For I have now been ill for
forty days, but I give thanks to God.' The brother went to the steward's
quarters and took a good light blanket and put it over him. But when he
saw the difference of the blanket, [Pachomius] said to him, 'Take it away;
I ought not to be different from the brothers in anything. I will manage
somehow or other until I depart from the body'" (*G1* 115).

From this story it can be seen that Pachomius could sometimes be
difficult to deal with. In this case his ideal of personal ascesis and the
equality of the brothers comes into conflict with his obvious needs as
a very sick man. In other words, he is not quite ready to *be served*, as
is proper for the sick. In a parallel account (*Sbo* 120) they bring him
a *worn* light blanket, and that is all right. At times it does seem that
Pachomius's notion of the radical equality of the brothers went too far.
For example, in one of his Rules we read: "In his house and cell, no one
shall have anything except what is prescribed for all together by the law
of the monastery: no woolen tunic, no mantle, no soft sheepskin with
unshorn wool, not even a few coins, no pillow for his head or various
other conveniences. They shall have only what is distributed by the
father of the monastery through the housemasters" (*Pr* 81). Although

one would not have to interpret such a rule literally, it is pretty clear that some of the brothers did just that.[20] And that, too, did not please Pachomius! On another occasion when he was sick, such was the case: "Another brother, sick to death, was lying in another cell nearby. He had been ill so long that his body was mere bones. He had asked the father of the monastery [the local abbot, not Pachomius] to be given a little meat, and it had not been given to him. . . . And when at the hour of the brothers' meal they brought [Pachomius] exactly what all the others had, he did not eat but said, 'Respecters of persons . . . do you not see that this man is a corpse? Why did you not take good care of him before he made his request . . . ? Are there no differences among sick persons?'" (*G1* 53). So it is obvious that, like St. Benedict (RB 34), Pachomius understood "absolute equality" to mean that each gets what he needs when he needs it. It is also characteristic of this rather fiery personality that he would go on a hunger strike himself until the emaciated brother was given a special diet. In other words, he would forego the standard ration until the needy brother got a supplementary ration.

Someone might wonder why Pachomius was sick so often. It may have been that he was too hard on himself—far more than he was on others. And he was probably harsher toward himself than was always prudent. Like many of the saints, he recommended prudence for other people, but himself practiced extraordinary asceticism. Many stories show him outdoing the brothers in asceticism. At any rate, Pachomius's personal practice of suffering service was part of a well-worked-out philosophy of Christian leadership. He did not hesitate to instruct his subordinates in this matter. Sometimes this pedagogy takes the form of a sort of folk wisdom: "The holy Pachomius did many things with [Theodore the Alexandrian] instructing him how to govern men. He would say, 'It is a great thing! If you see someone of the house negligent of his salvation, admonish him privately with patience. If he once gets angry, leave him until God moves him to repentance. It is just like when someone wants to extract a thorn from somebody's foot. He digs around it, and if it bleeds and is painful, it is better to leave it and put on it a softening plaster or something similar. Then after a few days it comes out by itself and easily'" (*G1* 95).

This story is not without a theological dimension, for it shows that God alone can move a person toward repentance. Indeed, for a superior

---

20. For his part, Heinrich Bacht, *Vermächtnis*, 184–85, does not interpret this precept literally, but notes that solidarity was more important to Pachomius than uniformity.

to move in too quickly and too forcefully may be a sort of proof of insufficient trust in God's power. As Theodore the Egyptian once put it, "Why did I not wait for the Lord to move him to free choice?" (*Sbo* 79). But this does not mean that such things happen easily or that they always happen at all. Besides developing the virtue of patience, a Pachomian superior was expected to go much further. A particularly poignant case was that of Silvanus, a young monk who was so undisciplined that Pachomius told him to go back home. But Silvanus put up such a howl at this that "then Pachomius was patient with him. He called a great monk named Psenamon and told him in the boy's absence: 'We know that you have labored in ascesis for a long time. Now, for God's sake, take this boy and suffer with him in all things until he is saved. You know indeed how I am occupied with many affairs concerning the brothers'" (*G1* 104). Here the theology of servanthood takes on a profound dimension of the imitation of the suffering Christ. It may not be enough merely to teach or give example. Even humble service may not be effective. At some point the Christian leader must be willing to take on the burden of the others and suffer for and with them.

> In the monastery of Phbow there were ten ancient brothers who, although they were chaste in body, often used to murmur and would not listen to the Man of God with faith. Since he was patient and loved their souls, especially the ones for whom he had been toiling for a long time, admonishing and exhorting them, he did not want to neglect them. He mourned for them before the Lord, humbling his soul with fasting, spending six days without food and up to forty nights without sleep. And his body became extremely lean and feeble. Then the Lord heard him and each one of them received the understanding to be healed from his error as much as possible. And this is how they died. (*G1* 100/*Sbo* 92)

Here we are given more insight into what Pachomius understood by suffering for others. He denies his own body food and sleep to the point that he is getting worn down. But he does not mind because he has been toiling with them for a long time. It is a rather remarkable glimpse into the workings of the ancient monastic mind. The father of this huge, sprawling body of brothers is not a remote, antiseptic administrator. Rather, he is down in the trenches, suffering with the troubled brothers.[21] But things did not always come out so well. In fact, this

---

21. Pachomius's mediatorship is discussed by Ruppert, *Das pachomianische Mönchtum*, 188–200.

same story appears elsewhere in the same document (*Sbo* 102) with a different ending. In this form the brothers are not converted from their murmuring. They die in their sins. In fact, this is a particularly sobering story because it makes it clear that these brothers were great ascetics, but full of pride.

Obviously such a pedagogy of monastic authority and obedience is extremely demanding, and it may be suspected that Pachomius did not master it once and for all. Probably he himself had to learn it by trial and error, as with the initial experiment we discussed above. One story that points in this direction is the so-called Draguet Fragment. In this episode two brothers get into a fistfight and Pachomius expels the instigator from the monastery. At that point, though, an old monk rises up and declares that he, too, will have to leave, for he is also a sinner. And then *all* the brothers begin marching out the gate! In response, Pachomius acts quickly, prostrating and begging them to return. Not only does he reverse his judgment; he goes much further by exclaiming that he was plain wrong in expelling a brother. The story concludes by saying that from then on he worked with them, no matter how bad they were.

It seems important to make at least three comments about this story. First, Vogüé has proven that it is not from the Pachomian tradition but from the desert of northern Egypt.[22] Second, it is not possible to have a successful human community without at least the *possibility* of definitive expulsion. Human sin is just too powerful a force to battle without such a sanction.[23] Third, the story has a kind of poetic truth about it in that Pachomius learned that force is not a very effective instrument in human relations, nor is it easy to reconcile it with the teaching of Jesus. We may have to discipline people, or even expel them, but we should only do so when all other means have failed, especially suffering love.

After we have gone through many stories about Pachomius it is still hard to categorize the man. In fact, unpredictability seems to be one of the primary characteristics of this saint. It certainly is an element that keeps the narrative of the *Life* interesting and evocative. This is no stereotyped hagiography that "paints by the numbers." Here is a saint who is ever surprising in his methods and responses:

22. "L'anecdote pachomienne du 'Vaticanus Graecus' 2091': Son origine et ses sources," in *De saint Pachôme à Jean* Cassien, 93–113.

23. See my article, "People Storage," *Cistercian Studies Quarterly* 26 (1991): 40–57, especially the conclusion.

> There was a small monastery about two miles to the south of Tabennesi. The father of that monastery would often come to see our father Pachomius because he was a friend whom he loved very much; and the words of God he heard from his mouth he would repeat to his own monks so that they might fear God's commandments. It happened that a brother of his monastery asked for a certain rank, and he replied to the brother, "Our father Apa Pachomius warned me not to do this because you are not yet worthy of that thing." That brother grew angry and dragged him along, saying, "Come, let us go to him, and he shall have to prove that to me." The other followed him in amazement and sorrow, wondering what was going to happen. . . . Then our father Pachomius took the father of that monastery aside and questioned him. . . . Then our father Apa Pachomius said to him, "Listen to me, give him [the office] so that by this means we may snatch his soul out of the enemy's hands." (*Sbo* 42)

Anyone familiar with monastic Rules and biographies will probably find this story astonishing. According to the standard wisdom, monks are *not* to be allowed to do as they please,[24] and especially not to have the offices they covet! This particular monk is displaying just about every monastic fault we can imagine, so we find it shocking that Pachomius advises that he be allowed to do as he wants. But of course it works; the man's eyes are opened to his own foolishness and he repents. In fact, he comes directly to Pachomius to thank him for teaching him a lesson. It is a remarkable monastic version of the old adage: "The only thing worse than not getting what you want is getting what you want."

In a passage I omitted, Pachomius can see that the man is so convulsed with anger that he has to diffuse that first before any conversion can take place. He lets the thorn fester a while before trying to pull it out. Yet we can hardly generalize from this episode as to how monastic authority should function. Rather, the story illustrates the profound discretion of Pachomius. Like the Desert Fathers, he has the ability to quickly size up a particular problem and prescribe an appropriate remedy.

24. For example, the harsh Rule of the Master (*The Rule of the Master = Regula magistri*, trans. from Latin by Luke Eberle; introduction by Adalbert de Vogüé; trans. Charles Philippi, CSS 6 [Kalamazoo: Cistercian Publications, 1977]), *Thema Pater* 40, states this philosophy in an extreme form: "See, therefore, that whatever we choose by our own will is patently unjust, and whatever is justly imposed on us against our will by the one who has command over us is accounted to our credit."

Earlier we have noted that Pachomius was a famous visionary, and no doubt this same clairvoyance helped him to deal with his monks. But at one point it got him in a great deal of trouble with the bishops of the district. He was summoned to Latopolis and forced to defend his visions. Indeed, the synod erupted into a riot, from which he barely escaped with his life. So it seems that not everyone appreciated this charismatic, unique monastic founder (*G1* 112).[25]

Theodore, the Perfect/Imperfect Disciple

Although Pachomius is the main protagonist of the *Life*, there is also a very important secondary character, and that in two respects. First of all, Theodore was the chief lieutenant of Pachomius, and the story continues on after the death of Pachomius to tell of the reign of Theodore. In addition to that, it is thought that the *Life* was written during the reign of Theodore and reflects his point of view.[26]

Like Pachomius, Theodore was also from the region of Sne to the south of Tabennesi but, unlike Pachomius, he was of a Christian family. Indeed, he was a kind of child-monk of whom are told many pious stories of precocious sanctity. Whether these are to be taken literally or not, it is certain that he came to Pachomius in his late teens. One of Theodore's chief traits was his rigorism. He was one of those monks who goes looking for hard observances, and he took the rules literally. In fact, he often wanted to go beyond the rules and had to be restrained by Pachomius. Here is one instance of that:

> During the Forty Days [of Lent], Theodore went to see our father Pachomius and asked him, "Since the Passover numbers six days during which our remission and our salvation were accomplished, ought we not to fast the [first] four days in addition to the two [others]?" He answered him, "The Church's rule is that we should only join together those two

---

25. James E. Goehring, "New Frontiers in Pachomian Studies," in *The Roots of Egyptian Christianity*, ed. Birger Pearson and James E. Goehring (Philadelphia: Fortress Press, 1986), 245, notes that *G1* 112 is the only version to record this strange, harrowing ordeal. He thinks it represents Theodore's distrust of visions. But Veilleux, "Monasticism and Gnosis in Egypt," *Roots of Egyptian Christianity*, 285 n. 68, argues that *all* fourth-century Egyptian monks were interested in visions, angels, and demons.

26. For a synthetic treatment of Theodore, see Ruppert, *Das pachomianische Mönchtum*, 209–32.

[days], so that we might still have the strength to accomplish without fainting the things we are commanded to do, namely, unceasing prayer, vigils, reciting of God's law, and our manual labor, about which we have orders in the holy Scriptures and which ought to permit us to hold out our hands to the poor." (*Sbo* 35)

This interesting passage goes on to say that great ascetics sometimes have others to serve them; it is not to be that way with this community! Asceticism does not come before our duty to the neighbor. Theodore is to keep to the church's rule of two days of fast for Holy Week so he will have strength for a balanced monastic life.[27] But we should also note that this was a *complete*, "black" fast from all food and drink. Another incident is more nuanced, but equally revealing of the character of Theodore, and of Pachomius's own practice of monastic authority.

Theodore's mother heard of him and she came with letters from bishops ordering the boy to be given back to her. Being given hospitality at the monastery of virgins, she sent the letters so she might at least see him. The father [Pachomius] said to him, "I hear that your mother has come for you and has brought letters from the bishops. Because of these letters, go to meet her and persuade her." The boy replied, "Tell me; if I go to see her as my mother, after being given such great knowledge, will the Lord not blame me in the day of judgment? For instead of becoming enough of a man to reform others, I will set up a stumbling block in the way of so many. The sons of Levi killed their own parents and brothers to please the Lord and escape the danger of his wrath. I too have no mother, nor anything of the world, for it passes." Pachomius said to him, "If you love God more than your mother, shall I prevent you? I shall rather encourage you. For, he who loves his father or his mother more than me is not worthy of me. This is perfection. And certainly our fathers the bishops will not be vexed when they hear about this, but will rather rejoice at your progress. But if someone meets his relatives not as his relatives but as members of Christ whom he loves as he loves all the faithful, he does not sin." (*G1* 37)[28]

Notice here the rather subtle back and forth of this conversation. At first Pachomius takes the common sense approach that mothers and

---

27. Lenten and Holy Week fasts were considered separate up to the middle of the fourth century. See Veilleux, *PK* 1, 273, note for *Sbo* 35.

28. Ruppert, *Das pachomianische Mönchtum*, notes that the literal interpretation of Luke 14:26 was common among the early monks. Moreover, Theodore teaches the same rigorism on this question in his Instruction 3.16 (*PK* 3: 102).

bishops cannot just be ignored. Theodore is advised to reason with his mother. But Theodore does not argue from common sense; he argues from Scripture. Indeed, to justify his intransigence he cites a bloodcurdling passage (Exod 32:27-28) about Levites killing their parents. Faced with this kind of radical biblicism and youthful idealism, Pachomius does not cite other, opposed biblical texts such as "Honor your father and your mother," nor does he simply fall back on his authority and order Theodore out to the gate. Instead, he agrees that Theodore should not go, since he is following not only the Pentateuch but the New Testament: "He who loves father or mother more than me . . ."

We see here something that pervades the whole Pachomius literature, namely, the profound respect for Scripture. Even though Theodore is still a novice, Pachomius accepts the fact that he has studied the Bible and applied it to himself. The *Apa* will not interfere with this direct response to God. The will of the superior is not the only source of revelation for the Pachomian monk; the Bible is equally important. Nevertheless, although Pachomius does not force Theodore to abandon his rigorist stance, he cannot resist adding an important qualification: "But if someone meets his relatives not as his relatives but as members of Christ . . . he does not sin." Clearly Pachomius is able to interpret Scripture with a maturity that knows how to pass by the letter to the spirit of the whole New Testament. Despite Theodore's youthful hardness, Pachomius recognizes in him real potential for leadership. And so he soon calls on him to give biblical conferences to the brothers: "'Stand here and speak to us the holy words of God.' Although unwillingly, he began to speak in front of all the brothers who stood, including our father Pachomius who listened too like the brothers. Immediately some among them, out of pride, were angry and returned to their houses without listening to the Lord's word. They said, 'He is a young one while we are ancients, and it is to him that he gives the order to instruct us!' In fact, Theodore was thirty-three the day our father made him stand to give the instructions, knowing that he was farther advanced than they" (*Sbo* 69).

Pachomius is well aware of their murmuring, and he does not hesitate to confront them. His point is one that anyone can understand: If the word of God is properly preached, what does it matter who preaches it? And Pachomius as always insists that he himself needs to listen like the rest: "And I tell you, I did not only pretend, but I was listening with all my heart, as one thirsty for cool water in summertime." At any rate, the prejudice against Theodore seems to have dissipated rather quickly. He was made a kind of special assistant to Pachomius, and the monks did not complain because they could see that he was a truly gifted leader.

Not only that, it seems that Theodore had a special charm about him that Pachomius himself did not have: "And whenever Theodore came to the monasteries, the brothers seeing him rejoiced. For as we have already said, he had great grace from the Lord. Our Father Pachomius was perfect in everything, but fearful and always mournful, remembering souls in torment. . . . Often after he had been very thirsty in the burning heat, he would take a pitcher of water to drink, but not drink enough to quench his thirst" (*G1* 91).

It seems, too, that Pachomius recognized that Theodore had certain relational gifts he himself did not possess. So he used him very cleverly to handle problem cases when he himself was unable to make headway. Sometimes the two of them conspired in elaborate ruses to trick troubled monks out of their obsessions or potential violations of their vows (*G1* 66–69). Perhaps Pachomius realized that the superior cannot always reach a given monk because the latter has an "authority problem." Rather than meet such cases head-on, he prefers to use the indirect approach of sending "*senpectae,*" much in the spirit of St. Benedict in RB 27.[29] But it is interesting to see that the *Life* recognizes that Theodore was a complex character: both hard and charming, both rigoristic and flexible. Sad to say, the partnership of Pachomius and Theodore did not remain peaceful to the end. In fact, they had a major conflict that serves as the chief point of drama in the *Life.* To put it succinctly, when Pachomius thought he was dying he suspected Theodore of plotting to succeed him:

> One other time it happened that our father Pachomius was ill, so ill that he was in danger of death. Then all the fathers of the communities and all the brothers who were at Phbow gathered about Theodore and said to him, "Promise us that, if the Lord visits our father, you will place yourself at our head and you will become our father in his stead. We must not become wretched and scatter like shepherdless sheep. For no one exists among us who knows his virtues as you." But he made them no reply at all, because out of his great humility he did not want the rank of a father or this world's glory. They proceeded to beg him again until he gave his consent. (*Sbo* 94)

But Pachomius did not die; he got well and summoned the leaders for a communal penance service, no doubt to induce Theodore to confess his own "sin." Theodore did not hide his "sin" but insisted he had not

---

29. See my discussion of RB 27.3 in *Benedict's Rule: A Translation and Commentary* (Collegeville, MN: Liturgical Press, 1996), 242.

instigated the "revolt." Nonetheless, Pachomius sentenced him to a long exile and penance. Not only that, when he really *was* on his deathbed he appointed a certain Petronius, and not Theodore, as his successor. Actually, there are other signs and hints in the text that Pachomius and Theodore had a fairly stormy relationship. At times the abbot rebukes and punishes him for lesser offenses, some of which appear to the reader to be rather minor and even nonexistent (*Sbo* 77). It often seems that he is being put in his place and taught humility.

At any rate, Petronius lived only two months as superior, dying of the same plague that killed Pachomius in 346 CE. He in turn appointed the timid young Horsiesi, who turned out to be quite unready for the heavy burden of authority thrust upon him. Soon enough he felt forced to call upon Theodore to assist him in governing, for there was a serious revolt of some of the monasteries that Theodore put down with characteristic vigor. Given the past history of Theodore, we might suspect that he would rule with an iron hand. No doubt he did, but we also find episodes in which this is qualified with a suggestion that Theodore had learned the art of governing well. He knew when to back off and when to intervene for the good of the brothers:

> On another occasion when one of the boats had fallen into disrepair, our father Theodore rebuilt it by order of our father Apa Horsiesi. When it came time to launch it in the water, the brothers started shouting loudly, like chariot drivers in a hotly disputed race—some shout, "We will be ready before you"; others reply, "No, we will." When our father Theodore saw the wrangling and the great commotion among them, the man of God cried out, ordering them not to quarrel over a matter in which there was no profit for their souls. But they paid no attention to him and our father Theodore, very much distressed, fell silent and cast his care on the Lord. (*Sbo* 192)

This is a story that did not make it into *G1*, and we might suspect that someone thought it implied that Theodore was weak. In fact, he lectured the brothers rather severely afterward, including this hilarious remark: "But let no one who hears me speaking misunderstand my language and say in his stupidity, 'If you die, will the world really become deserted because of you?'" No doubt someone *did* say that to Theodore, but apparently he had matured to the point where he could allow the monks to express themselves freely without it threatening his authority.

Rather than go further into the subsequent history of the Pachomian *koinonia*, which involved Horsiesi's return to power at the death of

Theodore (368 CE), it would be more worthwhile to spend some time examining Theodore more closely. In fact, a good deal of scholarly ink has been spilled over him, and some of it is worth thinking about. Since almost all of the Pachomian literature was produced in the time of Theodore, a typical modern approach would be to suspect that Theodore has shaped the material to suit his own interests. There may be a kernel of truth in this, since most hagiographers will inevitably impose their viewpoint on the material.

But with Theodore the case becomes more complicated, since he is not just an editor but a successor to Pachomius. What is more, we know that his succession was anything but peaceful. We might suspect that he would have had an interest in casting Pachomius in a bad light, but the truth is just the opposite. Theodore almost certainly glorifies Pachomius to bolster the community and his own position of authority within it. According to James Goehring, Theodore is engaged in the process of "routinization of charisma."[30] That is, after the death of the founder there was a need to move from Pachomius's unmatchable personal charism to institutions that can serve some of the same purposes. Thus the written Rule is a substitute for the personal rule of Pachomius. Of course, the suspicion is that Theodore "revises" Pachomius to bolster his own policies.

Goehring makes another point. He suggests that Pachomius himself created a problem in regard to the orderly succession of his authority. When he set aside Theodore it caught everyone by surprise and virtually guaranteed some kind of revolt. I confess that I get the same feeling reading between the lines. In political terms, the "ancient brothers," that is, the first who came to Pachomius, were especially unhappy with the choice of Petronius. He had lately joined the *koinonia* with his whole group of monasteries from downriver, and there is some evidence that they never were properly integrated into the Pachomian ethos. Theodore was the favorite of the "ancient brothers," and they finally got their way.

The surprising thing, though, was that as soon as Theodore took office he completely reworked the structure of the *koinonia* to undercut the power of the very people who put him into office! His method was to rotate the abbots of the communities twice a year, thus preventing any abbot from consolidating a power base. According to Goehring, Theodore had another agenda that tended to skew his picture of Pachomius: He was tied more closely to the bishops, and especially to Alexandria. He

30. "New Frontiers," (n. 25 above), 240ff.

was also less given to visions than his mentor. Consequently, he may have highlighted the Synod of Latopolis, where Pachomius was taken to task for his visions. Visions often make bishops nervous.

Another major scholar on Pachomius, namely, Armand Veilleux, thinks that there was a *Life* of Pachomius that originally did not represent the viewpoint of Theodore. At some later point a *Life* of Theodore was added to, or, better, superimposed on, that of Pachomius, thus creating a certain contamination. For his part, Adalbert de Vogüé does not agree with either of these scholars.[31] He denies that it is possible to disentangle a separate *Life* of Pachomius. But more important, he also denies that Theodore distorted the picture of Pachomius. He feels that the picture of Pachomius we have in the *Life* is so complex and multifaceted that it really does not serve anyone's ideology.

As a nonspecialist I would have to agree with Vogüé. Although there is no doubt that some later attitudes enter in, it is unlikely to me that anyone fabricated out of whole cloth the portrait of Pachomius we have here. It is precisely the rather quirky, unpredictable, unorthodox nature of the material that makes it so compelling. Pachomius is no artificial creation; he is the real item.

Pachomius and Orthodoxy

Although it is one of those special topics I said I would avoid, there is one Pachomian question we should take up, if only because it is causing current scholarly debate. In *G1* 31 we read this description of Pachomius's orthodoxy:

> Pachomius also hated the man called Origen, first of all because he was cast out of the Church by Heraclas, the archbishop of Alexandria, before Arius and Melitius, who had uttered blasphemy against Christ. He hated him also because he recognized him as a blasphemer, having heard that there were dreadful things in his writings, and because he had acted rashly against his own life. [Origen] had mingled things thought plausible with the true words of Scripture, to the ruination of the ignorant, just as a poisonous drug is mixed with honey. Therefore

31. "Saint Pachôme et son oeuvre d'après plusieurs études récentes," in *De saint Pachôme à Jean Cassien*, 115–48. As a matter of fact, this article was written a long time ago (1974) as a review of the doctoral theses of Ruppert and Veilleux. Since Vogüé denies that Theodore distorted the true portrait of Pachomius, one must assume he would also reject the theory of Goehring.

the great Pachomius emphatically ordered the brothers not only not to dare to read that man's writings, but not even to listen to his sayings. One day, having found a book of Origen, he threw it into the water and destroyed it, saying, "If the name of the Lord were not written in it, I would have burnt his blasphemies and nonsenses."

Of course, Origen *was* driven from Alexandria by the bishop, and some of his teachings *were* eventually condemned by the church. But that was only at the Council of Constantinople in 553 CE, two hundred years after the death of Pachomius. Origen was a speculative theologian, and Pachomius may have been particularly allergic to that kind of writing. But it has also been pointed out that only one manuscript contains this particular episode condemning Origen. Could it be a later interpolation?

In recent times, though, a far more serious doubt has arisen about Pachomius's superorthodoxy. To put it in a nutshell, a whole trove of Gnostic literature has been discovered right in the former Pachomian heartland at Chenoboskion. This is the so-called Nag Hammadi library, and it is as important in its own way as the Dead Sea Scrolls. Moreover, these Gnostic writings are wilder than anything Origen ever wrote. Many of them are quite incompatible with Christian doctrine. Therefore, imagine the surprise when the bindings were found to contain some "monastic" materials. There is a letter from a woman to some monks contracting for hay for her donkey, and the names of Pachomius and Paphnuti are mentioned in one letter. Putting two and two together, some scholars rushed to claim that these books were from the library of Phbow.[32] Veilleux soon rebutted these claims with a long article insisting that Pachomius and his monks were simple men who would have had no interest at all in these esoteric texts—even if they were orthodox.[33]

Other scholars, such as James Goehring and Henry Chadwick, are not so sure. They think it rather likely that these books *were* in the Pachomian library, although this does not imply that Pachomius or his

32. Thus John Barns, "Greek and Coptic Papyri from the Covers of the Nag Hammadi Codices: A Preliminary Report," in *Essays on the Hag Hammadi Texts: In Honour of Pahor Labib*, ed. Martin Krause, NHS 6 (Leiden: Brill, 1975).

33. See "Monasticism and Gnosis in Egypt," 291. After forty pages of careful and vehement argumentation against the likelihood that the Pachomians owned the Nag Hammadi library, Veilleux ends his essay with a section on the unity of Gnosis and monasticism. He thinks the monks would at least have respected the Gnostic search for truth.

monks were heretics.[34] Goehring suggests that doctrinal orthodoxy was not as important to the early monks as it was to the bishops. Of course, he knows that Athanasius did hide out with the monks when he was in exile, and certainly he was a fighter for orthodoxy.[35] And Theodore probably was more involved in that fight than Pachomius was, so he may have created *G1* 31.[36] We know that there were all sorts of different religious sects and monastic groups in the Nile Valley in the fourth century. How friendly they were to each other may be doubted, yet Goehring thinks he has evidence to show that sometimes they lived in the same community. Personally, I think Veilleux is still right, although he has not been heard from for a long time.

34. In his article "Monastic Diversity and Ideological Boundaries in Fourth-Century Christian Egypt," *Journal of Early Christian Studies* 5 (1997): 61–84, Goehring cites examples of orthodox and "heretical" (Meletian) monks living together in Egypt.

35. Samuel Rubenson, *The Letters of St. Antony* (Lund: Lund University Press, 1990), has argued on the basis of the *Letters* of Antony that the latter was in fact a theologically literate person who had assimilated Origen's work. It was Athanasius who, in the *Vita Antonii*, for his own reasons created the icon of the illiterate but wise Antony.

36. According to Veilleux, "Monasticism and Gnosis in Egypt," 287–88, *G1* 31 was written not only after the rest of *G1*, but outside the Pachomian milieu. It reflects a "strong antiheretical mentality."

Chapter Five

The Rule of Pachomius: I (Precepts 1–57)

The Rule of Pachomius, written in the middle of the fourth century, is probably the oldest monastic Rule in Christian history.[1] It consists of four parts, of which the Precepts (Pr.) are the longest and first.[2] These notes will deal with the first fifty-seven Precepts. They are not meant to be exhaustive, but merely to highlight the parts that interest the author and are judged to be of some relevance to modern Christians and monks.

In this study I am particularly dependent on two fairly recent scholarly publications. First, I have used the *Pachomian* Koinonia 2, a translation of the Rule of Pachomius published by Armand Veilleux, OCSO, in 1981.[3] This seminal work opened up the whole Pachomian literature to the Anglophone world. Anyone who wants to use my commentary in a studious fashion should secure Veilleux's translation as an accompanying text.

---

1. The translation given here is that of Armand Veilleux, *Pachomian Koinonia (PK)*, vol. 2 (Kalamazoo: Cistercian Publications, 1981). An earlier version of this chapter first appeared in the Australian monastic journal *Tjurunga* 66 (2004) 70–86. It is reprinted in modified form with permission.

2. In addition to the Precepts, there follow Precepts and Institutes; Precepts and Judgments; Precepts and Laws. Scholars argue about the original order of these four units, but there is no doubt that the Precepts are the best known and most significant part of the quartet.

3. *Pachomian Koinonia (PK)* 2 (Kalamazoo: Cistercian Publications, 1981).

Beyond that, I must give major credit to Heinrich Bacht, SJ, for his excellent notes on the Precepts, which he published in 1983.[4] A glance at Bacht's book shows that it is made up almost entirely of footnotes in tiny type—a daunting prospect for the casual reader! But for anyone who is stubborn enough to plow through this dense jungle of German *Wissenschaft*, the reward is a rich trove of careful and insightful research on the Pachomian Rule. One of the purposes of these chapters is to make this information available to the English-speaking world. The other purpose, of course, is to add my own insights into one of my favorite monastic texts.

The Preface of Jerome

In the year 404, St. Jerome received in his Bethlehem monastery a delegation of monks from Egypt. They were from an Alexandrian monastery called Metanoia (Repentance)[5] and they came to ask a favor. Would the famous scholar please translate their monastic Rule into Latin? This document, called the Rule of Pachomius, was originally written in Egyptian (Coptic) and then translated into Greek.[6] But they could not read either language, so they were at a great disadvantage.

4. Heinrich Bacht, *Das Vermächtnis des Ursprungs: Studien zum frühen Mönchtum. 2: Pachomius. Der Mann und Sein Werk* (Würzburg: Echter, 1983). See also Lisa Cremaschi, *Pacomio e i suoi discepoli: regole e scritti* ([Magnano] Qiqajon: Community of Bose, 1988).

5. Metanoia was the Christian successor to a famous pagan temple called Canopus, some twenty miles east of Alexandria. In 394, Patriarch Theophilus took over the site and brought in Pachomian monks from southern Egypt. By 404 some of these monks must have spoken Latin and not Greek, which was the *lingua franca* of Alexandria. Patriarch Athanasius had popularized Egyptian monasticism in the West some decades before, so many Latins went east to experience it. See Derwas J. Chitty, *The Desert a City: An Introduction to the Study of Egyptian and Palestinian Monasticism under the Christian Empire* (Oxford: Blackwell, 1966), 55ff.

6. The whole Pachomian Rule is extant only in the Latin translation of Jerome, the critical edition of which was published by Amand Boon, *Pachomiana Latina. Règle et Épîtres de St. Pachôme, Épître de s. Théodore et "Liber" de s. Orsiesius* (Louvain: Bureaux de la Revue, 1930). The Greek version used by Jerome has disappeared; the so-called *Greek Excerpts* were made at a later time for a different community. As for the Coptic original, fragments of it have been discovered, namely, of Precepts 88–130 and all the Precepts and Institutes.

In his preface, Jerome tells us why he gladly accepted their request. Besides doing them a kindness, he has his own reasons for undertaking this project. Foremost was his need to pull himself out of the grief he was experiencing at the death of his dear friend Paula.[7] He hoped that this translation project would restore his energy and zest for life. Jerome knew that Paula in heaven would be pleased that he was doing this project, since she was always the friend of monks and nuns. She and he were the cofounders of the Bethlehem monasteries, but Jerome knew she was really the foundation and support of them all.[8] He was a sort of scholarly recluse who was not a community man. Furthermore, the monks and nuns who survived her would benefit from having the Rule of Pachomius to guide their daily lives.[9]

Apart from these personal notes, Jerome's preface is not too remarkable. It is mostly a summary of the basic contents of the Rule that follows, and it contains several lists of items that may try our patience. A few of his remarks may need special interpretation, but by and large they are pretty straightforward.[10] Possibly he himself did not find the

7. Since we know that Paula died on 26 January 404 AD, we can assume that Jerome did this work later in that year. Her character is vividly described by Jerome in Letter 108, *PL* 32.878ff.

8. Paula was an immensely rich Roman widow whom Jerome introduced to the ascetical life in the decade before 385 when he lived in Rome. Together they came to Bethlehem, where they founded two Latin monasteries. Although it was Paula's money that made this possible, Jerome's letters indicate that her extreme asceticism and charity had caused her to run through the money by the time of her death. In fact, she left the convent with a considerable debt. See Heinrich Bacht, *Vermächtnis*, 71 n. 3.

9. Jerome had already described the cenobitic life to Paula's daughter, Eustochium, in Letter 22.35, written some twenty years earlier in Rome. That letter does not name the Pachomians, so we cannot presume Jerome knew the Pachomian Rule at that time. See Bacht, *Vermächtnis*, 75 n. 20. Since Eustochium became Paula's successor in 404, it is clear that she and the nuns already knew a good deal about cenobitic practice. Hence their possession of the Pachomian Rule would not be an entirely new revelation.

10. For example, Jerome twice in his preface (1 and 9) refers to an angelic revelation to Pachomius. There is a famous passage in the *Lausiac History* (*LH*) 32 of Palladius describing how the saint was the recipient of his monastic Rule from an angel. Yet it must not be assumed that Jerome is referring to Palladius; the latter only wrote in 419–20, many years after Jerome translated the Pachomian Rule. It could be that Jerome had access to the same legend about Pachomius that Palladius did. Veilleux, *PK* 2, 184 n. 4, suggests that both of

task too exciting because he admits that the monks from Egypt stayed around and prodded him to finish.[11] Once he got going, however, he must have worked rapidly, since he translated directly to a stenographer. Modern commentators consider him fairly accurate, but not scrupulously so.[12]

A Little Directory for the Postulant (Precepts 1–8a)

After a title that ascribes the Precepts to Pachomius, the text immediately plunges into practical details. The first eight numbers all seem to be addressed to a postulant,[13] and they instruct him on some very basic points. For example: Keep to the place in choir (*synaxis*) you are given among the *brothers* (Pr. 1); sit modestly in choir (Pr. 2); when you come into church, don't trample the reeds for plaiting (Pr. 4); do not gawk around in choir (Pr. 7); get up immediately from your prostration when you hear the hand signal (Pr. 6).

Probably the first thing that strikes us is the utter concreteness and plainness of these instructions! Rather than starting with a statement of theology or a memorable biblical verse, this Rule moves right into practical instruction. That may not be the ideal way to begin a monastic Rule, but we should remember that Pachomius had no models to follow:

---

them got their information from the *Life of Pachomius*, probably in the Greek version, chaps. 12 or 23. According to Veilleux, *La liturgie dans le cénobitisme pachômien au quatrième siècle*, Studia Anselmiana philosophica theologica 57 (Rome: "I.B.C." Libreria Herder, 1968), 138–46, the *Lausiac History* is not a particularly good source for an accurate idea of Pachomian monasticism.

11. It is sometimes said that Coptic-speaking monks may have come to Bethlehem to help Jerome with the work, using the Coptic text to help him understand the Greek. Jerome says nothing about that help, just that they urged him to get to work! He gives the name of one monk who was sent to him: Leontius. That is a Greek, not a Coptic name. Some scholars such as Bardy and Cavallera think Jerome himself knew Coptic, but then it is puzzling why he should be working from the Greek. No good scholar wants to translate a translation, but Jerome had no choice.

12. See Veilleux, *PK* 2, 8.

13. Adalbert de Vogüé, "Les pièces latines du dossier pachômien. Remarques sur quelques publications récentes," *RHE* 67 (1972): 26–67, at 48. It might be added that Pr. 1 calls the postulant a *rudis*, which Veilleux (*La liturgie*, 139ff.) thinks means a pagan, but Vogüé ("Pièces," 58–61) thinks means someone "unfamiliar with the Rule."

he was the first.[14] Furthermore, this Rule has several sections and we are not sure the Precepts were always first. But most important, Pachomius always assumes that these rules are merely practical implementations of the Bible itself.[15] In other words, the Bible is the basic Rule of the monk.

Yet even though these practical rules may seem rather irrelevant to our age, it is still surprising how they open up interesting questions. Take, for example, Pr. 6: "When the one who stands first on the step, reciting by heart something from Scripture, claps with his hand for the prayer to conclude, no one should delay in rising but all shall get up together." What are we to make of this? Apparently the Divine Office looked very different in those early communities.[16] In the first place, the Office was not primarily an exercise in which a group of people sang the Psalms from books; it was a more passive exercise in which everyone listened to someone recite or sing a psalm or read. Then, between these recitations, everyone rose and prostrated on the floor in silent prayer.[17] Furthermore, those who listened to the biblical recitations at the Office would themselves be plaiting reeds and grass into ropes and baskets.

Obviously this is a rather different approach to community prayer than what we know in the Latin church, and perhaps some aspects of it, such as the handwork, would be considered distracting and even disrespectful nowadays. But the key factor to notice is that the Divine Office for them was not primarily an active exercise in production but rather a contemplative event where one went to hear the word of God.

14. Pachomius died in 346, but most scholars think that parts of the Rule developed over time under his successors Horsiesi and Theodore. That would take us up to about 370, when the *Asketikon* of St. Basil was being written.

15. See Vogüé, Foreword to *PK* 1, xii.

16. Veilleux, *La liturgie,* 307–9, thinks that the community met only twice a day for prayer, at dawn and at dusk. Vogüé, "Pièces," 40, thinks they met more often.

17. There are varying interpretations of the prayer-pause between the psalms and the readings. Although the text seems clear enough, some scholars (e.g., Anton Baumstark, *Nocturna Laus: Typen frühchristlicher Vigilienfeier und ihr Fortleben vor allem im römischen und monastischen Ritus* [Münster: Aschendorff, 1957]) seem to think that Pr. 6 means that the *oratio* was a collect ending the silent period of prostration. Why, then, would the leader clap his hands to end it? The meaning must be that the *oratio* was the silent prostration, and the hand signal was for it to end.

And perhaps that necessitated some concomitant activity, such as weaving, to help one keep awake.[18]

Notice too that the leader recited Scripture "by heart," not from a book. No doubt it was easier that way in those dark days before electricity, but there is more to it than that. For Pachomius one of the most important monastic practices was the memorization of Scripture. Elsewhere he insists that the postulant not be admitted to the brotherhood at all before he has memorized the Psalms (Pr. 49). Only when he has done so is he equipped for a life of "meditation."[19] Consider this text: "As soon as he hears the sound of the trumpet, calling the brothers to the *synaxis*, he shall leave his cell reciting something from the Scriptures until he reaches the door of the *synaxis*" (Pr. 3). So whoever thinks that the Pachomians were lacking in love for the Bible is quite mistaken.

Rules for the Divine Office and Catechesis (Precepts 8b–22)

We have seen that in his Rules, Pachomius is content to regulate monastic life without expanding much on its spiritual significance. Thus in regard to the Divine Office, the public prayer of the monk, he has some very mundane rules. For example, in Pr. 9–10 he demands that those who come late to the prayers be subject to ritual penance, but less indulgence should be shown to those who come late to the evening *synaxis* than to those who come late in the morning.[20]

18. Veilleux, *PK* 2, 185 n. 4, goes further, noting that this plaiting work in choir is indicative of the close union between prayer and work in the Pachomian mind. In fact, the dynamic goes both ways, since they were also encouraged to pray at work: hence the memorization of biblical passages (Pr. 4).

19. "Meditation" did not mean the same thing for the ancient monks as it does for us today. Instead of mental cogitation, it involved the repetition of biblical texts that had been gotten by heart (Prs. 122; 139–140). This could be done all day long as one went about one's business (Prs. 3, 28, 59). It also implies that their work was generally simple enough so as not to demand intense concentration. Another term used in this regard is *ruminare* (Pr. 122), which refers to the chewing of the cud = reflecting on what was being recited. See Cremaschi, *Pacomio e i suoi discepoli*, 189 n. 4.

20. There is a good deal of controversy among scholars about the history of the Divine Office among the Pachomians. Veilleux, *La liturgie*, 297, claims that Pr. 9–10 refer to an early period in community history when there were two general *synaxes*, at morning and evening. Precept 121, as well as *Inst.* 14 and

It may surprise non-monastic readers to see how much these first monks cared about punctuality, but anyone who has lived a long time in a monastic community knows that habitual tardiness tends to lower general morale. Second, even though the Pachomians did not rise in the middle of the night for the Office, as did later monks, nevertheless the author realizes that some people have a very hard time getting up after a night of sleep. Hence the consideration and even indulgence in allowing them to come up to three psalms late without punishment.[21] What kind of penance was required for liturgical faults? A rather remarkable one: "If it happens that during the psalmody or the prayer or in the midst of reading anyone speaks or laughs, he shall unfasten his belt immediately and with neck bowed down and hands hanging down he shall stand before the altar and be rebuked by the superior of the monastery. He shall do the same also in the assembly of the brothers when they assemble to eat"(Pr. 8).

This dramatic "hangdog" gesture of humility has some interesting overtones. Obviously, loosening the belt is a sign of weakening,[22] but some scholars also think it was a relic of Pachomius's time in the military.[23] In the Roman army a person who was to be expelled from the ranks first had his belt loosened. However, the great Pachomius scholar Heinrich Bacht, S.J., denies[24] that the liturgical gesture has anything to do with "expulsion from the *militia Christi*" (Lehmann). For a long time

---

Leg. 10, seem to say that the evening office ("six prayers") was said separately in each house. This may indicate a later stage, when the communities were larger. If, however, one follows the chronology of Marie-Magdeleine van Molle, "Essai de classement chronologique des premières règles de vie commune connue en chrétienté" in *La Vie Spirituelle, Supplément* 84 (1968): 108–27, the Precepts were written last, thus making the custom of doing evening *synaxis* in the separate houses *earlier* than the custom of doing it in plenary assembly.

21. Most of the ancient Rules had legislation for tardiness at the Divine Office. See Corbinian Gindele, "Verspätung, Verzögerung und Kürzung im Gottesdienst der Magister- und Benediktusregel," *Revue Bénédictine* 86 (1976): 306–21; idem, "Die Satisfaktionsordnung von Cäsarius und Benedikt bis Donatus," *Revue Bénédictine* 69 (1959): 216–36.

22. Indeed, *Verba Seniorum* 10.115 explicitly says it meant that for the desert monks. In this regard, though, it is curious that the same monks loosened their belts when receiving Holy Communion.

23. Konstantin Lehmann, "Die Entstehung der Freiheitsstrafe in den Klöstern des hl. Pachomius," *Zeitschrift der Savigny-Stiftung für Rechtsgeschichte: Kanonistische Abteilung* 37 (1951): 1–94.

24. Bacht, *Vermächtnis*, 131 n. 48.

it was customary to connect Pachomius's monastic practices with his military experience, but it should be remembered that that experience was very short and painful.[25] If Pachomius consciously carried over any military customs, he meant to modify their meaning.

It is also worth noting that this dramatic, almost theatrical, gesture is probably at the origin of the Greek Orthodox custom of *metanie*, which figures so prominently in the prayer of the monks.[26] It does not involve the loosening of the belt, but bows and prostrations.

When we examine the Pachomian legislation on the *synaxis* or Divine Office closely, some of the details are not at all clear. Take, for example, Pr. 13: "Among the weekly servers from one house some shall not be chosen to stand on the step and recite something from Scripture in the assembly of all, but all of them, according to their order of sitting and standing, shall repeat from memory what has been assigned to them.' The point seems to be that a given house has to supply special monks to recite psalms in the general *synaxis*. Of these, *all* were to recite psalms in order, not just *some*.[27] But the Latin is obscure enough that a reputable scholar like Placid Deseille[28] comes to quite a different conclusion. He thinks this paragraph refers to the house *synaxis* (in the evening) and that it means that everybody recites, not just those who do so at the general *synaxis* in the morning.[29]

In Precepts 15–18 we seem to have a little subsection on the psalmody on Sunday or at the Eucharist. This psalmody is to be more festal than usual, and the way they achieve that is to make it antiphonal. In other words, there is alternation between the chanter and a chosen schola of cantors. That may not sound too festal to us, who normally

---

25. See *Coptic Life of Pachomius* (*Sbo* 7–8), in *PK* 1, 26–28.

26. Bacht, *Vermächtnis*, 130 n. 47.

27. This is the meaning also given in the German translation of Bacht, *Vermächtnis*, 84. Given the fact that it is possible to construe Pr. 13 very differently, it is surprising that Veilleux has no footnote for it in *PK*.

28. Deseille, *L'esprit du monachisme Pachômien, suivi de la traduction française des Pachomiana Latina par les moines de Solesmes* (Bégrolle-en-Mauges: Abbaye de Bellefontaine, 1968).

29. This is not the only time the French translation is erroneous. For Pr. 17, Veilleux has: "If anyone is missing when one of the elders is chanting, that is, reading the psalter, he shall at once undergo the order of penance and rebuke before the altar." The French, though, misreading an ablative absolute, has: "If anyone makes a mistake while chanting . . ." By definition the subject of the ablative absolute cannot be the same as the subject of the main verb.

use antiphonal psalmody, but it was more elaborate than their usual method of simply listening to a single chanter.

Although we are not exactly sure how they did Mass and Office on the weekend, it seems that the Pachomian community attended the parish Eucharist on Saturday evening.[30] They also had Mass at the monastery the next morning, and probably the psalms referred to here were sung at morning *synaxis* before Mass. There is no indication that they stayed up all night in a prayer vigil every weekend.[31]

In addition to liturgical worship, the Pachomian monks were deeply involved in the study of Scripture.[32] This study mostly took the form of catechetical instructions given by the superiors. From what we can tell, the abbot of the monastery gave three such instructions on Saturday and Sunday (*Sbo* 26), while the housemaster gave catecheses on Wednesday and Friday (Pr. 138). Even more interesting is the Pachomian custom of *discussing* among themselves what they have heard in the catechesis: "In the morning in the individual houses, after the prayers are finished, they shall not return right away to their cells, but they shall discuss among themselves the instruction they heard from their housemasters. Then they enter their quarters" (Pr. 19).

There is a certain amount of confusion about who gave instructions when,[33] but the very process of communal reflection on what has just been heard concerning the Scripture has a rather modern ring about it. However, anyone who has tried to promote this kind of ongoing discussion in the monastery knows it is not all that easy.[34]

30. *Sbo* 25, in Veilleux, *PK* 1, 47.

31. In his "Histoire des moines aux Kellia," *Orientalia Lovanensia periodica* 8 (1977): 187–203, at 194, Antoine Guillaumont says of the Desert Fathers that they had an *agapē* meal on Saturday evening followed by psalmody. Then at daybreak they had Mass.

32. My account of the catecheses is drawn from the synthesis of Cremaschi, *Pacomio e i suoi discepoli*, 94.

33. For example, in Pr. 19 it seems the words "from their housemasters" have been inserted by Jerome. At least it is not clear why the housemaster should be giving a catechesis at the general morning prayer. Regarding Pr. 20, Bacht, *Vermächtnis* (Veilleux, *PK* 2, 186 n. 20), thinks "by the housemasters" has been added by Jerome, and not to good effect. But Veilleux himself may stumble in these matters. For example, when he translates "meditate" in Pr. 122, Bacht thinks he should have written "discuss."

34. For years the present writer sponsored a Friday night discussion of the Mass reading for the upcoming Sunday, but the exercise was hard to maintain.

Work, Meals, and Sick-Care (Precepts 23–47)

Although Pr. 23–27 is a cluster on work, the topic is discussed in many Precepts outside of this section (58–66; 92; 111; 116; 123–25). This indicates that work was very important for the Pachomians, but it does not mean it was *all*-important. Because their work was highly organized, some scholars have concluded that the large Pachomian communities were little more than work camps.[35] It is true that economic concerns were of profound importance to the continuance of the community, but they were still secondary.

One way to keep monastic work within its proper bounds is to make sure it is done under obedience. Thus Pr. 23–24 insist that the superior keep control of this important area of life. Of course, authority had to be delegated, especially in a system where the work was so varied. But when monastic work becomes an autonomous enterprise the whole cenobitic system is in danger of collapse.[36]

Throughout these paragraphs the *minister* is a key official in the work system. He is the one who keeps people supplied, especially with reeds for plaiting. These reeds (*mattae*) had to be wet in advance to be pliable enough to plait, and they could only be wet three times before they began to rot.[37] This meant that a good deal of planning went into keeping the system functioning. Just as the reeds of the Nile were ubiquitous in Egyptian life, the plaiting of ropes, mats, cloth, cushions, and papyrus-paper was a constant activity for most of the people of the land. For the Pachomian monks it was combined with other seasonal work like farming, and also with various specialized crafts.

For one thing, it demands that someone give the "catechesis." If the other participants have not also done some previous study, the discussion tends to become one-sided. The practice of an American Benedictine abbot was interesting: he used to write out and distribute his conferences to the community. Then the actual "*synaxis*" would take the form of a discussion of his conference.

35. E.g., Emmanuel Amand de Mendieta, "Le système cénobitique basilien comparé aux système cénobitique Pachômien," in *Revue de l'histoire des religions* 152 (1957): 31–80, at 41.

36. The revolt against Abbot Horsiesi (*G1* 127) took the form of a move for economic independence by some of the monasteries. Theodore's method of regaining power and reuniting the community was to depose all the abbots and regain control for the head abbot over the economics of the whole *koinonia*.

37. Bacht, *Vermächtnis*, 143 n. 120.

Where the Pachomians excelled was in the rational planning of their work. This was necessary because for them work was not so much an ascetical exercise as a practical necessity to support the vast community.[38] One of the chief means of systematizing work is to conduct accurate inventory, and thus the arrangement in Pr. 27 for a weekly count of the production of each house. On a larger scale, the August meeting of all the monasteries featured financial accounting on the grand scale. By this means order and efficiency were ensured in a large, complex group.[39]

If the work system of Pachomius was more regimented than that of most subsequent monastic Rules, the arrangement for meals (Prs. 28–39) was not. It appears that the monks had two meals every day except fast days, at noon and evening, but not everyone was obliged to participate in the evening meal.[40] Further, some kind of sweets were handed out to those departing the refectory, to be eaten in one's own cell (Pr. 38). Since the monks were strictly forbidden to eat outside of mealtimes, this is a puzzling arrangement. Even more obscure is the fact that they received enough for three days![41]

Perhaps Pachomius was fairly liberal in the matter of communal meals because the peasants who came to him hardly knew how to eat properly at all! At least that is the impression we get from Pr. 31, which tells the housemasters to teach the monks how to eat "with manners

38. The classic example of work as an ascetical exercise would be that of the desert hermit who wove baskets all year long but burned them at the end. As a matter of fact, almost all the work done by the Egyptian monks, whether anchoritic or cenobitic, was sold for profit. Only rich people can afford to work for nothing but ascetic profit.

39. The Easter meeting of all the monks was primarily to baptize those who were catechumens. In August, however, the purpose was the less exalted one of financial audit. Still, Pr. 27 notes that the August meeting included the "forgiveness of sins for everyone." Some scholars (Ruppert, Veilleux in his early doctoral dissertation) think this means the reconciliation of quarrels. At any rate, more than just "business" was transacted in August.

40. According to Pr. 79 the monks could take a spartan meal of bread and salt in their own cells instead of coming to the evening meal. Bacht, *Vermächtnis*, 147 n. 134, says that this liberality scandalized the anchorites and that the scandal is still reflected in the Rule of the Master 28.3ff.

41. To add to the confusion, they were also to bring back "what was left over" to be mixed back into the main supply. Since we do not even know exactly what the "sweets" (*tragematia*) were that they were given, it is probably futile to speculate further on this point.

and mildness." This may also account for the rule that they were to eat with their hoods up, and not watch others eating.[42]

Even though there is nothing very remarkable about Pachomius's rules for meals, nonetheless a very important cenobitic principle does make its appearance here. In regard to the cooks, he says (Pr. 35) they "shall eat nothing but what has been prepared for the brothers in common, nor shall they dare to prepare special foods for themselves." This means that no one is to presume to make special arrangements for himself. And to ensure this, everyone is to *receive* what he needs from another, not take it for himself. Indeed, we read in the *Life* (*G1* 110) that Pachomius himself followed this rule to the letter.

In Pr. 39 the following corollary is stated: "No one shall give more to one than another has received." At this point some caution seems to be in order. As a principle for passing out sweets this rule might be acceptable, but on a broader scale it is not adequate. Even though cenobites have everything in common and do not help themselves, they still have different needs. If this rule of strict distributive justice were to be literally applied, those who need more would go wanting, while those who need less would have too much.[43] And in fact certain incidents in the *Life of Pachomius* show that this is not at all what he wanted.[44]

In many ways the rules for the care of the sick resemble those for meals. Since little was known about chemicals, ancient medicine was mainly concerned with special diets.[45] Yet the monks were so frugal

---

42. Bacht, *Vermächtnis*, 147 n. 136, says this was so that they would not know if others were eating or fasting. I had always assumed it was because Pachomius considered the very act of eating somewhat shameful, and therefore not to be observed. But he never manifests that kind of dualist rigorism elsewhere.

43. In RB 34, St. Benedict deals with just this problem, insisting that each one should get what he needs. This chapter is a sort of summary of many passages in the *Praeceptum* of Augustine, which discusses this question in great detail. Since Augustine had both rich aristocrats and poor but tough peasants in his community, fair distribution was a difficult issue.

44. In *G1* 51, Pachomius refuses special treatment from the brothers when he gets sick, but in *G1* 53 he is indignant when the nurses refuse special treatment to another monk who is sick. This shows a certain amount of conflict in the founder, whose ascetic background makes it hard for him to receive special care when he is himself sick.

45. In his preface (5), Jerome expresses his admiration for the fine, compassionate care of the sick that Pachomius offers. He understands it mainly as a more generous diet.

about what they ate that the relaxation of dietary rules for the sick had to be carefully articulated. In general the sick were allowed to drink some wine, and their food could be somewhat richer than the common fare. For example, sick monks in Egypt were given fish broth, something healthy monks did not eat (Pr. 46).

One of Pachomius's rules (Pr. 40) might seem to suggest that he distrusted the sick: "If some sickness is alleged, the housemaster shall proceed to the ministers of the sick and receive from them whatever is necessary." Since the Latin term *obtendetur* can mean to "feign," some translators think that is what is meant here.[46] But no other Pachomian text suggests that the legislator harbored the slightest distrust of the sick. In this regard he is unlike the Rule of the Master, and very much like St. Augustine, who taught that when one of the monks claims to be sick he is to be believed and treated specially.[47]

Yet special treatment for the sick does not include letting them do whatever they please. As the text quoted above shows, the sick person informs the housemaster, who then arranges with the infirmarians for his treatment. In other words, the sick people are cared for, but not necessarily on their own terms. They remain under obedience, which certainly has a realistic ring for anyone who has been in the hospital lately! Nor may the housemasters or even the nurses care for themselves when they are sick (Pr. 41). They too must be *cared for* by another and thus come under obedience.

We should not read back our own ideas of health care into ancient times, when medicine was incredibly primitive. It would be a mistake to credit Pachomius with establishing some kind of modern health clinic. Compared to St. Benedict, for example, Pachomius's sick-care system is still relatively undeveloped.[48] Still, Pachomius shows real compassion for the sick and does what he can for them by way of orderly arrangements.

Relations with the Outside World (Precepts 49–57)

In this section we find prescriptions for the treatment of new recruits from "the world" and other rules for various situations in which the

46. Thus Basilius Steidle, "Ich war krank und ihr habt mich besucht," *Erbe und Auftrag* 41 (1965), 189–206, at 191.

47. See RM 69–70; Augustine, *Praeceptum* 5.6.

48. For an overview of the ancient monastic Rules on care of the sick see *La Règle de saint Benoît*, introduction, translation, and notes by Adalbert de Vogüé, text by Jean Neufville (Paris: Cerf, 1971–77), 6: 1075–1109.

monks must interact with the people around them. It is such a clear-cut section that some scholars think it once existed independently before being integrated with the previous material.[49]

Precept 49, on the formation of new monks, is one of the longest and best developed chapters in the whole Rule.[50] While it never really proposes a "novitiate" in the later sense,[51] it nevertheless includes many valuable points that have been of great influence down through the history of monasticism. It does not answer all the questions we might want to ask about formation, but neither do any of the other ancient Rules. In his first sentence Pachomius says a mouthful: "When someone comes to the door of the monastery, wishing to renounce the world and be added to the number of the brothers, he shall not be free to enter." Why should he not be welcomed with open arms? Because he has come for a difficult purpose, a purpose he himself may well not understand.

First of all, he has come to "renounce the world." This idea was so basic to early monasticism that the Greek word *apotaktikos* (renunciant) was often used to mean "monk."[52] Precept 49 later explains that the specific renunciation of the monk regards his family and his possessions, but it is important to interject that to renounce these things is not the same as to *despise* them. That unfortunate interpretation came along later, and it has caused a great deal of trouble in monastic history.[53] Of course, the basic renunciation of the Christian monk is to forego

49. Fidelis Ruppert, *Das pachomianische Mönchtum und die Anfänge des klösterlichen Gehorsams* (Münsterschwarzach: Vier-Türme, 1971), 284, thinks that Prs. 50–57 were probably added onto the very highly developed Pr. 49, which could come from a later time, perhaps that of Theodore.

50. Actually, Pachomius discusses this topic three times. In Pr. 1 there is no formation at all, since the candidate is brought directly from the door to the choir. Precept 139 deals mainly with reading and memorization of the Bible. Compared to them, Pr. 49 is much more detailed and amounts to a veritable little treatise on monastic formation.

51. According to Irénée Hausherr, *Direction spirituelle en Orient autrefois* (Rome: Pontifical Institute of Oriental Studies, 1955), 112, quoted in Bacht, *Vermächtnis*, 157 n. 198.

52. See *G1* 24; *G1* 139; *Liber Orsiesi* 21, 27, 30, 47.

53. It can be seen in Denis the Little's Latin translation of the *Life of Pachomius*, found in *PL* 73:249. The Christian is asked to "renounce" the world at baptism, but that refusal is of Satan and all his pomps.

marriage, which is included in "family." But the cenobite also eschews private property as an impediment to community life.[54]

We have already noted that the memorization and rumination of Scripture was a key element of Pachomian monastic practice. Thus it is not surprising that the new monk is expected to "remain outside the door a few days and be taught the Lord's Prayer and as many psalms as he can learn." Precept 139 wants them to learn "twenty-two psalms or two of the Apostle's epistles or some other part of Scripture." Since many of these newcomers were illiterate, they were also expected to learn to read (Pr. 139). As an entrance requirement this was a hard trial for most of them, and a harbinger of the hard life they were undertaking.[55]

Even though renunciation was a big factor in early monastic ideology, it was not the whole story for Pachomius. One does not just come to renounce the world; one comes to "join the brothers." This is quite different from joining a guru or master, as was the case with the anchoritic novice. The operative word here is "brothers," an intensely communal word that occurs four times in Pr. 49.[56] Next comes a feature that is unique to this Rule, namely, an interrogation of the candidate's motives. Here, two impediments are mentioned as obstacles: (1) "Has he done something wrong, and troubled by fear, suddenly run away?" (2) "Is he

---

54. Many Precepts demand dispossession: 53; 81; 83; 98; 106; 116. *S1* 11 is a remarkable episode in the *Life of Pachomius* that describes his initial experiment in community formation. It seems he allowed the first recruits, probably former anchorites, to retain their own property as long as they supported the group from their goods. When these novices showed no signs of mutual obedience he drove them out. His next experiment demanded total renunciation as the cost of entry. This lesson was also learned the hard way by Augustine, who finally demanded full dispossession in his monasteries in Thagaste and Hippo.

55. Although many Rules decreed that newcomers not be granted easy entrance, it is not always clear how they were to be tested. RB 58.3 says they should be tested with "rebuffs" (*inuriae*) for four or five days, but one wonders how this was compatible with Christian charity. RM 90.2 suggests that the rebuffs be "feigned," but that is still vague. One also wonders if Pachomius turned down those who could not memorize. His own test with Palamon consisted in imitating the heroic asceticism of the master.

56. As Bacht, *Vermächtnis*, 158 n. 200, points out, this is one of Pachomius's favorite terms. In *Catechesis* 1, which is an adaptation of a text by Athanasius, Pachomius had added the word "brother" fifteen times, but the *Greek Excerpta* of Pr. 49 omits this word entirely. In *Sbo* 23 and *S1* 11–19, Pachomius is shown serving the novices, but he later learned that the novices should be tested in how well they serve the brothers.

under someone's authority?" The very fact that Pachomius is careful to scrutinize his candidates shows that he is aware that not everyone comes to the monastery for the right reasons. It also suggests that there were particular problems with monastic recruitment in Egypt.

If someone has done something wrong enough to cause him to run away, we can assume that it was a serious crime, not excluding murder. In fact, we know that some of the Desert Fathers were repentant sinners, fugitives from the law (*Lausiac History* 19). Apparently the law somehow allowed these men to live in the desert, but the Pachomian monasteries were not located in the desert; they were in the heart of the settled farmland along the Nile. Pachomius could not admit criminals.[57]

The second impediment that bars a person from this community is being under someone's authority. No doubt this refers to slavery, which was widespread in ancient times, but it could also have to do with the evasion of taxes. One of the reasons why the Pachomians were able to found large farms in the Nile Valley at that time was that other people were abandoning them. Taxes had become so oppressive that farmers were simply disappearing from the land, and no doubt some of them tried to join Pachomius's monastery.[58]

When the postulant had satisfactorily negotiated the short testing period he was ready to enter the community. This was effected by simply clothing him with the habit. In early Eastern monasticism "to put on the schema" simply meant to become a monk. According to Heinrich Bacht this was not so much a liturgical ceremony as a practical means of removing the last vestige of private property from the novice and

57. In her comment on this verse Cremaschi, *Pacomio e i suoi discepoli*, 100 n. 4, indicates that the problem was moral turpitude. In other words, Pachomius was not admitting homosexuals. At least that is the way I read the following sentence: "una vita moralmente disordinata, nel caso si rivellase impossibile sottoporre chi chiedeva di entrare a far parte nella communitá alle speciale vigilanza che Pachomio richiedeva in questi casi." Here she seems to refer to Pachomius's remark (*Sbo* 107) that he had turned down one hundred homosexuals in one year, not because they were hopeless, but because he did not have the time to devote to them that they would need. As for me, I don't think homosexuality is the kind of condition in which people are "troubled by fear, (and) suddenly run away."

58. For a good discussion of the social circumstances of the Pachomian foundation see James E. Goehring, *Ascetics, Society and the Desert* (Harrisburg, PA: Trinity Press International, 1999), 97–100.

replacing it with the property of the monastery. There is no explicit mention of vows in this Rule.[59]

After the magisterial Pr. 49, the following chapters on dealing with the world are less imposing, but they are still of considerable interest. The desert monks of Egypt were famous for their hospitality, and Pachomius surely shared that value.[60] Yet community life demands certain constraints on this openness to strangers, and most of the regulations in this section have to do with those restraints. For example, Pr. 50 forbids a monk to invite anyone to a meal but tells him to send the person to the guesthouse to eat. What could be more antithetical to the customs of the hermits, who went to great lengths to feed their guests? And what could be harder to observe for these monks who came from a culture where direct hospitality was the honor and privilege of every "great man"? Why was Pachomius so cautious in his openness to the world?

One factor may have been theology. Precept 51 is all in favor of bringing certain people such as priests and monks into the *synaxis* of prayers, "provided they are of the same faith." Probably this refers to orthodox believers as opposed to Arians, for this theological controversy was raging throughout the fourth century when the Rule of Pachomius was written.[61] But there were also other monks in Egypt who were not in communion with the Patriarch of Alexandria, and it is doubtful whether they were welcome at the prayers either.

59. Theodore, *Catechesis* 3.3.23 explicitly mentions monastic vows (*homologia*), and fifty years later Schenute has a written promise (*diatheke*) that must be signed (Cremaschi, *Pacomio e i suoi discepoli*, 103).

60. See Lucien Regnault, *Day to Day Life of the Desert Fathers in Fourth Century Egypt*, trans. Etienne Poirier, Jr. (Petersham, MA: St. Bede's Publications, 1999), 139–50. In fact, the Council of Nicea (325) instructed bishops to set up hospices, and it also recommended that those hospices be run by monks (Gian Domenico Mansi, *Sacrorum Conciliorum nova et amplissima collectio*, 31 vols. (Florence and Venice: 1758–98), 11.1006, quoted by Cremaschi, *Pacomio e i suoi discepoli*, 103–4).

61. In *G1* 138 the monks refuse to pray with an Arian official from Alexandria. As for the Meletian monks, they were not heretics but schismatics who did not accept Athanasius and the arrangements after the great persecution of Diocletian. Goehring, *Ascetics*, esp. 187–95, shows that they were very numerous and prominent in fourth-century Egypt. But the gulf between orthodox and Meletian monks may not have been unbridgeable, for sometimes they seem to have lived together. See Goehring, "Monastic Diversity and Ideological Boundaries in Fourth-Century Christian Egypt," *Journal of Early Christian Studies* 5/1 (1997): 6–84.

This same paragraph mentions that only the feet of "priests and monks" should be washed, which seems less generous than St. Benedict's rule that the feet of all, and especially the poor, be washed (RB 53.12-15). Yet Pachomius also received the poor for hospitality and even made special provision for them: "If seculars, or infirm people or *weaker vessels*, that is, women, come to the door, they shall be received in different places according to their calling and their sex." From the *Life of Pachomius* we know this meant that such groups had separate quarters, outside the main monastic compound.

That arrangement seems practical and thoughtful today, but it also caused some resentment, at least at first. When the community was still in its infancy all male guests lived among the monks. At some point Pachomius ended this arrangement and had guest quarters built outside the compound, which provoked an angry reaction from the Deacon of Tentyra. He accused Pachomius of violating Jesus' ethic of direct charity to all. But Pachomius did not back down, saying that he had some rough young neophytes in his ranks and he could not expose guests to them (*Sbo* 40)! The humor of this story should not blind us to the fact that this is in fact the first description of cloister in all of monastic literature.[62]

In Pr. 53–57 the monk's relation to his family is a main theme. An overview of these paragraphs may give the impression that Pachomius was determined to break, even obsessed with breaking, the family ties that bound his monks, but this is probably a false conclusion. It should be understood that family ties in his society were far stronger than in our postindustrial society. Families were extremely reluctant to "lose" a member, and they could exert enormous pressure to regain that member in one way or another. Those were healthy families, and we should not disdain them, but they were also an impediment to the monk's *apotaxis*.[63]

Still, compared to later monastic legislators Pachomius is really quite lenient about family relations. Precept 54 allows a monk to visit a sick relative, provided he is accompanied by a confrère. This is the so-called

---

62. Bacht, *Vermächtnis*, 170 n. 242.

63. Nowadays monasteries in traditional societies such as Africa operate within the same dynamics. For a discussion of the relation between ancient monks and their families see André Borias, "Le moine e sa famille," *Collectanea Cisterciensia* 40 (1978): 81–111; 194–217.

regula socii that became standard for most religious until recent times.[64] This same paragraph gets itself all entangled in worrying about whether the monk should eat with his relatives or not. Indeed, the question of food passing from family to monk seems to concern Pachomius very much.[65] But we should also recognize that Pachomius is fundamentally humane about the family question.

To illustrate the balanced approach of Pachomius we need only read *Sbo* 37. In that story the young monk Theodore absolutely refuses to see his mother when she comes to the gate. Pachomius suggests that, since she has brought a letter from the bishop, it would be best to go see her. Theodore then invokes the Gospel[66] to back up his decision, and Pachomius defers to the young zealot. Yet the reader gets the impression that he does so reluctantly, and in fact he later conspires to send Theodore out with a monk who insists on visiting his family (*Sbo* 63). Even though Pachomius is a Christian idealist, he tempers that trait with a good deal of realism.

64. Cremaschi, *Pacomio e i suoi discepoli*, 107, suggests that the biblical model is Mark 6:7, where Jesus sends out the disciples to preach "two by two." See also Pr. 56.

65. Families are still expected to feed their own in traditional societies. Even in modern Italy families often supply the diet for hospital patients! In some Third World hospitals, to lack this family support is to risk starvation.

66. Probably the fierce Luke 14:26: "Whoever comes to me and does not hate father and mother, wife and children, brothers and sisters, yes, and even life itself, cannot be my disciple." Biblical scholars often explain away "hate" as a substitute for "love less" because the Semitic languages cannot express nuance. Clearly there is no nuance in Theodore's interpretation of monastic *apotaxis*.

Chapter Six

The Rule of Pachomius: II (Precepts 58–97)

Work outside the Monastery (Precepts 58–66)[1]

The nine paragraphs in this unit[2] are all devoted to excursions outside the monastic compound. Most of the numbers refer to the activities of work crews going out daily, although a couple of paragraphs (namely, Prs. 64 and 66, which will be discussed below) may refer to longer journeys. Like most cenobitic monasteries, those of Pachomius owned fields outside the walls of the abbey itself. In this case the monks worked these fields, and so the Rule legislates for this part of their daily existence.

When one reads over this particular bloc of material, the impression one receives is of considerable rigidity on the part of the legislator. The monks are to march out to work in line; they are not to talk to each other; they are not to sit down without permission; at mealtime they are to wait to be served; they are to march home in order; and finally

---

1. The translation I followed for this work is found *in Pachomian Koinonia* (*PK*) 2, trans. Armand Veilleux (Kalamazoo: Cistercian Publications, 1981). The commentary that was most helpful was Heinrich Bacht, *Das Vermächtnis des Ursprungs*, vol. 2 (Würzburg: Echter. 1983). The material in this chapter was first published in *Tjurunga* 68 (2005): 81–96 and is revised here by permission.

2. I follow the division suggested by Lisa Cremaschi in *Pacomio e i suoi discepoli: regole e scritti* ([Magnano] Qiqajon: Community of Bose, 1988), 108.

they are to turn in their tools in good order. No wonder historians like Kassius Hallinger have labeled this Rule "militaristic."[3]

Recent scholarship has shown that Pachomius had no love for the military, of which he was but a brief and reluctant part.[4] But it must be admitted that in this section there is a strong emphasis on uniformity and discipline. The reason for this no doubt has to do with the fact that it was considered dangerous to the spiritual health of the monks to venture outside the monastic cloister.[5] The author seems to think the best prophylaxis for those who must work outside is the maintenance of the same discipline that prevails inside the cloister.

One way that the internal discipline is to be maintained comes through the strict observance of *statio*. Each monk must keep to his rightful place, in walking to and from the fields (Pr. 58, 59, and 65) as in all other things.[6] What is more, each house is to keep its place in the march. Even though they are superiors themselves, the work leaders are to consult higher superiors if they have to send a monk off to get something (Pr. 63).[7] Finally, if a superior has to leave the scene he must delegate his second to take command in his absence.

3. Hallinger was primarily a medievalist and no expert on ancient monasticism. Moreover, this conclusion was a mere sidebar in his massive doctoral thesis *Gorze-Kluny. Studien zu den monastischen Lebensformen und Gegensätzen im Hochmittelalter*, Studia Anselmiana; philosophica, theologica, 22–25 (Rome: "Orbis Catholicus," Herder, 1950–51), 781. Other scholars who have expressed chagrin at Pachomius's alleged militarism are Emmanuel Amand de Mendieta, Anscari Mundó, and Rudolf Hanslik.

4. See *Sbo* 7–8. Heinrich Bacht, on whom this article puts heavy reliance, resists the label of militarism at every turn in his magisterial commentary. The notes for this section of the Precepts are found in *Vermächtnis*, 2, 173–97.

5. RB 66 insists on strict enclosure: "If possible, the monastery should be situated with all necessities such as water, mill and garden contained within the walls so the various crafts can be practiced there. Then it will not be necessary for the monks to move about outside, which is certainly not good for their souls." But the fact is that throughout the history of monasticism monks have often *had* to go outside the walls for various necessities.

6. "Fields" are never mentioned in this section, but they are implied. In Pr. 59 passersby can talk to the monks, so apparently they are working outside. The Pachomian communities were not located in the Egyptian desert, but in the heart of the Nile Valley where they owned and worked extensive agricultural holdings.

7. Pr. 63 is the only member of this unit in which the Latin is not very clear. *Ductores fratrum in itinere si necessarium habuerint aliquem mittere,*

Silence is another aspect of internal monastic discipline that is to be carefully maintained by those participating in work crews. The monk is not to ask where the crew is going, and he is also not to talk during the march. While the group is at work the individuals are not to speak with each other, but they are to meditate on the Scriptures. Furthermore, if someone happens along and wishes to chat with the monks they are not to reciprocate, but all questions are to be directed to the "doorkeeper of the monastery" (*janitor monasterii*)[8] or the housemaster (*praepositus domus*).

The demand for almost total silence from the workers may strike us as rather harsh, but it can be interpreted in various ways. For example, Adalbert de Vogüé thinks it shows that although Pachomius is legislating for cenobites, his monastic ideal is really anchoritic. For him that would seem to preclude ordinary conversation.[9] But Pachomius does not merely demand silence; he wants the monks to meditate on Scripture while they are walking and while they are working. This is quite to be expected in

---

sine praepositi jussione non poterunt can either mean: (1) "If the leaders of the brothers on a journey have a need to send someone, they may not do so without the master's orders" or (2) "If the leaders of the brothers have a need to send someone on a journey . . ." Adalbert de Vogüé, "Les pièces latines du dossier pachômien," *Revue d'histoire ecclésiastique* 67 (1967): 26–67, at 30, opts for the first. Armand Veilleux, *PK* 2, 157, chooses the second. Bacht, *Vermächtnis*, 2, 98, probably holds the first view. Part of the problem lies in the term "leaders of the brothers" (*ductores fratrum*), which appears nowhere else in the Pachomian literature. They must be regular officials, because the same paragraph tells them to delegate to the next one in line (*in ordine*) if they themselves must leave. The *ductor* must be lower in the order than a *praepositus domus* because he has to clear his orders with him. Up to this point Prs. 58–62 have discussed work crews operating outside the monastery. Precept 64 applies to any Pachomian group functioning outside the compound. Based on these considerations, I prefer the first translation.

8. It does seem rather odd that the doorkeeper would accompany the monks out to fieldwork, but that is the obvious meaning here. Clearly, his role here is to shield the monks from unwanted interaction with seculars and not to admit the latter to the monastic group.

9. "'Comment les moines dormiront': Commentaire d'un chapître de la Règle de Saint Benoît," *Studia Monastica* 7 (1965): 25–62, at 41. Vogüé always emphasizes the solitary aspects of monasticism. While there is no doubt that monks always remain somewhat "alone in community," I do not believe it does justice to Pachomius to stress his eremitic training over his obvious wish to create an ideal Christian community with normal human interaction.

this author. Just as he wants the monks to do handwork at the common prayer (Prs. 2–5), so he wants them to pray during work.[10]

Finally, monastic discipline is maintained in meals taken outside the monastery. Although Pr. 64 is plainly not restricted to work crews, it certainly applies to them. Probably that is why it was included in this section even though it has wider application. When a group of monks must leave the compound they take a cook (*ebdomadarius*) with them. This monk does not actually cook but merely distributes cold porridge to the brothers.[11] For their part, they are not to help themselves, even to the water bucket (Pr. 64). That could be a real hardship for those doing fieldwork in the intense heat of Upper Egypt.

Washing Clothes (Precepts 67–70)

Surprisingly, four paragraphs of the Precepts concern washday. Of course, it is quite characteristic of this monastic Rule to enter into detail on mundane matters, but the whole subject of clean clothes is virtually untouched elsewhere in the early monastic literature. In fact, one sometimes finds the early monks positively glorying, on ascetic grounds, in dirty and unkempt clothes.[12] To judge from these four paragraphs, clothes washing was a regular communal exercise for the Pachomians. They did it together, as they did everything else together, marching down to the Nile every Sunday to wash their tunics.[13] It is not hard to

10. The vocabulary used here may not be entirely transparent. When Pachomius says the monks are to "meditate on something from Scripture" (Pr. 59), he probably does not mean they are to cogitate on a passage they have heard. Rather, they are to repeat in a low voice a biblical passage they have learned by heart. Note that in Pr. 60 "silence" (*silere*) is an alternative to this meditation! See Vogüé, "Les deux fonctions de la méditation dans les règles anciennes," *Revue d'histoire de la spiritualité* 51 (1975): 3–16.

11. In my view cold porridge (*absque coctione pulmenti*) points to long voyages in the Nile boats rather than fieldwork near the monastery. Of course, the fieldwork could have been too far from the compound to permit hot food being sent out to the brothers.

12. Thus Basil in Letter 2. But it should be added that this is a very early letter of Basil, written when he was in his "novitiate fervor." It is highly doubtful that this eminently practical and balanced bishop and monastic legislator would have glorified dirty clothes in his mature judgment.

13. Nor was it *ad libitum*. Precept 69 insists that anyone who "stays behind" should be sent with a companion to do his washing at another time. It is not permitted to linger by the river after the others have departed.

imagine that this could have degenerated into a pretty rowdy affair, so Pr. 69 demands that they maintain modesty,[14] and they are also to keep silent during the washing.

In an even more detailed fashion, Pr. 70 tells the monks exactly how to dry their tunics. They are not to leave them out in the sun after nine in the morning and they are to "lightly work them over" (*leviter mollientur*) when they are dry.[15] Linen tunics were expensive and quite perishable, so it was important to take good care of them. Thus even though it might have seemed a bit luxurious to some monks that the Pachomians washed their clothes every week, their care of the clothes set a good example of monastic poverty.

Besides insisting on proper care of the tunics, Pr. 70 makes it very clear that these were not private garments for the brothers. They are not to keep the one they have worn the past week and now washed, but turn it into the "second" of the house to be stored and redistributed. Since these were their most personal garments, we might think of this as an invasion of privacy, but in fact there are a few monastic communities even to this day where the members keep almost no personal clothes but take things from the general clothes closet as needed.

The alert reader may have noticed that the Pachomians did their washing on Sunday. Is this a typographical error? Not at all. The Catholic Church's prohibition of work on Sunday took a long time to develop. Some scholars point out that Constantine already banned work on Sunday in 321,[16] but Heinrich Bacht says that the early church did not connect its Sunday observance with Jewish sabbath prohibition from work until the sixth century in Gaul.[17] Certainly the ban on Sunday work was not official in the fourth century when the Precepts were written. Jerome, whose strong point was never consistency, lauds the cenobites in Letter 22.35 for not working on Sunday but praises the nuns of Bethlehem in Letter 108 for working hard on the same day. In his general study of this question for the whole church, Hans Huber

---

14. In fact, Pr. 69 tells them not to hitch their tunics up higher than is the norm (*statutum*). The ancients did not wear anything next to their skin under their tunics. This concern for modesty is repeated in Prs. 88, 89, 92, 93, and 96.

15. Apparently linen becomes hard and unwearable if it is not worked over after drying. See Bacht, *Vermächtnis*, 180 n. 320. In the fierce Egyptian sun it is not possible to wear wool, and the same sun will also destroy any garment left out to dry at midday.

16. Cremaschi, *Pacomio e i suoi discepoli*, 109.

17. Bacht, *Vermächtnis*, 178 n. 308.

notes that Pr. 67 was considered a classic proof-text for the acceptability of work on Sunday.[18]

Kitchen and Garden (Precepts 71–80)

Despite the title, this section is really about eating. The ingestion of food is a basic human need, and also a spiritual question. Briefly put, monks are supposed to be very careful what they put into their mouths and when. Their reasons for eating or not eating can be various, but they seem to fall into two categories: individual asceticism and social responsibility. Because Egyptian anchoritism focused largely on the first motive for fasting, the second is not too well known. Yet it is the main consideration in this section of the Precepts.

Thus the first two little paragraphs, which forbid the monks to help themselves to the vegetables in the garden and the dates in the palm grove, say nothing about personal discipline. Rather, they are concerned that such behavior will undercut the authority of the monks who have responsibility for these work zones.[19] This delicacy about protecting the authority of department managers is quite characteristic of cenobitic monasteries even to our own day, and it is interesting to see it operative at the very beginnings of the cenobitic movement.[20]

But even within the cenobitic ethos there are multiple reasons for observing self-discipline regarding food. Precept 73 warns the brothers not to sample unripe grapes or ears of grain before "they have been served to all the brothers together." Apparently there was a custom there of

18. *Geist und Buchstabe der Sonntagsruhe: eine historisch-theologische Untersuchung über das Verbot der knechtlichen Arbeit von der Urkirche bis auf Thomas von Aquin* (Salzburg: Otto Müller, 1958), 83. Further bibliography: Willy Rordorf, *Der Sonntag. Geschichte des ruhe- und Gottesdiensttage im ältesten Christentum* (Zürich: Zwingli Verlag, 1962) [English: *Sunday: The History of the Day of Rest and Worship in the Earliest Centuries of the Christian Church*, trans. A. A. K. Graham (London: S.C.M. Press, 1968)], and idem, *Sabbat und Sonntag in der alten Kirche* (Zürich: Theologischer Verlag, 1972).

19. The gardener is given the title *hortulanus*, but the palm-dresser is simply called "the one who has charge of the palms."

20. Obviously there can be abuses. Thus in RB 57 the craftsmen of the monastery are warned not to fall into the trap of thinking of themselves as a "gift to the monastery" (57.3). If they do they are to be summarily removed from their departments and not reinstated until they resume a sufficiently humble attitude.

communal sharing in the firstfruits of the monastic farm. For individuals to help themselves before the common celebration would be a violation of the common life.[21] The Pachomian discipline is meant to safeguard the community from the whims of the individual.

Although we have seen how the Precepts protect the authority of the department managers, they do not give them unlimited rights. In the kitchen, for example, the cook is not to taste the food before he distributes it to the community (Pr. 74). While this may sound severe and even unreasonable, it probably does not refer to tasting the food to see if it is properly seasoned.[22] Rather, it bars the cook from feeding himself before he has fed the rest of the community. The same holds true in the palm grove: Pr. 75 forbids the one in charge from sampling the dates "before the brothers have first had some."

But the next paragraph shows that the Precepts are not rigoristic in regard to food. When it comes to harvesting the dates, the crew that is gathered to do it should be given a few dates to eat for their trouble.[23] It is reassuring to see this ancient Rule tenderly taking care of the brothers and not slipping into the fanaticism about fasting that marred some sectors of early Christianity.[24] Since it was well understood that the use of food should build community and not undermine it, these monks

---

21. A comparison with Mark 2:23-28 is intriguing. In that episode the Pharisees complain that Jesus' disciples are violating the sabbath rest when they nibble on a few heads of grain. Jesus refuses to rein them in, insisting that "The sabbath was made for humankind, and not humankind for the sabbath." Thus he opposes humanitarian needs to the sanctity of the Law. But it would also be fair to say that the Pharisees were defending a reasonable custom.

22. The verb is *gustabit*. The notion of properly seasoning monastic food never comes up in the ancient monastic Rules, where the emphasis is on eating to live rather than living to eat. Nevertheless, when cooks ignore the art of preparing appetizing meals, monastic dining can become an area of tension and conflict.

23. Someone familiar with the Benedictine Rule will think immediately of RB 35.13, where the table waiters are offered a snack before the meal to tide them over until they can eat at "second table." Heinrich Bacht, *Vermächtnis*, 182 n. 340, wryly notes that this shows that Benedict was not the first, or the only, monastic legislator to exhibit humane concern for human weakness.

24. Some of the most zealous practitioners of asceticism in the early church were unable to keep clear of a dualistic fear and loathing of the body and the food needed to keep it alive. A classic study of this topic is Herbert Musurillo, "The Problem of Ascetical Fasting in the Greek Patristic Writers," *Traditio* 12 (1956): 1–64.

were careful not to destroy common work and morale with inappropriate fasting.

In a follow-up to the distribution of lunch to the harvesters, Pr. 77 rather surprisingly insists that the one who distributes the dates is not to take any for himself. It might seem commonsensical for him to do so, but the Rule requires him to take the crop to the general procurator, who will then give him some for himself.[25] The reason for this elaborate round dance is clear: no one is to feed himself! And that is the deepest principle of this whole section: no one is to take care of himself. The cenobite must take care of others—and allow others to take care of him.[26]

Admittedly, the detailed casuistry of the Precepts can sometimes come near the borderline of absurdity. Thus in Pr. 77 we find a warning against casual eating of fallen fruit, no doubt dates. The text is strong: "They shall not *dare* (*audebunt*) to eat them!" No, they must place them under the tree and pass on.[27] What is at stake here is probably not personal discipline but abhorrence of the possibility that any area of life would be completely *ad libitum*. For the cenobitic legislators, eating is also something that falls under the structure of obedience.[28]

25. The procurator here is called *dispensator*. This name did not persist in monastic history. In the Greek East the business manager was, and is, called *oikonomos*. In the West he is called *cellararius*.

26. This kind of thinking was put into radical effect by the founder himself. Although Pachomius was the abbot general of the whole congregation, he insisted on living in one of the houses with the brothers. Not only that: he subjected himself to the *praepositus domorum* of that house in obedience. Exactly how this convoluted system would work is not so important as the principle it inculcates. See *G1*, 110.

27. Actually, "pass on" is surprising and even anomalous. The Latin is clear enough: *in transitu*. Giuseppe Turbessi, *Regole Monastiche* (Rome: Studium, 1974), 116, thinks it means "on the path" but Bacht, *Vermächtnis*, 182 n. 342, thinks he is wrong. The trouble is that we are here in a context of harvesting and not simply "passing by." Bacht thinks that the Precept has conflated two separate rules that the *Excerpta Graeca* (Amand Boon, *Pachomiana Latina. Règle et Épîtres de St. Pachôme, Épître de s. Théodore et "Liber" de s. Orsiesius* [Louvain: Bureaux de la Revue, 1930], 177) keeps separate.

28. RB 43.18 is instructive in this regard: "If anyone is offered something by a superior and refuses it, then, if later he wants what he refused or anything else, he should receive nothing at all until he has made appropriate amends." Although it is not certain that this verse concerns food, it certainly looks like it.

Still, Pachomius does not completely eliminate personal choice in regard to eating. Indeed, Prs. 78–80 expressly allow the monk to eat in his cell rather than with the community. Precept 78 states the principle: "Let no one put away in his cell anything to eat, except what he has received from the steward." The next number makes it clear that this is a regular system of restricted diet. The steward is to make regular distribution of "loaves" of hardtack to those who have permission to eat alone. Moreover, this is not done as a "favor," but as a service to those who wish "to dedicate themselves to greater abstinence."

It could be said that this last provision does tend to undermine the communal practice of meals. Heinrich Bacht comments that it is absent from the *Greek Excerpta*, which were written for a later Pachomian house at Alexandria. No doubt that situation did not admit this kind of individual practice, which Bacht calls a "residue from anchoritism."[29] We might recall that Pachomius himself was first an anchorite and only later a cenobite, and it could be that he did not wish to eliminate the possibility of at least some individual choice in this matter of ascetic practice.[30]

Common Goods and Chastity (Precepts 81–97)

Precepts 81–97 are not a natural literary unit, but rather one of convenience. Within it there is one clear conceptual grouping concerning chastity (Prs. 92–97), but several lesser groupings as well: common goods (Prs. 81–83), enclosure (Prs. 84–86), and sleeping arrangements (Prs. 87–88). A few paragraphs seem to fall outside any obvious subunit, but they do connect to enclosure (Prs. 89–90) and chastity (Prs. 89, 91). Therefore my title for this section is somewhat arbitrary.

29. Bacht, *Vermächtnis*, 183 n. 345. He cites Alfred L. Schmitz, "Die Welt der ägyptischen Einsiedler and Mönche auf Grund der archäologischen Befund," *Römische Quartalschrift für christliche Altertumskunde und Kirchengeschichte* 37 (1929), 231, to the effect that the eating of the Eastern cenobites has never been successfully "domesticated." Even in 1929 some preferred to eat in their cells. Perhaps this has changed with the move in contemporary Coptic monasticism away from idiorrhythmic practices.

30. Certainly some accounts of the Pachomian monastic movement have lamented that it left no room for individual freedom. This view is disputed by Henri Delhougne, "Autorité et Participation chez les Pères du cénobitisme," *Revue d'ascétique et de mystique* 45 (1969): 369–94; 46 (1970): 3–32. And it certainly is not accepted by Bacht.

Precept 81 is a comparatively long paragraph on monastic possessions, couched in a curious double form that states first what the monk
may *not* have: "no woolen tunic, no mantle, no soft sheepskin with unshorn wool, not even a few coins, no pillow for his head or various other
conveniences." To an affluent modern reader this may look rather restric-
tive, but when the lawgiver lists what each one *was* given, it becomes
clear that the Pachomians did not practice extreme dispossession.[31]

More instructive for us is the rationale for this list, which is again
provided in a double form: (1) "No one shall have anything except what
is prescribed for all together by the law of the monastery." (2) "They shall
have only what is distributed by the father of the monastery through the
housemasters." Although the second principle might seem to open the
door to favoritism, the text goes on to specify precisely what the father
should distribute to each one.[32] He is to make sure the "common standard of the monastery (*commune monasterii lege*) is observed."

Some commentators[33] have noted that the emphasis in Pr. 81 is
on *community* of goods rather than on personal asceticism, as it is
in RB 33 and 55.[34] That is probably an accurate assessment, but we
might still ask a few questions about this common standard. Was it
applied with absolute rigor? in all situations? with no exceptions? The
Life of Pachomius indicates that the Founder practiced some flexibility
and common sense in these matters, although it took him some time
(perhaps a lifetime) to learn it. When he was sick, Pachomius refused
all special care, but he was outraged when another brother was denied

31. The standard of living was probably higher than that of the average
Egyptian peasant: "Two linen tunics plus the one already worn (thin), a long
scarf for the neck and shoulders, a goat-skin hanging from the shoulder, shoes,
two hoods, a belt and a staff." A glance at a similar list in RB 55 leaves a like
impression of frugality but not extreme abnegation.

32. See list in previous note. RB 34 seems to give the superior much more
discretion in this process: each is to get what he needs. This does not undercut
the value of a common standard, as is given in RB 55.

33. See Adalbert de Vogüé, *La règle de Saint Benoît*, introduction, translation, and notes by Adalbert de Vogüé, text by Jean Neufville, 7 vols. (Paris,
Cerf, 1971–77), 6: 912; Georg Holzherr, *Die Benediktsregel: eine Anleitung zu
christlichen Leben* (Zürich et al.: Benziger, 1982), 227.

34. RB 55.4, 10, and 14 repeat the key-word "enough" (*suffficit*), thus expressing a principle of moderation. RB 33, however, is a much more radical treatise based on the ancient theme of *avaritia*. Its claim is that private possessions
are a lethal vice to be extirpated.

special food by the infirmarians.[35] In my view St. Benedict goes well beyond Pachomius in RB 34, where he insists that what is needed is attention to individual *needs* and not standardization.

Precept 82 teaches that "no one shall have in his own possession little tweezers[36] for removing thorns he may have stepped on." In its present position this paragraph continues the discussion of the previous number. Precept 96 is on the same subject (pulling thorns), but it pertains to chastity and not common goods. Precept 83 forbids a monk who is transferred from one house to another (but within the same monastery)[37] to take with him anything but "what is mentioned above." So even though the cenobite does not *own* anything, he has a personal kit that only he uses.

The next subunit that presents itself could be labeled "enclosure." Precepts 84–86 presuppose a monastic philosophy of withdrawal from the surrounding society, with the enclosure wall serving as a protective membrane for the spiritual health and welfare of the inhabitants. At this point it needs to be repeated that the Pachomian monasteries were not in the desert, but in the heart of the Nile Valley, and thus close to the villages.[38] What is more, the monks went out regularly to farm and to trade by boat.[39] Given this proximity, it is not surprising that Pr. 84 does not want the monks strolling around outside the walls without

---

35. The story of the infirmarians is found in *Sbo* 48. This brother was suffering from severe malnutrition, yet the brothers refused to slaughter a goat for him. In his own case Pachomius repulsed the offer of a special light blanket on his deathbed (*Sbo* 120; see chap. 4 above). In this he exhibits a trait of many highly disciplined people who have trouble accepting care, and even love.

36. The term *mordax* is extremely rare. According to the authoritative *Thesaurus Linguae Latinae* it appears only here (Pr. 82) in all of Latin literature. *Mordere* means to bite.

37. The same principle would apply when the Pachomians were transferred from one monastery to another. See *Sbo* 144, where Theodore begins to rotate superiors on a six-month basis.

38. In *Sbo* 25, Pachomius sees that the local village (Tabennesi) is growing, so he builds a church there that the monks attend for Saturday evening Mass. It must have been an easy walk from the monastic compound.

39. As we saw above, Prs. 59–65 regulate the process of going to and from the fields for work. *Sbo* 132 tells of Theodore and two other brothers hearing of the death of Apa Petronios when they "were in the boat" at Alexandria. Apparently such long voyages on the Nile were routine. In fact, the community owned its own boats for transporting grain to the cities (see *Sbo* 192). Precept 86 speaks of "journeying by land and water."

permission. Nor does it permit them to circulate freely within the compound.[40] Of course, physical walls are no guarantee of enclosure if the monks do not internalize the value of withdrawal. Then they will carry tales with them to and from "the world," and they will also contribute to the gossip mills within the monastic community. Precepts 85–86 try to curb the general atmosphere of loquaciousness, which must have been a problem in that society.[41] Although it does not mention "silence," it was promoting this basic monastic value.

Precepts 87 and 88 both discuss sleeping arrangements, so they should be considered together. Precept 87 tells the brothers that whether they sleep in the cell, on the roof, or in the fields, they must use a sleeping chair (*sellula*).[42] Heinrich Bacht thinks these monks slept on reclining chairs to avoid deep sleep by lying flat.[43] I would respond that if the Pachomians worked as hard as the ordinary peasants such a practice would have ruined their health. As for their habit of sleeping on the roof or in the open, it can easily be explained as an attempt to cope with the intensely hot, dry climate of Upper Egypt.[44]

40. Vogüé, "'Comment les moines dormiront,'" 40, sees these regulations as a sure clue to the anchoritic origins of the Pachomian order: take care of your cell and your cell will take care of you. Bacht, *Vermächtnis*, 189 n. 382, agrees with him, but I would counter that RB 48.17-21 attempts to protect *lectio divina* from bored, gossipy, and wandering brothers. You need not be a hermit to require privacy and quiet for reading and prayer.

41. The same set of dynamics prevails in RB 67, a prohibition against discussing what one has seen on the road. Yet there *are* things happening around them that monks need to know. Nowadays the issue is complicated by the ubiquity of the mass media. For enclosed monasteries the question is how to use them without being destroyed by them.

42. Since the medieval scribes did not recognize *sellula*, and since *cella* appears elsewhere in the sentence, they changed *sellula* to *celulla*. This made no sense, but we are not exactly sure what a *sellula* was. For them to use it on the roof or out of doors it must have been light and portable.

43. Bacht, *Vermächtnis*, 191 n. 389. In his article "Agrypnia. Die Motive des Schlafentzugs im frühen Mönchtum," in *Bibliothek, Buch, Geschichte: Kurt Köster zum 65. Geburtstag*, ed. Günther Pflug, Brita Eckert, und Heinz Friesenhahn, 353–69 (Frankfurt am Main: Klostermann, 1977), Bacht assembles an array of ascetic strategies the old monks used to avoid sleep.

44. For a riveting account of how ferocious the heat can be in high summer in Egypt see Mark Gruber, *Journey Back to Eden* (Maryknoll, NY: Orbis, 2002), 198–203. When the thermometer hit 130° Fahrenheit even the Egyptian monks were virtually prostrate.

Precept 88 contains a number of ascetical restrictions on sleeping. "No one shall speak to another in the place where he sleeps." Although this text does not necessarily imply any sexual impropriety, it was interpreted by Schenute in that sense.[45] It should also be noted that Jerome's translation is already moving in that direction.[46] Apparently the Pachomian monks could have one or more roommates.[47] Also in an ascetic vein is the prohibition of Pr. 88 against eating or drinking during the night.[48] Precept 89 demands that they knock before entering the cell of another, which can be seen as a shield for modesty,[49] but also privacy. It would be a mistake, though, to interpret all the Pachomian rules through the lens of chastity. Precept 91 requires the monk to always wear his "goatskin and hood" to choir and table. Bacht plausibly suggests that this is aimed at common discipline, not modesty.

Precept 90 reprises Pr. 84, the prohibition against roaming about, except that now its scope has been narrowed. The brothers are not to "go in to eat at noon before the signal is given."[50] This could be construed as

45. Schenute of Atripe was the founder of a huge monastery (both male and female) in the same region of central Egypt as Pachomius. He ruled with an iron hand from 388 to 450 AD. In *De Vita Monachorum* 25 (CSCO Script Copt II.5), 4: 100, he uses this topic to introduce a whole series of warnings against sexual sins by cenobites.

46. "When he lies down to sleep, no one shall speak to another." Up to this point (Pr. 88) we have been following Jerome's translation, which is all we have. But from here on we have the Coptic original. Jerome makes silence a matter of time, not place. Presumably Schenute was using the Coptic version of Pr. 88.

47. *Lausiac History* 32 claims they slept three to a room; Cassian, *Inst* II.12, has one or two per room. Vogüé, "'Comment les moines dormiront,'" 391, would prefer private cells. One wonders if Palladius (*LH*) or Cassian had actually visited the Pachomian houses?

48. Although the Coptic forbids drinking upon rising, Jerome seems to make more sense: "If someone wakes up thirsty after he has retired, and it is a fast day, he will not dare to take a drink." Probably no medical adviser today would agree to this refraining from water in a hot, dry climate, and yet traditional Catholicism thought nothing of banning all hydration after midnight for communicants. And the medical people require the same regimen before certain tests!

49. The Precepts are generally concerned for modesty. See Prs. 2, 7, 31, 69, etc.

50. Jerome omits the words "at noon," which misses the reference to the "noonday devil," if it is there. Jerome also changes "in the village" to "in the "monastery," perhaps on the mistaken supposition that the former made no sense. But the village was in fact right outside the gate.

a reaction to a particular problem, namely, monks congregating outside the refectory door before mealtime. But Bacht[51] interprets it as a hedge against the notorious monastic problem of the "noonday devil." This refers to the tendency of a solitary monk to find the hours of the day growing very long, even endless. Although the Pachomians were not hermits, they sometimes plaited ropes and baskets in their cells. Since the noon meal was the first of the day, no doubt hunger was a factor here. But the real lesson is stability and perseverance in the contemplative life. Most modern commentators agree that Prs. 92–97 are a unit dedicated to protecting the monks from unchastity. This seems to be the case, even though the word "chastity"[52] is never mentioned and the regulations could seem fussy to the modern reader. Yet Schenute discusses many of the same details in explicitly sexual terms,[53] and we will also see that a careful reading of the *Life of Pachomius* shows that homosexual activity was a serious concern in fourth-century Egypt.

Precept 92 forbids a brother to "go to oil his hands in the evening unless a brother is sent with him." As Jerome makes clear, this activity is not cosmetic but practical: "hands rough from work." In fact, the plaiting of reeds is extremely hard on the hands. The real problem, however, is not with rough skin, but with being alone in the evening. As Pr. 56 indicates, no one was to move around alone (*nullus solus*). Yet most of the other infractions in this section happen with a second party.

The second half of Pr. 92, and Pr. 93 as well, deals with a subject that was touchy for all the early monks, namely, bathing. Actually what they objected to was total disrobing for any purpose. Of course, it was recognized that illness was an exception, but the prudish Jerome cannot resist adding that the sickness must be "obvious" (*perspicuus*). Needless to say, there must be no unauthorized bathing or anointing of another (sick) person (Pr. 93).[54] As with several of the issues discussed

51. Bacht, *Vermächtnis*, 193 n. 403. Perhaps the most famous expression of the syndrome of the "noonday devil" is found in Evagrius, *Praktikos* 12. A survey of the theme is found in Rudolph Arbesmann, "The 'Daemonium Meridianum' and Greek and Latin Patristic Exegesis," *Traditio* 14 (1958): 17–32.

52. Although Coptic Pr. 92 does have "immodestly" in regard to washing the body, Jerome's Latin has "naked" (*nudo corpore*).

53. The Abbot of Atripe (White Monastery) presents a long list of sexual sins in *De Vita Mon.* 25, given in Latin by Bacht, *Vermächtnis*, 194 n. 408.

54. It would not be hard to erect a large footnote of ancient monastic warnings against bathing, and especially in the nude: Jerome, *Ep.* 107.11; Horsiesi, *Catechesis* 2; Ps.-Athanasius. *De Virg.* 11. In our own time frequent

in Prs. 92–97,[55] the stricture against conversing at night in Pr. 94 is a reprise of Pr. 88. But if we are right that Prs. 92–97 are a group aimed at sexual purity, then the repetition is in a different key. At any rate, Pr. 94 forbids speaking in the dark, while Pr. 88 prohibits speaking in the bedroom.

With Pr. 95 we come to regulations that are obviously at war with homosexual activity. Precept 95 forbids the monks to sit together on a mat, but Jerome interprets this already as "sleep." Typically, Schenute spells things out: "Those who sleep two to a mat, or so close together that they touch each other or offend with lustful caresses, will be cursed."[56] Not surprisingly, many of the ancient Rules worry about young monks sleeping close to older ones.[57] Precept 95b is plain enough: "No one may clasp the hand or anything else of his companion; but whether you are sitting or standing or walking, you shall leave a forearm's space between you and him." This is sometimes known as the "rule of touch," which is interpreted by many of the ancient Rules as demanding a cubit of distance between persons.[58]

In Pr. 82 the monks were barred from having their own tweezers for pulling thorns; in Pr. 96 the action itself is regulated. But mutual aid is not completely excluded, for some thorns are hard to get out without

---

private bathing has become the norm in North America. But the ancient monks were probably reacting against the public bathing so dear to classical Greco-Roman society. Recently the pedophilia scandal has darkened the picture considerably.

55. So Pr. 87 and Pr. 95 both teach "one to a bed"; Pr. 82 and Pr. 96 are about pulling thorns.

56. *De Vita Mon.*, 21, *Opera* IV (CSCO Script Copt II.5), 74 Z 20.

57. Thus Bacht quotes Ps.-Anthony, *Reg. ad Mon.* 3 (PL 103.425A): "You are not to sleep on the same mat with someone younger than you." On the other hand, RB 22 wants the beds of juniors and seniors to be interspersed, so apparently it did not worry that the young would be preyed upon. But Benedict also wants each brother to have a separate bed, and he requires that a candle be kept burning until morning in the dormitory.

58. So Schenute, *De Vita Mon.*, 17, 57 Z 24, warns the older monks to keep their distance (i.e., one cubit) from the younger monks. Fructuosus of Braga (*Reg.* 17: PL 87.1107C) wants a cubit between the beds. Johannes Leipoldt, *Griechische Philosophie und frühchristliche Askese*, Berichte über die Verhandlungen der Sächsischen Akademie der Wissenschaften zu Leipzig, Philologisch-historische Klasse 106, 4 (Berlin: Akademie-Verlag, 1961), suggests that this regulation might be a residue of Pachomius's army experience, but Bacht, *Vermächtnis*, 197 n. 420, dismisses this as "naïve."

the help of another. Then one must call on the superior or his delegate for assistance. It may be hard for us to see the erotic dimensions of thorn-pulling, but there is no doubt that they were palpable to the early Egyptian monks.[59] The same must have been true for cutting hair, which seems innocuous enough but was also hedged with safeguards. Again, the cenobites need to give haircuts to one another, but not without authorization.[60]

After we have examined the details of Prs. 92–97 and have seen how they fit snugly into the fourth-century monastic discourse on chastity, we might still ask if Pachomius was not excessively cautious. Was homosexual activity so rampant in that society that he should have worried about its possible inroads into and effect on his community? If so, did he take any steps to keep homosexuals out of his monastery? In fact, there is a passage in the Coptic *Life of Pachomius* that can shed some light on these questions.[61]

According to *Sbo* 107, the brothers brought back three candidates from Alexandria to Pachomius at Phbow. The Father of the *koinonia*, however, was reluctant to accept one of these aspirants, calling him "darnel."[62] He knows by clairvoyance that the man has been a practicing homosexual: "He has been darnel since childhood because of the many impurities he has committed." Therefore, says Pachomius, he will have a very hard time observing the monastic regimen and he will also be tempted to involve the brothers in his vices. Nevertheless, Pachomius

---

59. Schenute thinks foot-handling can be unchaste (*De Vita Mon.* 21, 74 Z 16): "Whoever harbors filthy thoughts in his mind or nourishes erotic desires in his spirit when a thorn is pulled from his foot or he pulls one from the foot of his neighbor, he is to be cursed." For his part, Fructuosus (*Reg.* 17: PL 87.1107D) seems to regard unauthorized thorn-pulling as a threat to monastic obedience more than to purity.

60. This was not a matter of religious tonsure, which was unknown among the earliest cenobites, says Bacht, *Vermächtnis*, 198 n. 425. The salient aspect of hair-cutting (literally, head shaving), at least for this precept, is that it involves human touch. Of course, all human grooming has possible erotic dimensions.

61. *Sbo* 107; Veilleux, *PK* 1, 150–59. This is one of the longest units in the *Life of Pachomius*, which may witness to its delicacy. I have the impression that the author found it quite painful to discuss.

62. Matthew 13:25. "Darnel" is a British word for "weed." I will avoid the latter so as not to denigrate homosexuals.

decides to give this man a chance so as not to discourage the other two candidates from Alexandria.

Then Pachomius confides to the monk who brought the three men south that in fact he has turned away a hundred men like this during the past year alone![63] His interlocutor exclaims that he has thereby crippled the *koinonia*, but Pachomius retorts that in fact he has saved it from God's wrath. At this point the dialogue moves in an astonishingly "modern" direction with the superior asking the Founder what "darnel" really means. Does it mean these men are born evil? No, says Pachomius, they are able to choose, because they are made in the image and likeness of God:

> But then why deny them entry, asks the brother? To this, the Great Apa responds that if he accepts them, he must tell the brothers about their past. And if he does that, they won't pray for them but just tease and despise them. But Pachomius adds that he does not exclude them entirely: "For my part I sometimes accept one or two men of that kind and struggle with them very hard until I save them from the enemy's grasp. I must go to them often: night and day, until they are safe or else until the Lord visits them and they repose in Him. This I do in order to fulfill the words of the holy Apostle, 'Take pains with one another so that you may be saved.'"[64]

The Founder must not and does not neglect the rest of the brothers. Nor does he simply write off those homosexuals to whom he refuses admission, but strongly advises them to become anchorites and do special penance for their past sins. This is a sign that Pachomius is not "soft" on sexual vice. Indeed, he lays a very stringent regime on the man from Alexandria, but it is ultimately unsuccessful. After nine years of diligence,[65] the man begins to plot a seduction of one of the brothers. Pachomius again knows this by clairvoyance and immediately expels the man.

63. He also adds the interesting comment that the total population of the *koinonia* at that time was 360, which seems to contradict the vast numbers usually associated with the movement. Yet, it could be that this happened very early in the history of the movement, and the number of 360 may apply only to Phbow. See Veilleux, *PK* 1, 284.

64. Veilleux, *PK* 1, 155.

65. The author of *Sbo* 107 makes sure we know that the man's motives for penance were impure.

After my synopsis of this amazingly frank and nuanced discussion of homosexuality and its impact on the cenobitic community, the reader can easily imagine why the Rule of Pachomius spends so much time on these questions. They were very much part of the Egyptian cultural scene and needed to be dealt with vigorously. Even then, *Sbo* makes it clear that homosexual vice made its way into the *koinonia* and had to be extirpated from time to time.[66]

66. *Sbo* 108 tells of a visit of Pachomius to Tabennesi, where he immediately senses that some of the brothers have fallen into homoerotic behavior. He asks for divine guidance as to what to do with them and an angel with an unsheathed sword insists they be expelled forthwith.

Chapter Seven

The Rule of Pachomius: III (Precepts 98–144)[1]

Clothes and Books (Precepts 98–106)

In his Latin translation of Precept 98 we can see how Jerome has spiced up the original text of the Pachomian Rule. Since we have both the Coptic original and a Greek version of the same, we can observe a certain trajectory of interpretation at work. The Coptic speaks about clothing only, forbidding the monk to trade his garment for a better one without permission of the housemaster. But the *Greek Excerpta*[2] extend the prohibition to "trading down" for a worse piece of clothing, and Jerome adds the dramatic language of "dare" and "better/worse." Nor does the Coptic mention Jerome's *causa decoris* (= for decorative purposes).

Adalbert de Vogüé[3] has suggested that Jerome got his inspiration from Leviticus 27:10, where Moses forbids the Israelites from exchanging, for

---

1. A version of this chapter originally appeared in *Tjurunga* 71 (2006): 5–25 and is reprinted in edited form by permission.

2. Louis Théophile Lefort, "La Règle de S. Pachôme," *Muséon* 37 (1924): 1–28; 40 (1927): 31–64. Reprinted as "Les excerpta grecs" in Armand Boon, *Pachomiana Latina. Règle et Épîtres de St. Pachôme, Épître de s. Théodore et "Liber" de s. Orsiesius* (Louvain: Bureaux de la Revue, 1930), 170–82. Apparently Jerome translated a Greek version of a Coptic original; for the details see chap. 5 above.

3. "Deux réminiscences scripturaires non encore remarquées dans les règles de saint Pachôme et saint Benoît," *Studia Monastica* 25 (1983): 7–10. This reference comes from Lisa Cremaschi, *Pacomio e i suoi discepoli: regole e scritti* ([Magnano] Qiqajon: Community of Bose, 1988).

better or worse, an animal they have vowed to the Lord. While it may seem strange that a monk be forbidden to "trade down" on behalf of his neighbor, here is a case where monastic obedience overrides individual charitable impulse. Likewise, one of the constraints of monastic poverty is the loss of ability to donate to favorite causes.[4]

Mention of clothing at the end of Pr. 98 calls forth Pr. 99, which speaks of goat skins and hoods (*cuculli*). The former should be "fastened," and Jerome adds that they should "hang from the shoulders." Bacht[5] says the Coptic "fastened" is unclear, but perhaps the Rule does not want the wearer to have to keep the goat skin closed with one hand as do Muslim women who wear the *chador*. As for the hoods, they are to be marked with the "signs" of the monastery and the house. Those signs remind us of modern volleyball teams and their distinctive garb, which helps sort them out at tournaments. Bacht says such *signa* would have been useful at the great chapter meetings, where hundreds (maybe thousands) of Pachomians gathered. But he scoffs at Palladius's claim that all the Pachomians were divided into twenty-four groups according to "state of life and disposition." In Palladius's imaginative account each group was marked by a letter of the Greek alphabet.[6]

The next two Precepts are about the care of books. At a time when many people were still using scrolls, the Pachomians were using books (*codices*). Of course, these were handwritten and very costly, so they had to be well taken care of. Precept 100 enjoins the brothers to "bind up" (*ligatum*) the book when they go to prayer or meals. The Coptic just has "close," but Jerome is more graphic and accurate, for ancient codices had numerous strings for tying them shut.[7] We get more charming detail

---

4. See RB 33.2, "Whether monks should consider anything their own." This chapter prohibits the monk not from using community goods, but from freely disposing of them.

5. Heinrich Bacht, *Das Vermächtnis des Ursprungs*, vol. 2 (Würzburg: Echter, 1983), 199 n. 436.

6. *Lausiac History* 32, trans. Robert T. Meyer, ACW 34 (Westminster, MD: Newman, 1965). Cited by Bacht, *Vermächtnis*, 200 n. 438.

7. In fact, we have tangible proof of this with the trove of books found at Nag Hammadi in 1945. These Gnostic texts were buried very near the Pachomian center of Pbow, and some of the binding material appears to be of monastic origin. But it cannot be proven that the texts were from a Pachomian library. For discussion of this question see James E. Goehring, *Ascetics, Society and the Desert* (Harrisburg, PA: Trinity Press International, 1999), 208–16.

about the care of books in Pr. 101. It tells the assistant housemaster (*secundus*) to gather the books in the evening from the alcove[8] and shut them in their case. It is his regular duty to count them to see if any are missing. Books were so precious in those days that one did not risk leaving them unlocked at night.

Precepts 102 and 103 both deal with the monks' clothing, although the former discusses where to wear it, the latter talks about the care of garments. Precept 102 is somewhat surprising, since it prohibits the wearing of shoes (*galliculas*) and mantle (*palliolo lineo*) to the *synaxis* (Divine Office) and meals. In our culture "no shoes, no shirt, no service," but going barefoot was a regular feature of life in torrid Egypt. Perhaps the intent here was to remove all possible distinctions between persons at these common exercises. Even more surprising is the added phrase "either in the village or fields." Jerome has "in the monastery," not "in the village," but Veilleux notes that there was not that much difference for the Pachomians.[9] After all, they built their monasteries in deserted villages. As for the fields, Pr. 61 prohibits the monks from wearing their mantles out there. Like Benedict's monks,[10] Pachomius's cenobites sometimes prayed in the fields.[11] Since they probably wore shoes of some sort for heavy fieldwork, these had to be removed for the brief, periodic prayers.

Precept 103 is one of those rules that have given Pachomius a bad name for micromanagement: the mantle is not to be left to dry in the sun until the noon meal. Actually, the care of clothes was of considerable importance for the ancients, since clothes were handwoven and easily ruined by carelessness. Precept 70 had gone into greater detail about leaving the mantle to dry too long in the fierce Egyptian sun. There the limit was 9 a.m., not noon, as here. But Pachomian *Institute* 6 allows the garment to be dried for two full days in the sun. Perhaps they are talking about different times of the year.

The conclusion of Pr. 103 is not surprising, but probably is not as clear as it could be: "The one who neglects all these things shall be

---

8. The Coptic has "alcove," but Jerome has more: "The books which are in the window (*fenestra*), that is, the basket of the wall (*risco parietis*)." Some of the cells of the northern Egyptian hermits that have been excavated have blind window wells that were apparently used for bookcases.

9. Note to Pr. 90, *PK* 2, 189.

10. RB 50.1-2.

11. Precept 142.

rebuked." This may seem to refer to the treatment of clothes,[12] but all the commentators think it covers the whole sweep of Precepts 49–103A. At Pr. 48 there is an almost identical summary. Veilleux considers the Precepts that remain (104–144) to be a "complementary section," that is, a loosely organized addendum.[13] Vogüé disagrees.[14]

In Precept 104 we see Jerome's tendency to elaboration given free rein. The Coptic is very laconic: "No one shall take a shoe or any other object to oil it but only the housemasters" (Veilleux); Jerome: "No one shall dare to take on boots or anything else that needs oiling or fixing, except the one assigned to this task or the housemaster." Probably there is no distortion here, but Jerome's addition does broaden the principle of "proper channels." There is no doubt that work in the *koinonia* was highly specialized, but one wonders if *all* repairs had to be done by a specialist or cleared by a superior? The Coptic focuses only on oiling, apparently an important act of maintenance in the superdry climate of Egypt. If only a superior, not a specialist, controlled the oil, perhaps it was a question of power. Again, Jerome dramatizes by adding "dare."

The housemaster is the focus of the next two numbers as well. Precept 105 has to do with a brother who is injured, but not so badly as to be bedridden. The housemaster should get him what he needs for his recuperation, whether a garment or some oil, and he should get it from the steward. Jerome dramatizes all this, and perhaps distracts, by introducing the verb "has been wounded," which sounds ominous. But he has dropped the mention of oil, which may connect Pr. 105 to Pr. 104 in the Coptic. At any rate, the injured man is not to go into the storeroom and help himself. No, everything is to be done through official channels. One receives what one needs from God's representative.[15]

---

12. Jerome almost certainly understands it that way: "If anyone neglects one of the abovementioned things . . ." He also has "out of contempt," which is lacking in the Coptic. Jerome's writing is full of dramatic conflict, which reflects the life of that irascible church father.

13. *La liturgie dans le cénobitisme pachômien au quatrième siècle*, Studia Anselmiana philosophica theologica 57 (Rome: "I. B. C." Herder, 1968), 126ff., 129ff.

14. "Les pièces latines du dossier pachômien," *Revue d'histoire ecclésiastique* 67 (1967): 26–67, at 37 et seq.

15. Both Latin and Coptic add that whatever remains of his sick-equipment is to be returned upon recuperation. This principle of "return to discipline" is also observed in the Rule of Benedict: Upon cure, the sick return to the regular diet (36.9); travelers return special garments when they get home (55.14);

But it is not enough just to get what you need from someone else. In fact, Pr. 106 adds an important qualification: "No one should receive anything from another unless the housemaster[16] approves it." Bacht notes that this is a generalized version of Pr. 98, which prohibits the trading of clothes. Here, though, the question is not trading but the giving of gifts among monks. Although that practice may seem to promote Christian charity, it may also create a parallel economy of patronage in the monastery.

Boundaries (Precepts 107–112)

The next several numbers (Prs. 107–112) mostly deal with lines not to be crossed. The first Precept, 107, actually refuses to allow a boundary to be erected: no one is to lock his bedroom door. The Coptic permits the superior (Jerome: *pater monasterii*) to provide a lockable bedroom, which Jerome elaborates with his typical casuistry: "except because of someone's age or sickness." What neither of them explains is the purpose of the ban on bedroom locks. Vogüé [17] thinks it is a guard against violations of poverty. Bacht, however, feels that the subtext is chastity.[18] Since Pr. 109 is also on chastity, this seems more likely.

Precept 108 forbids anybody but the farmers[19] from entering the stables. The issue here may not be just one of good order. Bacht points out that stables had to be on the banks of the Nile, and hence outside the monastic compound.[20] Actually, the reference may be a bit more general, for *villa* can refer to any farm building, not just stables. Yet any such building would probably be outside the compound. Veilleux translates the Coptic as "stables," which the "herdsmen" alone may enter.[21]

---

guestmasters return to the regular work program when there are no guests (53.18). The message for both Benedict and Pachomius is that cenobites do not construct private kingdoms.

16. The Latin has just *praeposito* without the addition of *domus*. But it is doubtful that another official is meant. *Excerpta Graeca* 45 has *pater* (= abbot).

17. "'Comment les moines dormiront': Commentaire d'un chapître de la Règle de Saint Benoît," *Studia Monastica* 7 (1965): 25–62, at 44.

18. *Vermächtnis*, 203 n. 466.

19. Jerome has typically spelled this out: "shepherds, herdsmen, and farmers." One wonders if there was much herding of animals in the intensively farmed Nile Valley.

20. *Vermächtnis*, 204 n. 470.

21. *PK* 2, 162.

Precept 109 can seem puzzling to the modern urbanite: "Two men shall not sit together on a bare-backed donkey or on a wagon-shaft." In fact, "wagon-shaft" is just a guess, since *mrêh* appears nowhere else in Coptic literature.[22] At any rate, the meaning of this Precept is not transparent. Bacht rejects the idea that Prs. 108–109 are to be associated with prohibitions of the early church against cruelty to animals.[23] Much more likely, he thinks, is Veilleux's emphasis on Pachomius's anxiety to banish homosexuality from his monasteries.[24] The link between sexual aberration and cruelty to animals seems to me to be not entirely implausible.

The next Precept (110) is also about animals, and about boundaries as well: If one arrives at the monastery riding a donkey, he should dismount and lead it in. This sounds obvious until we recall that Egyptian monasteries were, and still are, more like walled villages than our large, fortresslike buildings. Two possible explanations suggest themselves: (1) The *Life of Pachomius* claims he never rode a donkey, except when he was sick; instead, he went on foot with "thanks and humility." (2) Dismounting could be a sign of respect for the holiness of the monastery. Certainly the fact that Jesus rode a donkey, not a horse, had overtones of humility (see Matt 21:5).

Boundaries are certainly the subject of Pr. 111, which has to do with the workshops. No one but the workers may visit the shops, with the exception of superiors, and even they should only go there for business, and never before the daily meal except in case of serious necessity. Although it is not too clear to me, it seems that if something is needed *during* the meal, the abbot sends the weekly server to fetch it.[25] Whatever the precise details, this Precept has to do with the seriousness of work for the Pachomians. They were a numerous community who lived strictly by the sweat of their brows, not by alms or state subsidies. Like all serious workers, they did not appreciate casual visitors. Nor were community members free to appropriate whatever they pleased from the shops.

The final department where monks are not to go without permission is the "place of the breadboards." This is a Coptic phrase that escaped Jerome; probably the Greek he was translating already muddled it. He

22. *PK* 2, 109 n. 109.
23. *Vermächtnis*, 204 n. 473.
24. *PK* 1, 281 n. 2 on *Sbo* 88.
25. One of the problems here is the shift of personnel. Why is a different official sent at different times? To make it even more confusing, the Coptic has "man of name" for housemaster.

has "without permission of the superior." He makes the prohibition for "the cell of another." That squares with Coptic 112B, but 112A is about the bakery. As Pr. 116 will show, regulations for the baking crew were very precise, but the point here is simply to keep visitors out. Once again, Jerome heightens the drama with "no one shall dare," which contributes a sexual tension that is missing from the Coptic.

The Bakery and Other Questions (Precepts 113–117)

The remaining Precepts appear to be something of a random addition. There may be a connecting link or links, but I do not see them. The first directive (113) is quite general: "No one shall take anything on trust from another man, not even from his own brother." Although some commentators think this is a question of lending and borrowing, it is a little different. *Commendatum* (Jerome) means "surety": one is not to become the trustee for anything for anyone, even one's sibling (*germano*). For a cenobite to do so is to resume an economic autonomy that he has set aside at profession.

Eating in the cell or private room is the target of Pr. 114: "No one is to eat anything in his cell." Jerome has considerably concretized this Precept with "not even the least apple or anything like that." This makes the regulation more memorable but appears to forget the fact that Prs. 37–38 allow numerous exceptions to this rule. There, the brothers are given some kind of snacks on leaving the refectory. These are not to be eaten until one arrives at the cell (Pr. 38: *ad domum perveniat*). Apparently this could be a good deal of food, for it sometimes lasted three days. All of this tends to undercut an absolute prohibition.

Precept 115 is a bit longer and more complex. If a housemaster needs to be gone for a while, another housemaster from his tribe[26] should take over for him. In this case the Coptic original is not clear, and Veilleux thinks that Jerome's addition of "another" helps to clarify the situation. Bacht, however, complains that Jerome has still created confusion by speaking of "the other" housemaster, as if there were only two per

---

26. "Tribe" is a Pachomian category that does not get much use. It must include more than one house, but less than the whole monastery. The Coptic has "the housemaster of his tribe," which would mean that the same title is used for the superior of the house and the tribe. Fidelis Ruppert, *Das pachomianische Mönchtum und die Anfänge klösterlichen Gehorsams* (Münsterschwarzach: Vier-Türme, 1971), 306, thinks this is a symptom of the secondary position of "tribe" in the Pachomian structure.

tribe.[27] What is the substitute housemaster to do? "Everything in which the second may need him." Apparently the second could not give catechetical instructions, for the substitute is to give "fast day instructions, one in his own house and another in the house of his fellow master." These were the biblical instructions given on Wednesdays and Fridays in all Pachomian monasteries. From Pr. 19 we know that these biblical *catecheses* were not only heard but also discussed by the brothers of each house after morning prayers.

If we ask why the *secundus* was not to give instructions, the reason was not his lack of orders. Very few of the Pachomians were priests. But apparently one of the qualifications for housemasters was precisely the ability to exegete Scripture.[28] Pachomius almost caused a revolt among the veteran monks when he had the young Theodore give instructions (*Sbo* 69).[29] In the confrontation that followed, Pachomius insists that he did not appoint Theodore for his seniority but for his biblical wisdom.

Back to the bakery, or rather the bakers (Pr. 116). This Precept has a special heading, indicating the importance of baking in the Pachomian system. This is clearer still for the Regulations of Horsiesi, which devote no fewer than seven paragraphs (39–45) to the baking process.[30] Baking for a large community in the days before mechanization required many hands. Therefore the potential for noise and disorder was considerable. The *Life of Pachomius* (*SBo* 74 and 77)[31] relates an incident in which Pachomius punishes Theodore for allowing the brothers to chatter during the baking at Tabennesi.

27. Jerome speaks of the superior of "the other" (*alterius*) house leaving, and "another" (*alius*) replacing him. So, strictly speaking Bacht, *Vermächtnis*, 207 n. 496, is right. But I think Jerome is clear enough here.

28. Veilleux, *PK* 2, 190 n. 115, points out that monastic *catechesis* in Egypt was based on an Alexandrian model. The famous lay leaders of the Catechetical School of that city, especially Clement and Origen, were accustomed to give biblical teachings in church on Wednesdays and Fridays. See André Turck, "Catéchein et *Catéchésis* chez les Premiers Pères," *Revue des sciences philosophiques et théologiques* 47 (1963): 361–72.

29. *PK* 1, 191. In fact, Theodore went on to become one of the greatest leaders of the *koinonia*.

30. The Regulations, which are given by Veilleux in *PK* 2, 210–14, are ascribed to the second successor of Pachomius (Horsiesi). As with the Precepts, with which they largely agree, they are a compilation of rules developed over an extended period.

31. *PK* 1, 97–98 and 100–1.

In order to fill the vacuum left by their silence, the monks are to "recite together" until they have finished. Jerome makes it clear that what they recite are "psalms and Scriptures." The Coptic here is more laconic: they are to "meditate" (*meletan*). This was in fact the ancient monastic form of meditation, where one memorized biblical passages for just such a purpose: to recite them during the working day. Often these were murmured privately in a low voice, but here in the bakery they were sung in unison. Apparently baking was considered a quasi-religious act.[32]

Even though many brothers were needed to do the baking, it did not take everybody. Precept 116 says that only "authorized personnel" are to be in the bakery during the mixing and cooking.[33] Otherwise, people are not to loiter[34] around the bakery when it is operating in high gear. The brothers probably did not loiter around the bakery out of idle curiosity; they were hungry. The Regulations of Horsiesi (41–42) indicate that nibbling the "crusts" in the bakery was a powerful temptation for the whole community. Anyone who has struggled to practice fasting downwind of a bakery will understand this perfectly.

Sailing and Psalming (Precepts 118–122)

The next two numbers (Prs. 118–119) concern boats and sailing. Since most of the Pachomian monasteries were located on the very banks of the great river Nile, it is not unusual to find sailing regulations in this Rule.[35] Not only did the Pachomian boats move between the monasteries of the congregation, which were as much as a hundred miles apart, but they also delivered grain and other commodities to the port of Alexandria, some four hundred miles downstream. Later the boats had to be pulled back upstream by beasts or men on a towpath.

Jerome starts Pr. 118 with this introduction: "the same discipline applies to the boats." He might mean that those who go sailing are not

32. Bacht, *Vermächtnis*, 207 n. 501.

33. The mixing of the dough (*ad miscendam farinam*) is an addition of Jerome, but the detail is also found in the Coptic version of the previous Precept.

34. Veilleux's translation of the Coptic in *PK* 2, 163. Jerome has *residebit* (twice), which seems a rather colorless word for this flamboyant writer.

35. Canopus was on the Nile, but in the eastern suburbs of Alexandria. Therefore it is no surprise that its version of the Rule, namely, *Greek Excerpta*, lacks Prs. 119–126.

free from monastic discipline, or that boats are only to be used with permission of the superior, the message of the previous number. The two things are not so different. Probably there was a temptation to escape the grind of common life by a little cruise. And life on board ship, especially on long voyages, could undermine monastic discipline.

Beyond the basic need for permission, the big concern on board ship was where to sleep. On long trips they certainly docked at night and no doubt slept on board. But for some reason, perhaps hygiene, they were not to sleep in the hold. We do not know why, and neither did Jerome, who makes up for his ignorance with a plethora of detail.[36] Probably the sleeping arrangements are another example of the Pachomian worry about sexual misconduct. That also applies to the last sentence of Pr. 118, which bars laymen from sleeping in the boats. They are not barred from riding from port to port, just from spending the night among the brothers. As for women (*vasa inferiora*: weak vessels), only permission from the local abbot could allow them to ride with the monks, much less sleep with them. To understand all this better, it should be pointed out that in ancient times there were no passenger boats. People had to hitch rides on cargo boats as the opportunity presented itself. No doubt the monks did the same, so it would not do to bar others entirely from the boats of the monastery.

Precept 120 is a single sentence about the stove: "No one shall light a fire in his house before the brothers have been so commanded." Bacht thinks the reference is to the judgment of the housemaster.[37] Jerome shifts the condition: "unless it be in common for all." One wonders if Jerome knew what the Pachomian houses looked like, for he had never visited their monasteries in the far south of Egypt. Surely the individual cells had no stoves; rather there was one stove per house. Although Egypt is usually hot, it can get cold in winter, and even today there is no central heating. Precepts 5 and 22 speak of communal stoves.

The next Precept (121) has to do with discipline at evening prayers. What is not permitted is coming late, mumbling, gossiping, or laughing. The problem here is where evening prayers were held and where

---

36. This is the opinion of Bacht, *Vermächtnis*, 210 n. 219. Jerome forbids sleeping in the *sentina* (hold) and *interiore parte navis*. He further elaborates that the brothers should sleep on the *transtra* (crossbanks for rowers) and *tabulate* (floorboards). Jerome specifies the general prohibition against unauthorized boating with "undoing the rope." He also adds "not even a skiff (*lembum*)." Bacht claims that this latter term was from the Dalmatian coast, where Jerome grew up.

37. Bacht, *Vermächtnis*, 111 n. 525.

one was to do penance for these peccadillos. According to Veilleux[38] the Pachomians prayed Vespers, called "the Six Prayers," in their separate houses before retiring. But other scholars, notably Vogüé,[39] have resisted this interpretation, holding that there was a plenary Vespers, followed by more prayers in the separate houses. Bacht agrees with Vogüé on this point.[40] A full discussion of this question must take several texts into account. What can we learn from Pr. 121 alone?

To judge from Veilleux's translation of the Coptic, there probably were two sets of prayers: "The one who arrives late for one of the Six Prayers at evening . . . shall do penance in his house during the Six Prayers." If there was only one service of prayers, why mention them twice or why mention the house? As for Jerome, he does not mention the house, but he does talk of the "rest of the prayers." Still, he also speaks of an infraction during "one of the Six Prayers," so "the rest" could refer to the same series.

Precept 122 is also about spiritual practice in the house. Now the practice is "rumination" on what they have heard from their housemasters. "Rumination" in the Pachomian literature often refers to individual repetition of memorized biblical texts, and that is what the Coptic suggests here. But Jerome has considerably filled out this laconic Precept: "When they are sitting in the house, no one may speak of anything worldly; but if the housemaster has taught something from the Bible, let them reflect on it together."[41]

Obviously Jerome thinks there was colloquy on biblical and spiritual matters in these houses. But if it happened, it was not formal discussion as in Pr. 19. Here they are "sitting in the house," no doubt plaiting ropes or baskets. These people did not sit idle. Veilleux rejects Jerome's expansion. He points out that the Coptic says "they shall not speak," with the object of "speak" illegible. Still, the appearance of pious discussion among the first cenobites is attractive to modern critics, and most of them have sided with Jerome's translation of this Precept.

---

38. *La liturgie dans le cénobitisme* pachômien, 296–302.

39. "Les pièces latines du dossier pachômien," *Revue d'histoire ecclésiastique* 67 (1972), 26–67, at 57–58. For Vogüé the decisive text is the title of the Precepts and Laws: "about the Six Evening Prayers and the Synaxis of the Six Prayers which is made in each house."

40. Bacht, *Vermächtnis*, 211 n. 529.

41. My translation. As it stands, *inter se ruminant* could mean either "within themselves" or "between them." The real issue is the Coptic, which I do not have before me—and could not understand if I did!

Work and Funerals (Precepts 123–130)

There then follow two numbers beginning with *nemo*, "no one." In Pr. 123 no one is to start working after the instruction by the housemaster until the latter gives the go-ahead.[42] Although the connection to Pr. 122 is clear, the issue now is not meditation or discussion, but work. Apparently some people are eager to get to work as soon as possible, but the Rule tries to put a brake on this. The implication is that the housemaster will make sure there is a decent interval between spiritual exercises and mundane life. Since the Pachomians famously plaited reeds *during* meditation, and even during the Divine Office,[43] it is important to distinguish that from what is at issue in Pr. 123. Here, it is a matter of the end of meditation and the start of work as such. Jerome makes this a bit more explicit, for in addition to the Coptic "plait or draw water" he adds "any work."[44] Again, it is unseemly for monks to rush off to work—unless they have to.

Another way to put this is to say that monastic, cenobitic work is not autonomous, but under the control of institutional authority. This is seen again in the next Precept (124): "No one (*nemo*) shall take soaked rushes without [the permission of] the weekly server of the house." Now the official is not the housemaster, but the principle is the same: one does not work alone, for work as such is under obedience as is any other facet of monastic life. The plaiting of reeds among the Pachomians was highly organized, requiring disciplined cooperation. Even when monastic work is highly specialized and individual, as with much modern work, it is never "a separate kingdom."

To give this teaching some teeth, Pr. 125 sets out sanctions for infractions of the rules for work. Again, the rushes for plaiting are a matter of concern: one must not soak them a third time.[45] What is more, clay jars are to be handled carefully and not broken. If someone violates these

---

42. Jerome has dropped the introductory reference to the housemaster's instruction, thus making the need for permission to work somewhat meaningless.

43. Precepts 5, 7, and 12 all discuss plaiting during prayer, so the matter is up front, at the very headwaters of the Rule.

44. Actually, the Coptic itself is clearer: "they shall not go out to the water-wheel." One can hardly do that during meditation. Jerome has "carry around vessels full of water." See Bacht, *Vermächtnis*, 213 n. 539.

45. Apparently too much soaking and drying would rot the reeds. See Bacht, *Vermächtnis*, 143 n.120. Precept 26 spells out the need for the steward to supply the workers with material in such a way as to avoid waste.

principles he is to do penance at the Six Prayers in the evening. Bacht thinks the lesson here is monastic poverty: the goods of the monastery are *God's* goods.[46] That may be true, but following Pr. 124 this number makes sure that the treatment of goods is kept firmly under monastic authority. Life in a large commune can become careless. Where nobody owns anything there is the temptation to treat goods carelessly.[47]

Although Pr. 126 has no immediate connection to its preceding number, it is like Prs. 123–125 in treating of goings-on in the separate houses: after the Six Prayers (Vespers), every monk is to go to his cubicle to sleep, and no one is to leave his cell during the night without necessity. Without fully reopening the discussion as to whether the Six Prayers were said or sung all together or on a house-by-house basis,[48] we might note that Jerome says they are to "disperse" (*separantur*) for sleep. Although it is not decisive, *separantur* suggests a general *synaxis* outside the house.[49] Bacht plausibly suggests that chastity is the reason why the Pachomians slept alone.[50]

Precept 127, like its predecessor, features the verb *dormire*, but now it means "death" and not "sleep." The Coptic reads: "When a brother dies among the brothers, they shall all together accompany him to the mountain."[51] Jerome does not mention the mountain, perhaps because he does not understand Egyptian topography very well. The "mountain" refers to the rock cliffs lining the Nile Valley on both sides; people were buried in rock-cut tombs to remove the corpses from the annual

---

46. Bacht, *Vermächtnis*, 213 n. 247. A famous example is seen in RB 31.10: "He will regard the utensils and goods of the monastery as sacred vessels of the altar." Bacht points to additional texts: Basil, Short Rules 143, *PG* 31.1177B; Cassian, *Inst.* 4.19, SC 109, 148.

47. RB 46.1-4 reveals Benedict's rejection of material sloppiness. He rages at seemingly minor faults, probably because they were a particularly intractable problem in his monastery.

48. See the remarks on Pr. 121 for more on this problem.

49. It does not help our understanding of the Precept that it is missing from the Coptic. Veilleux thinks this may be a copyist's error caused by *homoeoteleuton*; since Pr. 125 ends with "Six Prayers" and Pr. 126 starts with the same words, this may be so. See Veilleux, *PK* 2, 191 n. 126.

50. See Bacht, *Vermächtnis*, 214 n. 553.

51. The *Life of Pachomius* (Sbo 205–207; PK 1, 255–260) describes the funeral of Theodore in great detail. There was an all-night vigil; at dawn the body was wrapped in linen; Mass was offered; the body was carried to the mountain with psalmody; a solemn burial followed.

flood-waters. The remark that "all together" walk to the burial is not meant casually but literally.[52] This and the next three Precepts all stress uniformity and discipline during the burial ceremony.

First, every monk is to walk in this procession to the tomb. Of course, the superior may permit someone to stay behind, but Pr. 127 insists this is the exception. This utter seriousness about burials no doubt reflects an Egyptian culture that expended enormous resources on embalming and vast tombs.[53] The Pachomians did neither, but they were still part of the same culture. Nevertheless, some may be too weak to make the trip to the cliffs or may have to turn back for the same reason. Precept 129 orders the infirmarian to remain at home with the sick.[54]

Not only is everybody to walk to the tomb, they are to walk together. This is actually only stated explicitly in one short Precept (130): "No one may walk ahead of his housemaster and leader." Bacht admits it is not certain that this Precept actually goes with Prs. 127–129 on burial.[55] But it seems clear from the copious remarks on disciplined psalmody at funerals in this whole section that they had to walk together to sing together. There is nothing like a straggling procession to kill a hymn or psalm.

Of course, a good way to maintain musical unity[56] is to follow a leader. First of all, they should not start a psalm without being or-

---

52. Jerome says "all" accompany the body, which is not as strong as "all together." To judge from what follows, "all together" (Veilleux) is a more plausible translation.

53. This seriousness comes through in the writings of Schenute (*De Vita Mon.* 12, *Opera* IV), who, if he found a monk who had skipped a burial, forced him to *crawl* to the grave if he could not walk. One hesitates to associate Pachomius with that kind of fanaticism.

54. Jerome has seriously garbled this Precept. He claims the sick must make the trek to the burial. Yet he arranges for them to have an assistant (*ministrum*) with them to aid them. He then expands the last sentence of Pr. 129 to include a general principle: whenever the monks travel they should be accompanied by an infirmarian in case they should fall sick. This is not incongruent with Pachomian practice, but it is still not the point here. See Basilius Steidle, "Ich war krank und ihr habt mich besucht," *Erbe und Auftrag* 41 (1965), 189–206, at 194.

55. Bacht, *Vermächtnis*, 216 n. 575. The Coptic ms. breaks off at this point, which greatly hampers our possibility of critical insight.

56. Precept 128 ends with this demand: "They shall not neglect to respond, but shall maintain unison." Jerome elaborates a bit: "they shall keep together in tempo and pitch."

dered.[57] There is a suggestion that the psalms were led by a cantor. If so, one should not neglect to respond to him (Pr. 128). This kind of arrangement, with stereotyped responses, greatly simplifies the tricky business of walking and singing in unison. Finally, the Coptic has this note: "Proceeding to the mountain they shall not sing psalms two by two." This seems cryptic to commentators, but tandem-psalming could create overall cacophony.

Various Sanctions (Precepts 131–137)

From the specificity of the funeral procession (Prs. 127–130), Pr. 131 turns to the more general case of the monk who loses something.[58] The Pachomian Rule is surprisingly hard on this point. There is no suggestion that those things happen to the best-intentioned people; one should keep looking; the item will turn up.[59] No. One is publicly corrected before the altar, and the matter does not end there. If one has lost a piece of personal clothing, one is to go without it for three weeks before it is replaced.

What should we think of this severe attitude toward what looks like a mere foible? Probably it is a facet of the general Pachomian concern for communal poverty. Many numbers of the Precepts address this issue, so it must have been a constant concern.[60] The Pachomians were not poor; far from it! Some scholars suggest that affluence eventually became the cause of their downfall.[61] Nevertheless, they seem to have realized that material carelessness can be a special problem in large cenobitic communities, where small infractions can add up to a major problem.[62]

57. Schenute also prohibits freelance psalming at funerals (*De Vita Mon.* 12, *Opera* IV). Jerome extends this prohibition to "adding psalm to psalm" (Pr. 127); in other words, one does not cease when the leader ceases.

58. Actually, the first sentence of Pr. 131 is not about losing things: "No one may stay out of his rank." In its content it seems to continue Pr. 130, but in its generality it goes with what follows. Thus it forms a kind of bridge.

59. Precept 132 does reflect some pragmatism: whoever finds a lost item should hang it in front of the meeting hall for three days so the loser can reclaim it.

60. Bacht, *Vermächtnis*, 216 n. 578, points to Prs. 4, 26, 70, 100, 103, 125. As we noted earlier, Benedict is equally merciless to those who lose or break things.

61. See William Harmless, *Desert Christians: An Introduction to the Literature of Early Monasticism* (New York: Oxford University Press, 2004), 137.

62. The writer once heard of a large monastery where personal expenditures became fairly massive. The response of authority was swift and tough: everyone was put on a strict budget, which had to be submitted a year in advance.

Our present throwaway society needs comparable sanctions. As for the punishment, correction before the altar is typical of the Pachomians,[63] but the three-week deprivation is not. It is important to note that this is a case of people losing personal items. If they do, they must go without those same items for their penance.[64] We seem to have here a case of punishment fitting the offense.[65] No doubt this has considerable pedagogical value, but it often becomes hard to carry out. When somebody loses his or her glasses, do we wait three weeks to buy a new pair?

The next Precept (133) is even more general than its predecessor. Now the topic is punishment, and who should administer it. The criterion is whether the matter has been put into writing or not.[66] If it has been spelled out (that is, what penalty follows what offense) the housemaster should carry it out. But if it is a "new thing" that has not been codified, the matter is to be referred to the head of the monastery (*principem monasterii*).

The thinking here seems straightforward enough: the lower official can carry out a set policy, but where there is no written precedent a higher official is called on. Why? Because more creative discretion is called for; indeed, one may be establishing a new precedent. Although it is not stated here, we may presume that the matter could go even further: if the offense were grave enough, surely it would have been referred to the father of the whole *koinonia* on his periodic visits. Although this precept circumscribes the authority of the housemasters and makes them mere functionaries regarding punishment, we should not conclude too much from this. We have seen that the housemasters gave frequent catecheses,

---

63. Precept 8 arranges for similar rebukes in the oratory and dining room for faults committed there. Although items were usually not lost in church, people were rebuked there, no doubt, because everyone gathered there.

64. Precept 131 says they are to go without "until the penance has been performed." According to Bacht, *Vermächtnis*, 217 n. 581, the penance here is precisely the three-week deprivation. Another, though clumsier, reading would be to have two kinds of penance: (1) rebuke before altar and (2) three weeks of deprivation.

65. The Rule of Benedict has many penalties, but few fitted to the offense. RB 43.19 is an exception: if someone refuses food or drink offered by a superior, he should be refused when he does want it.

66. Bacht, *Vermächtnis*, 217 n. 584, notes that this precept betrays the time of its origin, for it presupposes a written Rule. Most scholars place such writing after the death of Pachomius (d. 346) and in the reigns of Theodore (d. 368) and Horsiesi (d. 380).

which certainly required more wisdom than would be expected from a functionary.[67] This precept does not undermine the considerable authority of the Pachomian housemasters. Similarly, a modern physician does not lose authority or prestige by referring cases to a specialist.

There follows a little Precept that seems to be an intrusion, for Prs. 133 and 135 speak of correction, but Pr. 134 does not. In fact, it speaks of mud! Literally, "no one shall make mud in the house without him." It appears that the reference here is to remodeling a house,[68] which is not to be done without the permission of the head of the monastery. Then Pr. 134 adds a sentence that probably generalizes on the mud principle: "Every new matter shall be decided by him." We notice that this dictum really continues the thinking of the previous Precept.[69]

We have noted that Pr. 135 continues the subject of penalties. Now, however, the issue is not who imposes the correction, but how it is to be carried out. The ritual is simple and dramatic: one stands ungirded (unbelted) in the *synaxis* liturgy and the dining room. This is actually a repetition of what is laid down in Pr. 8, except for the *metanies* (bows). Unlike some monastic penalties, there are no blows here. But the penalty was not negligible. For ancient people, public shaming was a regular feature of life. That does not mean they liked it, but it would not have crushed them the way it would the modern psyche.[70]

Precepts 136 and 137 are also about punishment: now the offense is specific and so is the penalty. If a monk leaves the monastery without permission, he is of course to do penance. But that is not enough: he is not to return to his former rank until bidden to do so by the superior. That this is a serious matter seems plain from another clue as well: "If

---

67. Actually, Pr. 133 speaks of "all punishments and teachings" (*cunctis increpationibus et doctrinis*), but this phrase seems to translate a single Coptic term (*spo*), which refers to character education. The Greek *paideia* is much the same.

68. Veilleux has a curious rendition here: "No one shall make abode in a house without his permission." It would be convenient to think his version is based on the Coptic, but all he has is the Latin.

69. The word *novum* is the same in both. Bacht, *Vermächtnis*, 215 n. 599, objects that this sentence could preclude all initiative on the part of the ordinary monk. Indeed it could, and so could a text like RB 5.12: "They prefer to walk according to the judgment and command of another." Like Bacht, I do not believe Pachomius wanted robots, nor did Benedict.

70. See my article, "The Healing of Shame in the Rule of Benedict," *American Benedictine Review* 53 (2002): 453–74.

one leaves the community of brothers . . ." This is not just a matter of leaving the compound, but a breach of the brotherhood.[71] It does not say these people were formally abandoning monastic life, but unauthorized absences can have that cumulative effect.

To underline the gravity of this fault, Pr. 137 resolutely applies it to superiors: if a housemaster or procurator[72] is out overnight without leave, he does not resume his place without explicit permission. Again, general penance is not enough;[73] one can lose one's rank by violations against stability. It does look as if this Precept is a reaction to real violations. No doubt monastic officials had more reason to leave the compound than other monks, but the Rule does not want that to be a pretext for lax behavior.

Studying God's Word (Precepts 138–142)

Precepts 138–142 are about monastic study of the word of God. We have seen that the Pachomians listened to frequent biblical catecheses. In Pr. 138 there is a directive about what the monks are to do after the teaching sessions. In fact, this is the third time the topic is discussed in the Precepts. Like Pr. 19, Pr. 138 tells the brothers to discuss what they have heard; for its part Pr. 122 instructs them to meditate on it, presumably silently. Bacht considers Pr. 122 particularly significant because we have the Coptic original.[74]

Still, Pr. 138 makes a very strong statement about discussion: "they shall be *forced* to discuss"![75] Lying behind this surprising injunction is the

---

71. The term used here is *communio*. Bacht, *Vermächtnis*, 218 n. 593, points out that this is the only time the word occurs in all the Precepts. That is rather odd, because it must render the basic Pachomian Coptic term *koinonia*. At least that is the judgment of Veilleux, *PK* 2, 192 n. 136.

72. *Dispensator*. This official is rare in the Precepts but is seen in Prs. 77–78.

73. In fact, the word used is *paenitudine*, not *paenitentia* as in Pr. 136. Bacht, *Vermächtnis*, 219 n. 599, thinks it means an expression of regret, not an act of penance. Regret is the first meaning given by Albert Blaise (*Dictionnaire Latin-Français des Auteurs Chrétiens* [Turnhout: Brepols, 1954], s. v. *paenitudo*), but he also lists texts from the Gelasian Sacramentary and Pope Siricius, where it clearly means an act of penance.

74. *Vermächtnis*, 219 n. 602.

75. The Latin is unambiguous: *necessitate cogentur*. Veilleux has "they must absolutely" (*PK* 2, 166). Even though his rendition is weaker, Veilleux may

fact that disciplined discussion is hard work, and some people may at times wish to avoid it. This is reflected in the fact that few, if any, subsequent cenobitic Rules arranged for this kind of dialogue. The ascetic dimension of discussion may also be suggested by the final sentence of Pr. 138, which wants discussions to be held on the fast days, that is, Wednesdays and Fridays. Also, it is curious that these conferences by the housemasters, and not those of the abbot on the weekends, *must* be discussed.[76]

Precept 139 is also about learning Scripture, but now one does so by memorization and reading, not discussion. Pachomius is adamant that his monks learn to read. If they cannot, how can they memorize biblical passages for meditation? We quote the whole passage: "Whoever enters the monastery uninstructed shall be taught first what he shall observe; and when, so taught, he has consented to it all, they shall give him twenty psalms or two of the Apostle's epistles, or some other part of Scripture."

The "uninstructed" (*rudis*) here is someone who does not know the rules for monks.[77] This person has passed the initial interrogation of Pr. 49 and has been admitted to formation (*ingressus*) but needs instruction on the rules before he can make a mature choice. He needs more than that: to be a successful monk he needs to know Scripture, and so he is given some biblical texts to memorize.[78] This is not the only time a Pachomian is asked to memorize: in Pr. 49 the newcomer is given two psalms, and in Pr. 140 the monk is urged to learn the whole Psalter and the whole New Testament by heart.[79] We must remember that none

---

be closer to the intended meaning, for the Precept is probably addressed to the monks, not the superiors.

76. The number of catecheses, and their giver, is somewhat garbled. Precept 20 says the housemasters are to give three catecheses, but Veilleux (*PK* 2, 186, n. 20), invoking *Sbo* 26 and many other texts, says Pr. 20 must refer to catecheses given on weekends by the abbot, not the housemaster.

77. In his earlier work (*La liturgie*, 199ff.), Veilleux thought that *rudis* meant "pagan." But Vogüé ("Pièces," 59–60ff.) showed that although *rudis* does mean pagan in Pr. 49, here and in Pr. 1 it means simple Christian. Veilleux (*PK* 2, 166) now agrees with Vogüé. See Bacht, *Vermächtnis*, 220 n. 609.

78. Bacht has the words [to memorize] in brackets. I assume this is his editorial clarification, and it is helpful. Veilleux does not have it.

79. Bacht, *Vermächtnis*, 223 n. 619, thinks the feat of memorizing the Psalter was fairly common for monks, but the New Testament could take a lifetime. The ancient memory was much more active than the modern one, but people can still memorize vast quantities of what really interests them.

of this was done for its own sake, but out of love for Scripture and to promote contemplation.

With all this, we might assume that Pachomius required literacy for entrance, but that was not the case. Precept 139 goes on to arrange reading lessons for the illiterate.[80] These lessons are not leisurely: one "stands before" the teacher three times a day to learn "letters,[81] syllables, verbs, and nouns." Moreover, the monk is to learn to read "very studiously with all gratitude," a surprising requirement, but perhaps just the positive aspect of the final sentence: "He shall be compelled to read, willingly or not!"

Now the truth comes out: some monks did not *wish* to read![82] That was true in the fourth century, and it is true today. Some monks are by nature activists and are practical persons. Further, the ambient culture can be more or less conducive to reading. For example, some have predicted that the Internet will eventually put an end to books. It behooves a modern monastery to think carefully about its requirements for literacy.

Precepts 141–142 may seem to shift gears abruptly, speaking as they do of unauthorized absences from "praying and psalming" (that is, the

---

80. Whether or not illiteracy was common in fourth-century Upper Egypt can be disputed. Bacht, *Vermächtnis*, 221 n. 614, strongly denies that the cultural level of the Pachomians was low. He opposes two older scholars: Emmanuel Amand de Mendieta, "Le système cénobitique basilien comparé au système cénobitique pachômien," *Revue de l'histoire des réligions* 152 (1957): 31–80, at 37ff, 53ff.; Gustave Bardy, "Les origines des écoles monastiques en Orient," in *Mélanges Joseph de Ghellinck* (Gembloux: Duculot, 1951), 293–309, at 300.

81. *Elementa syllabae* is sometimes taken as "elements of syllables," but Bacht, *Vermächtnis*, 221 n. 616, shows this is incorrect. Indeed, the four elements are exactly what was learned in a formal curriculum. Apparently the author of Pr. 139 attended such a school; probably Pachomius or Theodore did so at Esneh. In his classic work *Histoire de l'Éducation dans l'Antiquité* (Paris: Éditions du Seuil, 1965); English: *A History of Education in Antiquity*, trans. George Lamb (New York: Sheed and Ward, 1956), 330–31, Henri I. Marrou cites Pr. 139 as an example of how people were taught to read.

82. Nevertheless, it would not be wise to overstress this strong demand of Pr. 139, for it occurs only this one time in all of Pachomian literature. See Ruppert, *Pachomianischen Mönchtum*, 129. It is interesting to note St. Benedict's attitude toward monks who cannot or will not read: They must not bother others trying to do *lectio* (RB 48.18) and should be given some work to do on Sunday if they cannot read (RB 48.23). If they cannot write their profession documents, they should at least "make their mark on it" (RB 58.20).

Divine Office).[83] Yet it is not always possible to be there, and Pr. 142 deals with situations when this is the case. When a monk cannot pray with the community he must still "not neglect the times of prayer and psalmody." The reasons why one cannot join the common prayer are myriad, but none of them removes the personal obligation from the individual.[84]

Relations with Nuns (Precepts 143–144)

Then, so near the end, the Precepts take up a completely new topic, namely, how the monks are to relate to the neighboring convent of nuns.[85] Although this is a rather long and detailed Precept, the contents can be easily summarized: contacts between monks and nuns are strictly controlled. First, an experienced monk is sent to live with the nuns as their chaplain.[86] But Pr. 143 is mostly about visits of other monks to the nuns.

It might surprise us that such visits were allowed at all, but in fact they were only permitted to relatives: "mother, sister, daughter, some

---

83. Precept 141 has "psalming and praying," while Pr. 142 reverses the order; Pr. 141 adds a third member, "the Collect." The *Greek Excerpta* consolidate all of them into "the common prayer."

84. Precept 142 attempts to symbolize the many reasons for private recitation of the Office by listing cases: "whether he is on a boat, in the monastery, in the fields, or on a journey, or fulfilling any office whatever." The *Greek Excerpta* of Prs. 141–142 rework this into a more logical order: "None of those who are involved in service, whether in field or cloister, shall seek an excuse to miss the common prayer." This shows that the determining factor is *service*, not place.

85. Precept 143 starts out with the words "Let us speak of nuns," which suggests a new topic, but some editors have concluded it was written by someone else. Holstenius [Lukas Holste], in his *Codex Regularum* (Paris, 1663), illustrates this by placing Pr. 143 at the end of the Laws and suggests that it is not Pachomian at all. But *Sbo* 26 shows that Pachomius actually did found a convent for his sisters, and it lays down similar rules for engagement. Furthermore, Armand Boon, *Pachomiana Latina*, assures us that Pr. 143 appears in most of the best manuscripts.

86. This chaplain is a *senior*, but in cenobitic jargon that refers more to wisdom than to age. *Sbo* 27 says that Apa Peter was the first chaplain. He was "seasoned with the salt" of wisdom, which he needed for biblical preaching to the nuns. *Sbo* 27 also informs us that Pachomius wrote a separate Rule for nuns, which is no longer extant.

relatives or cousins, mother of his children."[87] But there must be some "evident reasons" to see them, and the monk must be accompanied by another monk of "proven age and life." In addition, the visit must be cleared by both the abbot and the chaplain of the nuns. And then the latter shall meet the visitors, and the three of them will meet with the nun.[88] No mention is made of the female superior.

Faced with such a thicket of cautions, we might get the feeling that Pachomius had a problem with women. Perhaps in a different social context he might have been less defensive, or he might have devised some sort of coed monastery. Perhaps, but he could only respond to the world he knew. The fact is that monks throughout the ages have maintained an extremely guarded stance toward all women. Given the recent revelations of clerical violations of celibacy, such an approach will probably have to continue.

And so we come to the final paragraph of the Precepts (144). We would expect a conclusion,[89] and that is what we get: "Whoever transgresses any of these commands shall, for his negligence and his contempt, do penance publicly without any delay so that he may be able to possess the Kingdom of Heaven." Three things catch our notice: First, the Precepts are primarily a rule of life, the violation of which brings sanctions; second, the approach is subjective. What is punished is bad will, which must be atoned by good will. Third, the whole purpose is eschatological—to gain heaven.

---

87. Some of the Pachomians, however, refused to see their relatives when they called. When Pachomius's sister Mary came to him, he would not see her, but he agreed to set up a convent for her (*Sbo* 27). In *Sbo* 37, Theodore's mother comes to visit him, but he will not see her. Pachomius tries to talk him into visiting her but praises Theodore for his strong stand.

88. There is some unclearness about this sentence. Veilleux has: "They shall meet [the virgins] and with them see those whom they need with all discipline and fear of God." Bacht, however, has [the visitors] in parentheses, and he construes "those whom they need" to be the nuns. Since *quas* is feminine, Bacht seems right.

89. Precepts 48 and 103 also threaten sanctions against anyone who flouts the Precepts, and so they are often regarded as endings as well, but of subsections. Vogüé, "Pièces," 35, calls Pr. 144 a true conclusion. He thinks it shows the Precepts are a self-contained unit, not lacking the other parts of the Rule, namely, Institutes, Judgments, and Laws.

Chapter Eight

Monastic Issues in *The Life of Augustine* by His Disciple Possidius

Introduction

When Possidius, the bishop of Calama in the North African province of Numidia, sat down to write his *Life of Augustine* (*VA*) in the third decade of the fifth century, the golden age of the church in those parts was near its end.[1] At the Vandal invasion of North Africa in 428, Possidius and the other bishops of Numidia had fled to Hippo for safety and there they attended the deathbed of Augustine (*VA* 31). Since he describes the scene, we know that Possidius wrote *VA* after 428, and probably before the year 437, when he was definitively driven out of Calama by the Vandal chief Genseric.[2] At that point he disappears from recorded history.

---

1. A version of this chapter first appeared in the *American Benedictine Review* 38, no. 2 (June 1987): 159–77. It is reprinted, with revisions, by permission. The text of the *Life* I have used for this article appears in *Vita di Cipriano, Vita di Ambrogio, Vita di Agostino*, ed. Antoon A. R. Bastiaensen, intro. by Christine Mohrmann (Milan: Mondadori, 1975); hereafter *VA*. The text is also found in PL 32.33–66. The only English translation I know is by Sr. Mary Magdeleine Mueller in *Early Christian Biographies*, FC 15 (New York: Fathers of the Church, 1952).

2. Marie-François Berrouard, "Possidius," *Dictionnaire de Spiritualité* 12 (1985), cols. 1997–2008.

Possidius was well placed to write Augustine's life, since he had been his disciple and friend for forty years (*VA* 31.11). He had joined Augustine's lay monastery at Hippo in the early 390s, had taken Holy Orders and moved to the clerical monastery after 395; then he finally became a bishop in his own right. As brother bishops, Augustine and Possidius saw a good deal of each other on both an official and friendly basis. Although Augustine urged his former pupil to make his own decisions as a bishop of the church,[3] it is clear that Possidius was dependent on him throughout his career.

Before he wrote the *Life of Augustine*, Possidius had already exercised devotion to his deceased mentor in a different kind of literary work. In his last years Augustine had spent a good deal of time reediting the vast corpus of writing he had done over a fifty-year span. This reworking took the form of *Retractationes*,[4] that is, corrections of points he now saw differently. Evidently he was anxious to leave a literary legacy and, as Possidius himself notes, "He always ordered the church's library to be carefully preserved for posterity" (*VA* 31.6).

Shortly after the saint's death, Possidius himself set to work to carry out Augustine's wishes about the library of his works. The bishop of Calama, no doubt in a kind of act of faith, for he had every right to fear that the Vandals outside the gates of Hippo would eventually burn and pillage the town, carefully listed each book in the collection. This annotated list has come down to us under the name *Indiculum*.[5] Although Possidius has provided posterity with these two precious documents about Augustine, that is not to suggest that the bishop of Calama was a

3. "On the matter of the ordination of him who has been baptized in the party of Donatus, I cannot exercise the authority of your office" (Letter 245.2; CSEL 57, 583). Berrouard, "Possidius," notes the following instances of dependence: In 403, shortly after he became bishop, Possidius was attacked and beaten by a gang of Circumcellions. Augustine urged him to take the Donatist bishop, Crispinus, to court and debate him (*VA* 12.7); in 408, after the cathedral at Calama was besieged by pagan mobs, Augustine insisted that Possidius seek redress from the emperor in Ravenna, which he did (Letter 91.10); finally, Possidius accompanied Augustine and Alypius to Mauretania in 418 as papal legate (*VA* 14; Letters 190.1 and 193.1, CSEL 57, 137–38, 168).

4. PL 46.5–22. This work is often printed along with *Vita Augustini* as in *Opuscula Sancti Possidii episcopi Calamensis: Vita sancti Augustini et Indiculum librorum eius*, ed. Angel Custodio Vega (Escorial, Spain: Monasterium Escurialensis, 1934).

5. See previous note.

writer. He was simply a disciple to a great man, who took up the task of writing his biography and bibliography when no one else seemed ready or able to do so. His *Life of Augustine* is in no sense a great book, but a rather pedestrian one written by a simple, practical person.

The excellent critical edition of the *Vita Augustini* recently published by A. A. R. Bastiaensen,[6] which includes a helpful commentary, has shed light on certain aspects of Augustine's life that may be of interest to students of ancient monasticism. Although Augustine rarely used the word "monk," and his Rule has been claimed by the canons regular and friars rather than the monasteries of Western Christianity, he was nevertheless a real monk in his attitudes and instincts. So was his biographer, Possidius,[7] who gives the monastic element its due proportion in the narrative of Augustine's life.

It is true, of course, that Augustine's pastoral duties kept him out of the monastery for most of his life. It is also true that his ideas about the monastic life were not exactly the same as those of the Egyptians, who are often considered the founders of Christian monasticism. In this sense Augustine offers an alternative, minority view. Nonetheless, since Augustine was one of the principal sources of the Rule of Benedict, his approach to monastic life ought to be of perennial interest to Benedictines, especially those who share the circumstances of his busy urban existence.

Conversion to Christianity/Monasticism

According to Possidius, Augustine turned toward ascetical and monastic life immediately after his conversion to Christianity in Milan: "Thus, by extraordinary divine assistance, Augustine received the saving doctrine of the Catholic Church and the divine sacraments through the ministry of the great and illustrious prelate, Ambrose. From the bottom

6. See n. 1 above.

7. In the very first lines of his Preface, Possidius betrays his lifelong commitment to monasticism: "Under the inspiration of God, the Creator and Ruler of all things, and mindful of my *purpose* whereby through the grace of the Saviour I resolved to *serve* faithfully the omnipotent and divine Trinity, I have striven both formerly in my life as a layman and now in my office of bishop, with whatever talent and eloquence I possess, to help toward the edification of the true and holy Catholic Church of Christ the Lord" (*VA* Preface 1). The two italicized words, *propositum* and *servire*, are technical terms for the religious life in fourth-century parlance. They will be discussed later in this chapter.

of his heart, he soon abandoned every hope that he had in the world, with no further desire for wife, children of the flesh, or worldly honors. He determined, instead, to serve God in company with his *servants*" (*VA* 1.6–2.1).

The modern reader may be struck by the claim that Augustine moved so quickly from conversion to Christianity to conversion to "super-Christianity," namely, religious life. "Servant of God" may not mean monk in the strict sense, but it certainly refers to a separate and elite group in the church in the fourth century.[8] To someone conversant with Augustine's own autobiography (*Confessions*), however, it is quite clear that Possidius has not got the monastic conversion too early but too late. It happened even *before* Augustine's conversion to Christianity.[9]

This rather glaring error has caused Hans-Joachim Diesner[10] to question Possidius's reliability as a historian, but that does not seem to be a necessary conclusion. Possidius is telescoping his account of Augustine's early life because he does not wish to repeat what has already been treated in great detail in the *Confessions* (*VA* Preface 5). In the interest of brevity it was much more convenient to place the conversion to monasticism after the general conversion rather than explain how they could be reversed.[11]

Christine Mohrmann agrees that Possidius has garbled the account of Augustine's conversion, but she is not so certain the error lies in chronology. In her opinion the claim that "an eager longing to become proficient in religion was stirred up within him" (*VA* 1.5), which is placed before the baptism by Possidius, may well be a reference to

8. "Thus, when Alypius and Augustine arrived in Carthage, in late 388, they already belonged to an ill-defined, but quite recognizable, group of men: they were *Servi Dei*, 'servants of God' . . . . These *Servi Dei* owed their position in the Latin Church less to any connexion to organized monastic life, than to the pressure of a fashion in perfection . . . . a [*Servus Dei*] was a dedicated layman, determined to live, in the company of bishops, priests and noble patrons, the full life of a Christian." Peter Brown, *Augustine of Hippo* (Berkeley: University of California Press, 1967), 132.

9. Thus Pierre Courcelle, *Les Confessions de saint Augustin dans la tradition littéraire; antécedents et posterité* (Paris: Études augustiniennes, 1963), 612ff. Upon hearing of the life of St. Antony of Egypt, Augustine and Alypius expressed interest and sympathy (*Confessions* VII.vi.14).

10. Diesner, "Possidius und Augustinus," *Studia Patristica* 6 (1962): 350–65.

11. *VA*, Commentary, 347.

an ascetic conversion. She also notes that Possidius's use of "soon" (*moxque*) between the baptism and the turning to monastic life should not be taken too literally. For Mohrmann, Possidius's real mistake is to think that Augustine was converted to Christianity from Manicheism. For her the true issue was intellectual: Augustine was converted from Platonism.[12]

One might ask whether Possidius has not purposely deferred Augustine's turn toward religious and monastic life so as to dissociate its later development as clearly as possible from heterodox ascetic groups. If Augustine embraced monasticism when he was still a Manichee, that could open the way to charges that his Christian monasticism was still tinged with unorthodox elements. We will see that both Augustine and Possidius were at pains to allay any such suspicions.

Another text from the conversion period that has bearing on our subject is one concerning Monica: "His mother, sole living relative, clung to him and exulted more over his *resolution to serve God* than she would have over the hope of natural offspring" (*VA* 3.3). We have already seen that "Servant of God" was a technical term for "religious" at that time. In addition, "resolution" (*propositum*) had a more precise meaning than can be seen in translation. It is like "Servant of God" in that it refers to a life fully dedicated to the things of God and his church, but it seems to have the further connotation of *structured* religious life.[13] In fact, within a very few years Augustine would write a Rule for the monastery he founded in Hippo.

Tagaste, a Home Monastery

About a year after his conversion Augustine returned home to North Africa from Milan, where he had been a teacher of rhetoric. Possidius makes this return immediate, thus omitting a long visit to Rome and the death of Monica at Ostia. His description of Augustine's time at his

---

12. See Mohrmann, general introduction to *VA*, xlix–l.

13. Ludovic T. Lorie, *Spiritual Terminology of the Latin Translations of the Vita Antonii: with reference to fourth and fifth century monastic literature* (Utrecht et al.: Dekker & Van de Vegt, 1955), 101. Lorie puts great emphasis on the fact that words like *propositum* are clues that show how Western monks habitually made Eastern charismatic monasticism into a life of law and order. In addition to *VA* 2.3, *propositum* occurs six more times in the text; Preface 1; 4.1; 11.2; 11.4; 15.7; 31.7. Mueller translates these variously with words connoting "lifestyle" or "monastery." *VA* 3.1-2: my own translation.

hometown of Tagaste is also laconic: "After he had received the grace [of baptism], he decided to return, with his fellow townsmen and friends who like him were serving God [as religious] to Africa and his own home estate. When he arrived there, he lived almost three years on the property which had already been divested. He lived there for God with those who were united with him in fasting, prayers and good works; he meditated on his law day and night."[14]

The fellow townsmen and friends here referred to include Augustine's son, Adeodatus, and at least Alypius and Evodius, two other men from Tagaste who had been with Augustine in Milan and who shared in his conversion and experiments in communal living at Cassiciacum, a suburban estate. We know that another very close associate, Nebridius, also returned to Africa at this time, but not to Hippo. After about three years (388–391) Augustine moved to Hippo, where he became a priest and the founder of another monastic community.

The details of the communal Christian life lived at Tagaste are not clear. For example, Mueller translates a key phrase as follows: "He lived there for nearly three years, but then renounced his property and joined those faithful. . . ." This rendition makes it sound as if Augustine only embraced religious poverty after leaving his estate and joining another group.[15] Bastiaensen, however, remarks that the adverb *iam*, although vague, must mean "soon" here; that is, soon after his arrival back at the home estate he divested himself of his goods.[16] Another suggestion about this difficult passage comes from André Mandouze, who thinks that *alienates* should be read with what follows, namely, *cum his qui eidem adhaerebant*. The effect of this would be to associate the others in the community with Augustine's newly undertaken poverty.[17]

---

14. *Ac placuit gratia cum aliis civibus et amicis suis Deo pariter servientibus ad Africam et propriam domum agrosque remeare. Ad quos veniens, et in quibus constitutus ferme triennio et a se iam alienatis, cum his qui eidem adhaerebant Deo vivebat, jejuniis, orationibus, in lege domini meditans die ac nocte.*

15. In order to read the text thus she must make the phrase *et a se alienatis* into an adversative, which seems to me unwarranted.

16. *VA*, Commentary, 349. Two other references to this same event are too vague to help us establish the precise situation: Letter 126.7 and *VA* 5.1, 7-8, which reads: "Augustine had formerly (dispossessed himself) when he returned home from overseas."

17. André Mandouze, *Saint Augustin, l'aventure de la raison et de la grâce* (Paris: Études augustiniennes, 1968), 206ff. Bastiaensen objects to this reading on textual grounds.

In direct contradiction to this last interpretation is Georges Folliet, who thinks there was a sharp difference between Augustine's experience at Tagaste and what happened later at Hippo. In his view that difference lay precisely in the matter of poverty: at Tagaste, Augustine was the only one in the community to shed his goods; at Hippo this became the norm, and so Possidius could call the latter community a "monastery" in the strict sense.[18] Folliet also judges that the Tagaste communal experiment was still a search for philosophical leisure such as Augustine had sought at Cassiciacum. He notes that Augustine's writings from this period (388–391) feature the phrase *deificari in otio* ("to become godly in leisure"), which is a trademark for the Platonic search for the perfect life of a contemplative philosopher.

Christine Mohrmann[19] wonders whether Folliet has not created too sharp a cleavage between the community life lived at Tagaste and that pursued at Hippo. In her view community is a more primary value than poverty for Augustine (and Possidius). She thinks that the element of "conviviality" runs like a thread from Augustine's earliest experiment in community right through Tagaste, the Hippo lay monastery, and on to the bishop's house in Hippo. We will have occasion to expand on this topic at a later point.

Along this same line, Peter Brown lays heavy emphasis on Augustine's lifelong need for friendship. He was a man who needed constant communion with those he loved, but the Tagaste period brought him much suffering in this regard: "Much had changed in the past three years. When Augustine arrived in Hippo in the spring of 391, he was a lonely man, entering middle age, who had lost much of his past and who was groping, half-consciously, for new fields to conquer."[20]

In fact, there had occurred two deaths during this period that were traumatic for Augustine: first, that of his friend Nebridius, who had settled on his own estate near Carthage. Augustine had refused to visit him shortly before his death, so this may have caused him some guilt.[21] It was also at this time that Augustine's son Adeodatus died at a young age. Brown has remarked on the astonishing fact that Augustine never mentions this event in his intimate autobiography, *Confessions*. It

18. Georges Folliet, "Aux origines de l'ascétisme et du cénobitisme africain," *Studia Anselmiana* 46 (1961): 25–44, at 36. Peter Brown, *Augustine of Hippo*, 132, calls this article "sound and differentiated."

19. *VA*, Introduction, lvii.

20. Brown, *Augustine of Hippo*, 137.

21. Letter 10.1.

cannot have failed to mark the father deeply. Finally, Brown's reference to "new fields to conquer" is plausible. Augustine was a great leader in search of a wider field of endeavor, whether he knew it or not.

Personally, I tend to think that the Tagaste community was already a monastic one. After all, one of its members was Alypius, and his later history was quite as monastic as that of Augustine. He became bishop of Tagaste after Augustine's departure, and there are good reasons to think that he maintained a monastic community. After Alypius became bishop, Paulinus of Nola wrote to him of the *monasteriis Carthagini, Thagastae, Hipponis regione*.[22] Moreover, Luc Verheijen thinks that Alypius wrote the Ordo Monasterii, a document traditionally associated with Augustine but apparently written for the monks at Tagaste.[23]

The Garden Monastery at Hippo

The story of Augustine's ordination at Hippo is well known. Possidius tells it in the ancient manner as the struggle of a saintly soul to flee from the awesome burden of sacred orders, but he also lets us know that the reasons for the choice of Augustine were not simply mystical ones. The church of Hippo needed a vigorous and articulate spokesman against its public enemies, namely, the pagans, Manichees, and Donatists. The old bishop, Valerius, was not up to the polemical and rhetorical task, so he even took the unusual step of having his new *presbyter* preach in public.

But Augustine was not about to abandon his monastic lifestyle altogether: "Soon after his ordination as presbyter, Augustine founded a monastery within the church, and began to live there among the servants of God according to the rule and custom established by the holy Apostles. The principal regulation of that society specified that no one should own anything, but that all things should be held in common and distributed according to personal needs. Augustine had formerly done this when he returned home from across the sea" (*VA* 5.1). This monastery "within the church" (*intra ecclesiam*) was actually located in the precincts ("garden") of the Hippo church, an arrangement that Bishop Valerius gladly agreed to.[24]

---

22. Letter 3.6.
23. Luc Verheijen, *La Règle de saint Augustin*, 2 vols. (Paris: Études Augustiniennes, 1967), 2, 142ff.
24. Sermon 355.2.

Luc Verheijen, the principal modern expert on Augustine's monastic writings, considers the reference to the Acts of the Apostles in this quotation of capital importance for the history of Augustinian monasticism.[25] He points out that Possidius combines Acts 4:32 and 4:35, "no one should own anything, but all things should be held in common and distributed according to personal needs," to describe the poverty practiced by this community. This apparently casual combination of two closely connected biblical passages, a procedure entirely in the ancient manner, is in fact a verbatim quotation of *Praeceptum* 1.3, from what is commonly called the *Rule of Augustine*. But what is so unusual about a disciple like Possidius quoting his master? Surely he was well imbued with the monastic teaching of Augustine embodied in his famous Rule.

Yet traditional scholarship has not usually admitted that the *Praeceptum* was written for the Hippo lay monastery at all. A nearly identical form of it for female religious is found in Letter 211, and this has been thought to be the original text. If that were true, the *Praeceptum* would be a subsequent version for men, probably not written before the later years of Augustine's episcopate.[26] But Possidius's exact quotation of the *Praeceptum* and his association of that text with the Hippo lay monastery proves to Verheijen's satisfaction both that Possidius really was a monk of that monastery and that the *Praeceptum* was indeed the Rule followed by Augustine's garden monastery in Hippo.

In *VA* 5.1, Possidius seems to refer to the Rule of Augustine when he says that the monks there lived "according to the custom and rule set down by the Apostles" (*secundum modum et regulam sub sanctis Apostolicis constitutam*), but Verheijen does not think that *regulam* here refers to Augustine's Rule.[27] It probably is another example of the Western tendency, noted previously, to see all things connected with religious life as matters of law and order.

25. Verheijen, *Règle*, 1, 418 and 2, 89ff.

26. In his second volume (pp. 7–85) Verheijen traces at great length the history of the interpretation of the *Rule of Augustine*. He shows that a certain "softness" in that Rule caused commentators to think that it must have been written for women. It also enabled them to cast aspersions on it to the effect that "real monks" would have to add a good deal of austerity to Augustine's prescriptions.

27. Verheijen, *Règle*, 2, 8–9.

The Bishop and His Clerical Monastery

In the year 397, Valerius died and Augustine was elected his successor. At that point the new bishop moved out of the garden monastery into the episcopal residence. He explains why he felt this move was necessary: "I became bishop and saw that the bishop must extend careful hospitality to those who arrive or are passing by. If the bishop does not do this he is called inhuman. Yet if that custom were permitted in the monastery, it would be indecent. And therefore I wished to have with me in the bishop's house a monastery of clerics."[28] Possidius does not mention Augustine's change of residence, but he gives a rather full description of the new situation:

> As the divine teachings prospered, the clerics of the church at Hippo, who had served God in the monastery with Holy Augustine, began to be ordained. Consequently, the truths taught by the Catholic Church, as well as the manner of life practiced by the holy servants of God, became more celebrated day by day. To insure peace and unity, the church eagerly began to demand bishops and priests from the monastery that had been founded and strengthened by the zealous Augustine. Later, the request was fulfilled. The most blessed founder gave about ten men, holy and venerable, chaste and learned, to various churches, some of them being quite prominent. Like him, those holy men who came from that community increased the churches of the Lord and also established monasteries. As their zeal for spreading God's word increased, they in turn supplied other churches with brethren who had been elevated to the priesthood. And thus, because of their number, the teaching of the church's salutary faith, hope and charity became known to many people. This was true not only throughout all parts of Africa but even across the sea, by means of Greek editions and translations. So, too, we read, "The wicked saw it and was angry." Gnashing his teeth and fainting away. The servants, however, as we read again, were peaceable toward those who hated peace, and acceded willingly to any discussion. (*VA* 11)

Before we comment on details of this important chapter it should be pointed out that Mueller's translation seems to misconstrue the first sentence. Her rendition makes it seem that the members of the clerical monastery began to be ordained, as would be the normal progression of a class of seminarians today. But the text actually says the monks, presumably from the garden monastery, began to be ordained clerics: *in monasterio Deo servientes ecclesiae Hipponiensi clerici ordinari coeperunt.*

---

28. Sermon 356.3: my translation.

Perhaps the translator was misled by the fact that in his discussion Possidius passes from the garden monastery to the clerical monastery so silently and effortlessly that one hardly notices the move. Likewise, we can assume that he made the same transition in real life, but there is no explicit acknowledgment of this. No doubt his reticence is partly due to natural modesty, for he rarely refers to himself in *VA* except in the Preface and at the very end (*VA* 31.10-11). Yet there appears to be no great difference and certainly no contradiction in his mind between the monastic and the clerical vocation. Whereas in the Eastern Church there was often resistance on the part of monks to ordination ("beware of women and bishops!") and Augustine himself tried to avoid ordination (*VA* 4), now the monks seem to pass almost naturally from the purely monastic state to clerical orders.

One case that suggests the fluid boundary between the monastic and clerical states in Hippo is that of Firmus, a convert whom Possidius discusses in *VA* 15. After this merchant entered the church as a result of one of Augustine's sermons, he also joined one of his monastic communities: "Firmus adhered to the manner of life of God's servants" (*VA* 15.7). The term employed there is *Servorum Dei*, the same as is used elsewhere for lay monks. Yet the clerical members of the bishop's clerical community are also called *conservi* (*VA* 15.1), and since Possidius himself was a clerical monk when the Firmus incident occurred, it seems to pertain to the clerical house.

Later, Firmus was employed by Augustine as a messenger with letters to Jerome in Bethlehem, and he seems to have made several trips back and forth between Hippo and Palestine.[29] Possidius notes that Firmus was later ordained: "Having been called and constrained by God's will, he entered upon the office of presbyter in another region" (*VA* 15.5). This implies that he was not ordained in the Hippo monastery, and also that he was not too eager to be ordained.[30]

---

29. Peter Brown, *Augustine of Hippo*, 370, n. 2, suggests that this is the same Firmus who later acted as a literary agent for Augustine. Letters 81.1 and 82.1 name a Firmus as messenger in the year 404. Around the years 416–418 he reappears as the bearer of Letter 172 from Jerome to Augustine. Firmus is also mentioned in several other letters of Augustine, where he is called *frater et presbyter*. Probably he was ordained in Palestine.

30. *Dei voluntate petitus et coactus*. Of course, Firmus may have been a cleric of lower rank previous to this. Further, the claim that he was reluctant for priesthood may be a pious convention.

Possidius is, however, quite explicit as to why so many monks were ordained: because of the progress of the church (*proficiente porro doctrina divina*). But this statement is not in itself crystal clear. Did the actual numerical growth of the African church require more clergy? Or could it be the other way around, namely, that the promotion of the church required a certain kind of clergy? Perhaps these men were needed for the apologetic defense of the church, just as Augustine himself had been needed. At any rate, we learn that "about ten" of the clerics living a monastic life with Augustine were chosen to be bishops in their own right. We have the names and cities of seven of them: Severus of Milevus, Evodius of Uzalis, Profuturus and Fortunatus of Cirta, Urbanus of Sicca Veneria, Peregrinus of Thenae, and Possidius of Calama.[31]

Possidius makes it sound very much as if the influence of "The School of Augustine" spread far and wide, even to the ends of the earth. The bishop of Calama and others maintained clerical monasteries in their own episcopal residences: Augustine often writes to "Bishop X and the brothers who live with you, Augustine and the brothers who live with him send greetings." But we know nothing of the third generation claimed by his comment: "As their zeal for spreading God's word increased, they in turn supplied other churches with brethren who had been elevated to the priesthood" (*VA* 11.4). As for "Greek translations and editions," only two of Augustine's anti-Donatist works were translated into that language. The Greeks were not interested in the provincial polemics of North Africa.[32]

In *VA* 11, Possidius actually tells us rather little about the kind of life lived in the clerical monastery of Hippo. His only comment in this regard is that the members lived in "continence and extreme poverty" (*continentia et paupertate profunda*). In a sense this is a somewhat puzzling remark, since "extreme" poverty does not seem to have been a hallmark of Augustine's monasticism. In Sermons 355–356, where the bishop of Hippo is outraged to discover that one of the priests has left a will, his complaint is not so much that frugality has been violated, but that community of goods has been betrayed. The Rule of Augustine devotes a good deal of space to common goods.

31. Othmar Perler, *Les Voyages de saint Augustin* (Paris: Études augustiniennes, 1969), 156, citing the Maurists.
32. *VA*, Commentary, 374.

A Traumatic Occurrence

Sometime after the year 397, Possidius became bishop of Calama, an important town about forty miles south of Hippo. We know that Megalius, the previous bishop of Calama, died in 397, but we are not sure if Possidius replaced him immediately.[33] Calama was a dangerous place to be bishop in those days. In 403, Possidius was personally beaten up by a gang of Circumcellions, and in 408 the church building was besieged by angry pagans.[34] The first of these events is more pertinent to our present study:

> In this connection we must not fail to mention what the illustrious Augustine accomplished for the glory of God against the above-mentioned rebaptizing Donatists, through his ardor and zeal for the house of God. On one occasion, one of the bishops [Possidius] whom he had given to the Church from the clergy of his monastery, together with several priests, visited the church at Calama. [No doubt this refers to a rural visitation: tr.] This diocese was under his care, and in the interest of the church's peace the bishop had used all his knowledge in preaching against the heresy. Accordingly, in the middle of the journey he fell into an ambuscade. Although he escaped with all his companions, their animals and baggage were stolen. The bishop himself was left seriously injured and wounded. (VA 12.1-4)

The Circumcellions were bands of zealots who roamed the countryside, harassing the Roman government and the Catholic Church. Possidius here identifies them with the Donatists, but they were a special group, perhaps corresponding to the monks of the Orthodox party.[35] Naturally Possidius was deeply marked by this violent experience.

---

33. Augustine, writing in 403 in *Contra Cresconium* III.46, 50, calls Possidius *hesternus tiro*, a "new recruit" to the episcopate. We do not know if Calama lay vacant for some years or whether there was an interim occupant. Perhaps six years seemed a short interval to Augustine.

34. This event took place on 1 June 408 and is described in Letters 91.8 and 104.4, 17.

35. Some scholars like Hans-Joachim Diesner ("Possidius und Augustinus," 357ff.) and W. H. C. Frend, *The Donatist Church, a Movement of Protest in Roman North Africa* (Oxford: Clarendon Press, 1952), see the Circumcellions as rural guerillas revolting against oppressive socioeconomic conditions. Peter Brown (*Augustine of Hippo*, 217), however, sees the conflict as primarily religious.

Indeed, his entire book is colored by his hatred of Donatism in all its forms, but there also seems to be a particularly monastic element in his polemic. In *VA* 10.1 he notes that the Circumcellions were a "strange group of men, perverse and violent, who professed continency." This looks bland enough, but the Latin may have more of an edge to it: *velut sub professione continentium ambulantes.* Is Possidius suggesting that the Circumcellions may claim to be monks but really are not true monks? We know, for example, that they were sometimes accompanied by young women and thereby laid themselves open to criticism.[36]

Christine Mohrmann suggests that *ambulantes* may be a criticism of their wandering habits, as indeed it might be if they were roving bandits. But another one of her comments is much more important for an overall assessment of Augustinian monasticism. She notes that although Augustine and Possidius often use the term *monasterium*, they rarely ever use the corresponding word *monachus*.[37] Could it be that the violent and outlandish condition of the Donatist monks had brought this name into bad repute? It is true that Augustine did write a treatise entitled *De Opere Monachorum*, but that book is very critical of the Circumcellions. At any rate this is an interesting thesis to which we shall add more data in our last two sections.

A Jaundiced View of Asceticism

We noted earlier that Possidius says little about the actual manner of life in Augustine's clerical monastery when he discusses its founding in *VA* 11. Yet as bishop of Calama he spent a great deal of time with his colleague at Hippo, so it is not surprising that he includes remarks about the lifestyle at Hippo in a later chapter. First, there is this comment about clothing: "His clothing and footwear, and even Augustine's house furnishings, were modest yet adequate—neither luxurious nor too plain. In such matters, men have the habit either of arrogantly displaying or of degrading themselves; in either case 'seeking not the things which are of Jesus Christ, but their own'" (*VA* 22). We note again the theme of moderation. For Augustine and his disciples it is not enough that one avoid ostentation, for exaggerated frugality is also a pitfall and perhaps a more dangerous one for monks. Augustine himself sometimes

---

36. Augustine, *Contra epistulam Parmeniani* II.9.19; III.3.18 (PL 43; CSEL 51); *Contra litteras Petiliani* II.88.195 (PL 43; CSEL 52); Letter 35.2 (PL 33).

37. Mohrmann, *VA*, Introduction, lvii.

comments on the need for "decent" clothing for the clergy.[38] Elsewhere he discusses the more subtle problem of ascetics who carefully affect disorderly clothing in order to create an impression.[39]

Bastiaensen questions whether Possidius really grasped the second point fully,[40] since he only applied the adjective "arrogantly" to the ostentation (*iactare se insolenter*) and not to the degradation. Nevertheless, Possidius does seem to agree with Augustine's general wariness of extreme asceticism.[41] Unlike many of the early monastic texts, *VA* extols not ascetical rigorism but prudent moderation. This attitude applies to food as well as clothing:

> Augustine, however, as I have said, held the middle course, deviating neither to the right nor to the left. His table was frugal and sparing, although, indeed, it sometimes included meat, herbs and vegetables, out of consideration for guests or the sick. Moreover, he always had wine, because he knew and taught as the Apostle says, "every creature of God is good, and nothing is to be rejected that is received with thanksgiving; for it is sanctified by the word of God and prayer." Moreover, he always showed hospitality. At the table itself he preferred reading and discussion to mere eating and drinking, and against the pest of human nature he had the following inscription carved on his table: "Whoever slanders the name of an absent friend may not as guest at this table attend." Thus he warned every guest to refrain from unnecessary and harmful tales. When, on one occasion, some of his closest fellow bishops forgot that warning and spoke heedlessly, Augustine became exasperated and sharply rebuked them, declaring that either those verses should be removed from the table or he would leave in the middle of the meal and go to his room. Both I and others who were at the table experienced this. (*VA* 22.1-2, 6-7)

Possidius claims that the fare of Augustine's table was not marked by rigorism. There was sometimes meat and always wine, but the author

38. Sermon 356.13. Sermons 355 and 356 (PL 38–39) are a long, impassioned discussion of the poverty of the clerical monastery in Hippo. Augustine pleads with the congregation not to undermine the morale of the clergy by inappropriate gifts.

39. *De sermone Domini in monti* II.12.41 (PL 34).

40. *VA*, Commentary, 412.

41. Augustine was well aware of the rigorous asceticism of monks in both East and West. This is quite clear from his *De Moribus Ecclesiae Catholicae et de Moribus Manichaeorum* I.13, 65–33,70 (PL 32).

makes it quite clear that these are relaxations that need explanation: the meat is for the guests and the sick; the wine is explained scripturally. Perhaps the standard against which this diet is compared is the garden monastery of Hippo, where, for example, it is probable that wine was available only at Saturday and Sunday meals.[42] But prudence and moderation were not the only motives behind the comments in *VA* 22. Michele Pellegrino argues that Possidius is carefully distancing Augustine's monastic lifestyle from any connection with Manichean dualism and its loathing of the material world.[43] This purpose seems certain, since the biblical quotations brought forward in *VA* 22 are precisely the ones used by Augustine to refute the Manicheans.[44]

The most compelling part of *VA* 22 is the charming story told by Possidius about the conversation at Augustine's table. It is not hard to picture the gathering of his protégés and the conviviality that such reunions often provokes. Yet the old mentor is not afraid to reassert his moral domination over the proceedings. Again it should be noticed that conversation at table was not the general monastic custom, nor was it practiced by the monks of Augustine's garden monastery. *Praeceptum* III.2 prescribes the public reading of Scripture at table so that the soul as well as the body might be fed. No doubt the bishop's table saw enough guests that public reading was not very practicable, yet one wonders whether Augustine did not prefer good and holy conversation even to Scripture reading. Peter Brown has taught us not to underestimate the need Augustine had for friendship: "Augustine needed the constant response and reassurance of a circle of friends: both to know that he was loved and to know that there was someone worth loving, encouraged him greatly to love in return: 'I must confess I throw myself headlong upon their charity, especially when I am depressed by the tensions of the world.' At this time he found no difficulty in calling a friend 'half of my soul' (*Conf.* IV.vi.11). His idea of friendship, a complete harmony

---

42. At least that is the arrangement prescribed in Ordo Monasterii 3.2 (critical text, Verheijen, *Règle*, 1, 148–52). Verheijen thinks that OM was followed at Hippo, even though it was written for the monks of Tagaste by Bishop Alypius. Later, Augustine wrote *Praeceptum* to supplement OM at Hippo.

43. Michele Pellegrino, *Possidio, Vita di S. Agostino. Introduzione, teso critico, versione e note*, Verba Seniorum IV (Alba: Paoline, 1955), 218.

44. *Contra Fortunatum* 22 (PL 42; CSEL 25.1); *Contra Faustum* VI.7-8; XIV.11 (PL 42; CSEL 25.1); *De Natura Boni* 34 (PL 42; CSEL 25.2). See *VA*, Commentary, 413.

of minds and purpose, was ideally suited to maintain a tight group of dedicated men."[45]

A Curious Miracle

A final window into Augustine's monastic vision as presented by Possidius in his *Vita* comes at a rather unexpected place in the narrative. In an account that is otherwise devoid of miracles,[46] Augustine does manage to perform one on his deathbed: "Likewise, when he was sick and confined to his bed, a certain man came with a sick relative and asked him to lay his hand upon him that he might be cured. Augustine replied that if he had any such power, he certainly would have first applied it to himself. Thereupon the visitor replied that he had had a vision and in his sleep he had heard these words: 'Go to Bishop Augustine, that he may lay his hand on him, and he will be healed.' When Augustine learned this, he did not delay doing it and immediately the Lord caused the sick man to depart from him healed" (*VA* 29.5).

It is hard to suppress a guffaw at Augustine's remark that if he could cure people, he would cure himself first. Somehow that rings true from the deathbed of a great saint. It is not something that the simpler Possidius would have made up or said himself. In fact, we can almost sense that Possidius found it hard to record such things about his revered master, but his sense of honesty made him do so.

When we study the broader context of this question, the passage becomes even more impressive. First of all, Possidius was a great devotee of the miraculous. Marie-François Berrouard[47] points out that when the bones of St. Stephen were discovered in Palestine in 415, Possidius made sure that Calama got some relics. These were duly enshrined and the place became a center of pilgrimage for that reason.[48] But Augustine's

---

45. Brown, *Augustine of Hippo*, 200–1.

46. Christine Mohrmann, *VA*, Introduction, xlvi, thinks Possidius is trying to employ the classical *vita* genre in the manner of Suetonius rather than the hagiographical style of, say, Jerome in his lives of Hilarion and Paul. The hagiographical genre relies on miracles to produce an effect on the pious reader. Mohrmann is able to detect a somewhat Suetonian structure in Possidius's account, but she acknowledges that the bishop of Calama was not skilled enough to make it work well.

47. Berrouard, "Possidius," col. 2004.

48. Augustine acknowledges this fact in *De Civitate Dei* XXII.8.21-22 (PL 41; CSEL 40).

interest in miracles in the last chapters of *De Civitate Dei* was something that occurred only in the very last years of his life. By that time people he trusted like Paulinus of Nola, and no doubt Possidius, had convinced him that God was working directly in human affairs in the fifth century. For most of Augustine's life, however, he was extremely reserved about miracles, which is not surprising in someone so committed to the rational life.[49] It bolsters the historicity of Possidius's account that he has refrained from involving Augustine in his own fascination with the miraculous.

Christine Mohrmann has derived an interesting corollary from Augustine's lack of interest in miracles: she thinks it indicates a corresponding lack of connection with Eastern monasticism. An interest in miracles was generally an Eastern Christian phenomenon that was only transmitted gradually to the Western part of the church. Since this transmission was largely accomplished by means of the monastic hagiography, such as the *Life of Antony*, Mohrmann concludes that Augustine must not have been much influenced by Eastern monasticism.[50]

Conclusion

In Augustine's monasticism and Possidius's account of it we find an interesting variant within the ancient tradition. Unlike most other monastic systems and outlooks, this one is marked by an undisguised interest in active ministry as well as a deep distrust of extreme asceticism. This case alone warns us not to stereotype monastic origins: different circumstances throughout the early church produced rather different monastic responses. Rather than repeat the outworn cliché that all Christian monasticism finds its ultimate root in Egypt, we need to admit that the situation was much more diverse. Monasticism sprang from the indigenous churches and adapted itself to the soil it grew in.

The evidence of Possidius's *Vita Augustini* makes it clear enough why Augustine was chary of extreme asceticism: his bad experience with the Manichean dualists taught him that hatred of the body invariably leads to corrosion of the spirit. Possidius's own difficulties with the Donatist

49. See Pierre Courcelle, *Recherches sur les Confessions de saint Augustin* (Paris: E. de Boccard, 1950), 144ff.

50. Even before his conversion Augustine knew of Eastern monks like Antony (see *Confessions* VII.vi.14), but his philosophic mind was not attracted to the miraculous element in that story. He was moved by it as an example of conversion.

Circumcellions also color the picture, causing him to project an abhorrence of all forms of fanaticism, including the monastic variety, on his subject. Yet a glance at the Rule of Augustine and his other monastic writings shows that the African doctor was by no means blind to the values of discipline.

Still, Possidius shows plainly that the thing that led Augustine to cenobitic monasticism was not his need for ascesis but for *philia*: Augustine needed friends and he needed a life of conviviality. He knew from Scripture and from his own experience that "it is not good for the human to be alone." This was the characteristic form that monasticism took under his creative genius. For him all other aspects of monastic life must serve community. Whether or not this squares with other monastic philosophies, it must at least be admitted that it proved to be a very hardy and adaptable approach for the church at Hippo. While some of the ascetic practices of the garden community had to be left behind, the bishop and his clergy were still able to pursue community to a considerable degree. Their common meals and practice of communal goods are an impressive witness to the life of monastic charity that prevailed in that house.

Chapter
Nine

Praeceptum: The Rule of Augustine

Introduction

The writing of this Rule, called *Praeceptum* (*Pr.*), probably took place in 397 AD.[1] At that point Augustine decided it would be disruptive for him to continue living in the monastery, so he moved to the bishop's house. His formal monastic life was over. It probably lasted no more than ten years or so. The life of a busy bishop was hardly compatible with monastic seclusion. Still, Augustine had very strong communal instincts and he was not about to abandon this value.[2] So he made the clergy of Hippo live in a common house with him, like it or not. Not all of them found it to their liking.[3]

---

1. Virtually the same Rule has come down to us in another form in Letter 211, addressed to the convent where his own sister had been superior. Down through the ages the feminine form, with an admonition added (211.1-4) was considered the original, but the research of Luc Verheijen, *La Règle de saint Augustin*, 2 vols. (Paris: Études augustiniennes, 1967), and others has proven conclusively that the masculine form came first. Because Augustine's Rule is quite refined and sensitive, some have disparaged it as "feminine," but that is now considered an insensitive and inaccurate judgment.

2. See Peter Brown, *Augustine of Hippo* (Berkeley: University of California Press, 1967), 137. Throughout Augustine's life he exhibited a strong need for friendship and company. See *Confessions*, IV.VI.11; Brown, *Augustine of Hippo*, 200–1.

3. Possidius, *Vita Augustini* (*VA*) 22.1-2, 6-7 (PL 32.33), denies this community was "ascetic." Rather, it was aimed at fraternal charity. Although there

As for the Garden Monastery and the monastery at Thagaste, it seems that they perdured after he left. In fact, they became the beginnings of a flourishing monastic life throughout North Africa. Yet this flowering was not destined to last long, for the Vandal invasions of the 430s severely impacted it as well as much else in the North African church. Although the Rule has been tremendously influential in the subsequent history of religious life for both men and women, in itself it is rather short and incomplete. Fortunately, though, we can flesh it out with other monastic writings of Augustine.[4]

For example, the Rule says almost nothing about the Divine Office. That lacuna was taken care of historically by affixing another document called Ordo Monasterii (OM) to the beginning of the *Praeceptum*.[5] The Ordo Monasterii was probably not written by Augustine, but by Alypius, his successor as the superior of the Thagaste community. Augustine's own community at Hippo followed much the same pattern of the Office, which Alypius seems to have copied from the monks of Palestine.[6]

On the subject of work, the Rule has more to say (*Pr.* 5.2), but Augustine also wrote a considerable treatise on monastic work in 401 when he was a bishop.[7] "The Work of Monks" was addressed to the monks of Carthage at the request of Aurelius, the patriarch. He sought the opinion of Augustine because the bishop of Hippo was considered the greatest African authority on monastic life. Indeed, he was the *founder* of North African monastic life.

The general problem at Carthage, it seems, was that some monks were espousing the Messalian doctrine that monks should not waste

------

is no indication that this group followed the *Praeceptum*, it was followed in subsequent history by orders of mendicants and canons who did not consider themselves monastic. That has led some to deny that the *Praeceptum* itself is a monastic Rule.

4. This section is largely drawn from Adalbert de Vogüé's survey of Augustine's monastic writings given in his *Histoire littéraire du mouvement monastique* (Paris: Cerf, 1996), 3: 149–245.

5. OM is found in PL 32.1449; there is a critical edition and English translation in George Lawless, *Augustine of Hippo and His Monastic Rule* (Oxford: Clarendon Press, 1987), 74–79.

6. Vogüé, *Histoire littéraire*, 3: 149–72.

7. *De Opere Monachorum*, PL 40.547; CSEL 41; English translation in Augustine, *Treatises on Various Subjects*, ed. Roy J. Deferrari; trans. Mary Sarah Muldowney and others, FC 16 (New York: Fathers of the Church, 1952), 323–96; see Vogüé, *Histoire littéraire*, 3: 231–45.

their time working; they should spend all their time in prayer. Other Christians should support them. Even though this same position was held by the monks of St. Martin at Marmoutier, who were the first monks in the West, Augustine wanted no part of it. In fact, this treatise is quite relevant to modern monasticism since it deals not only with manual labor but also with apostolic work. Augustine assumes that urban monks will be called on as spiritual counselors, so he offers his opinion on how they should handle that work, which he encourages.

Not surprisingly, Augustine is not opposed to monks being ordained. He himself was, and so were many of the monks of the Garden Monastery. In Letter 48, to the monks of the island of Capraria, Augustine urges them not to refuse orders when the church needs them.[8] As with Gregory the Great, he is constantly bemoaning the *otium* he lost when he was ordained—but also demanding that other monks not refuse ordination. While these are the major writings of Augustine on monasticism, he talks about it in numerous other treatises, letters, and sermons. Of course, Augustine wrote voluminously, and he wrote well. Therefore with him, as with someone like Basil the Great, we are able to go to his other writings to supply the background for his teachings: in short, the *Praeceptum.*[9]

Praeceptum

Basic Structure

Although *Praeceptum* is not a long document, perhaps one-fourth the length of the Rule of Benedict, it is not a concise one. Rather, it is what might be termed "discursive," that is, a rather elaborate, even wordy discussion of a few points. It makes no claim to be a complete legislative program for every aspect of monastic life, but it does address certain points that must have been of great importance to Augustine when he wrote it. Nevertheless, these practical discussions, whether of poverty or celibacy, are really not the main point of *Praeceptum.* Instead, they are illustrations of the main point. To put it another way, they are

---

8. Ibid., 3: 219–23.

9. This is done very well for us by Luc Verheijen, the greatest modern expert on Augustine's monasticism. Not only has he produced the critical edition of the *Praeceptum,* but he also has written definitive studies on virtually the whole of the Rule. Much use will be made here of his collected studies: *Nouvelle approche de la Règle de saint Augustin,* 2 vols. (Bégrolle-en-Mauges: Abbaye de Bellefontaine, 1980).

means to the end or purpose of the monastic life. It is easy to forget that, since they take up such a disproportionate amount of space and the main theme takes up so little.

The main theme is seen in the very first chapter. The monks or nuns are to live together in love; that is the reason they have come together. That is the very purpose of their common monastic life. This point is made in *Pr.* 1.2 and 1.8 to form an inclusion. The intermediate material quickly plunges into a preoccupation of Augustine, namely, how the rich and poor monks are to share goods. But that is simply a practical implementation of "love one another."[10]

After *Pr.* 1, Augustine spends the next six chapters expounding on different practical questions of communal living. These discussions are rather rambling and disorganized, but there is a constant insistence on the main point, namely, the need to live together in love. Moreover, these subjects are treated with a good deal of sensitivity and insight. Everything is done to promote loving interpersonal relations among the monks. Finally, in *Pr.* 8 he returns to his major theme, the need for monks to live in love. So we have a major inclusion with *Pr.* 1 concerning love. In *Pr.* 8, though, a wonderful new concept is introduced, that is, "spiritual beauty." But at this point we only need to insist on the fact that *Praeceptum* begins and ends with love. That is the main teaching of this great theologian, Augustine of Hippo.

A Key Text: Acts 4:32-35

First, we need to quote the beginning of *Praeceptum*: "The chief motivation for your sharing life together is to live harmoniously in the house and to have one mind and one heart seeking God."[11] Although we will

---

10. *Ordo Monasterii* also begins with the command to love. In that document, however, the biblical text is not Acts 4:32a but rather Matt 22:37-40: "You shall love the Lord your God . . . and your neighbor as yourself." Note that OM and Matthew mention the love of God first, and this serves as a lead-in to a discussion of the Divine Office, which comes already in OM 2. *Praeceptum* 2 will also discuss prayer to God, but it immediately takes up interpersonal relations: your neighbor as yourself. See Vogüé, *Histoire littéraire*, 3: 154–56.

11. This short passage actually alludes to two biblical texts: Psalm 67:7: "live harmoniously in the house," and Acts 4:32a: "and to have one heart and soul seeking God." The fact that Augustine begins with Scripture is very important. He does not just use the Bible to embellish the text; the text is rooted in Scripture and is in fact deeply biblical. All translations of *Praeceptum* given here are from Lawless, *Augustine of Hippo*, 81–108.

comment extensively on this text in what follows, I think it worthwhile to pause here and consider the overall importance of starting with this kind of communal statement. Here at the very beginning of his Rule, Augustine insists on the importance of mutual love and unity in cenobitic monastic life. In contrast, we can compare the Rule of Benedict, which begins with a fine, uplifting prologue. This is inspiring and energizing, but essentially an exhortation to an individual. The communal theme is not strong at the beginning of Benedict's Rule. Even though RB 1 does claim that it is aimed at cenobites, it is less than clear in its preference for them over anchorites.[12] Indeed, it is only toward the end of RB that communal matters become the main focus. Not so with Augustine: community is the great concern from the very beginning.

Augustine's call to community is not made in general terms, but in reference to the Bible. He quotes one of the most famous New Testament teachings on Christian community life, namely, Acts 4:32a. Since he often uses Acts 4:32-35 in connection with monastic life, it is best that we quote the whole passage here: "The community of believers was of one heart and mind, and no one claimed that any of his possessions was his own, but they had everything in common. With great power the apostles bore witness to the resurrection of the Lord Jesus, and great favor was accorded them all. There was no needy person among them, for those who owned property or houses would sell them, bring the proceeds of the sale, and put them at the feet of the apostles, and they were distributed to each according to need."

As we have seen, Augustine uses Acts 4:32a to begin his Rule: "to have one heart and soul, seeking God." We can note right away that he has added "seeking God" (*in Deum*) to the text, which is something we will need to look into. But the text he does quote, "one heart and mind," is certainly an evocative way of speaking of unity of persons. Yet we also know that Augustine himself took a long time to understand that text correctly. In a specialized study of this question the great Augustine scholar Luc Verheijen has shown that Augustine first interpreted "one heart and one mind" to mean that *each individual* Christian achieved personal integration because of the Resurrection.[13] In other words, he saw nothing communal about this statement.

12. See Terrence G. Kardong, *Benedict's Rule: A Translation and Commentary* (Collegeville, MN: Liturgical Press, 1996), 42–45.

13. See Verheijen, *Saint Augustine's Monasticism in the Light of Acts 4:32-35* (Villanova, PA: Villanova University Press, 1979).

From our advantageous position of hindsight we might wonder how that could happen. It did so largely because of Augustine's personal intellectual history. He was greatly influenced by the Platonist thought of Plotinus, who achieved great spiritual advancement but was not a Christian. One of Plotinus's famous descriptions of the goal of philosophical/religious life was "The alone with the Alone." In short, his main interest lay in the reunion of the individual soul with the One God.

As for Augustine, it is also true that he showed a keen interest in community life from an early age. As we have seen, he experimented with his friends in philosophic communes even before he was baptized a Christian. But it does also seem that his Platonism was so dominant that it blinded him to the "obvious" meaning of *anima una et cor unum* (one mind and one heart). At any rate, Verheijen shows that Augustine still misused this text ten years after his baptism and right up to the point when he was made a bishop.[14] And yet when he wrote the *Praeceptum*, shortly thereafter, he finally got it right.

Verheijen is able to pinpoint the "conversion" of Augustine on this question. It seems that Paulinus of Nola, a bishop in southern Italy and literary friend of Augustine, wrote to him on the occasion of his ordination as bishop (397 AD) to congratulate him. In his letter (*Ep.* 30 in the Augustinian dossier), Paulinus asks Augustine to receive his messengers just as if they were of "one mind and one heart" with the sender. Clearly, then, Paulinus understood the text correctly. In his return letter (*Ep.* 31), Augustine has seen the light; he uses the text the same way. If nothing else, this little episode in the tangled history of exegesis shows that preconceived notions can blind us to the obvious meaning of the word of God, or any other word from another person.

When we say that Augustine was temporarily confused about the meaning "one mind and one heart," we do not mean to suggest that he was a shallow or confused thinker. Far from it! In fact, he was one of the most powerful theological intelligences ever to study the Bible. So we should not be surprised that he eventually was able to plumb the depths of "one mind and one heart." Thus Augustine is able to set this formula for human unity in its proper theological framework, namely, the trinitarian life of God. Here is an attempt at a summary: The three divine persons are a unity of love. If the Spirit could weld the early

---

14. For example, *Ennarationes in Psalmos* 4:10, written when he was a priest (395–397), invokes the phrase *cor unum* to speak about recollection—the centered heart.

Christians into one mind and heart, that was only because the Spirit comes out of the fundamental divine unity of persons.[15]

At this point we have gone beyond the moral level. Augustine is not just urging us to get along with each other. He is telling us that the unity we do have is only possible through divine grace; it is not humanly attainable. It is not just a matter of improved group dynamics; the Spirit is working in us by means of the Eucharist, Scripture, and so forth. Let us quote another text: "And the Lord says to the Father regarding us: May they be one, as we are one. And in the Acts of the Apostles: the multitude of believers was one mind and one heart. Therefore, glorify the Lord with me, and let us exalt his name together (*in unum*). For one is necessary, that supernal one, the one where the Father and the Son and the Holy Spirit are one . . . And he does not lead us to this one unless we the many have one heart."[16]

We should pay particular notice to the last sentence, which speaks about Christ leading us to the Father. This is no offhand remark, but the whole theological thrust of the argument. The Holy Spirit unites us into one whole, one body, in order to bring us to the Father. Since the Spirit and Son and Father are one, we must be one before we can be brought to them. This is the significance of those two little words in *Pr.* 1.2. We know that Augustine deliberately changed *in Domino*, which was what Paulinus wrote, to *in Deum*. There seems to be no doubt that Augustine wants to show that this is a dynamic process. In other words, the unification the Holy Spirit is working in us is not just "in the Lord," but "toward God." The goal of community is reunion with God.

This might seem to undercut the great emphasis of Augustine on community itself. After all, we said above that the purpose of monastic life is mutual love. Perhaps we could say that this is the earthly purpose; the heavenly purpose is to bring us to God. Not that we will cease to love each other in heaven, and not that our mutual love is a mere instrument for individual salvation: now the whole process is not closed in upon itself but opens out to God. It is aimed at eternity; it is eschatological. It starts with God and ends with God. What is more, we, each of us, belong to God more than we belong to ourselves or to each other. There is no contradiction here: we do belong to each other, but first we belong

---

15. *Letter* 238.16 (CSEL 57.545ff. = PL 33.1044D); see Luc Verheijen, *Nouvelle approche de la Règle de saint Augustin* (Bégrolles-en-Mauges: Abbaye de Bellefontaine, 1980), 39–40.

16. *Sermon* 103.4 (PL 38.614ff.).

to God. The God-centeredness of the *Praeceptum* is accentuated by the
end of *Pr.* 1 as well. Here again, mutual love is aimed at divine worship:
"Live, then, all of you, in harmony and concord; honor God mutually in
each other; you have become his temples." As we noted in the remarks
above on structure, this exhortation to charity forms a frame with *Pr.*
1.2. We might note, though, that the form is a little different in *Pr.* 1.8.
In the first member we had "one mind and heart toward God." Here we
have "honor God in each other."

Variations on Acts 4:32-35

Luc Verheijen notes that we can pretty well reconstruct Augustine's
entire monastic thought by following his remarks on Acts 4:32-35. Here
we will follow this advice by tracing these ideas in various Augustinian
writings. In fact, we will be following Verheijen's own notes.[17] We recall
that some of the North African monks did not want to work, claiming
that the Bible itself tells Christians to "pray always." Therefore they
preferred to beg.[18] Augustine, however, wants monks to make their
own living, or at least to work at it. But he also believes that they are
deserving of help from the Christian population. In this they are like
the first apostolic community of Jerusalem, who voluntarily espoused
poverty in the name of the Gospel.[19] Paul felt they deserved the alms
of Christians everywhere.

Augustine notes that some of the monks need help because they are
aristocrats who have given up everything to become radically poor. In
this they are like some of the first Christians: "They live like this not
because they are better educated, as many think, but because having
been brought up for a soft life, they cannot bear manual labor. Perhaps
there were many such in Jerusalem. For it is written that 'they sold
their goods and laid the proceeds at the feet of the Apostles, so that
they might distribute them as there was need.' Because they were found

17. This material is taken from Verheijen, *Nouvelle approche*, 76ff.:
"L'utilisation monastique des Actes des Apôtres 4, (31) 32-35."

18. This philosophy was typical of the Messalians of Syria, and indeed some
historians speculate that Christians of that bent may have migrated to Carthage.
In general Augustine thinks that the work of monks should be spiritual, that
is, pastoral. But he never favors strict contemplation without any work. For an
overview of "The Work of Monks," see Vogüé, *Histoire littéraire*, 3: 231–45.

19. *De Op. Mon.* 16; Verheijen, *Nouvelle approche*, 88. Besides invoking
Acts 2 and 4, Augustine refers here to 2 Cor 8:9-10, where Paul speaks about
collecting money in Greece for the impoverished Christians in Jerusalem.

useful to the Gentiles . . . the Apostle says that the Gentile Christians are their debtors."[20]

The question of aristocratic monks who still need concessions is an important one in the *Praeceptum* and we will take it up in due time, but here we might ask a historical question: Did the Jerusalem community actually embrace voluntary poverty? It depends on what we mean by poverty; if we mean "total dispossession," it seems they did not. Even though Acts 4:32-35 seems to say that they all sold their possessions and pooled them in a common fund, a closer reading of that text indicates that was not the case. We should note the RNAB translation of 4:34, which is very accurate: "There was no needy person among them, for those who owned property or houses would sell them, bring the proceeds of the sale," and so forth. Notice the verb "would sell" in this verse. The text does not just say "sold," but "would sell": sometimes someone "would sell" something and donate it to the community to alleviate hardship among them. It was not a case of everybody selling everything. We should also pay attention to the motivation, which was not dispossession or asceticism, but practical charity.[21] To say this does not mean there is no teaching on voluntary poverty in the New Testament. It just means that Acts 4:32-35 is not the place to find it.

But Augustine does not feel that the historical element is most important in the famous text of Acts. He knows that it is the spirit that counts, and in this regard there is no doubt that the motivation of the first Christians was communal. In his *Commentary on Psalm 132*, he notes that the opening verse of that psalm was the basic inspiration of the community: "Behold how good and how pleasant it is for brothers and sisters to live together!" And yet even though the Jerusalem community lived according to this ideal, he laments that monks, who are vowed to do so, often do not. But real monks live in mutual love; indeed, their very name implies that they must: "Why then should we not use the term 'monks' when the psalm says, 'See how good and how pleasant it is for brothers to dwell together in unity'? *Monos* means 'one,' but not any kind of 'one.' One person may be present in a crowd; he is 'one,' but one with many others. He can be called 'one' but not *monos*, because *monos* means 'one alone.' 'But where people live together in such unity

---

20. *De Op. Mon.* 21. My translation.

21. Writing in *The Jerome Biblical Commentary* (Englewood Cliffs, NJ: Prentice Hall, 1990), 44.36, Richard Dillon says that the statement in Acts 4:34 is a generalization built on the single historical case of Barnabas narrated in 4:36-37.

that they form a single individual, where it is true of them, as scripture says, that they have but 'one mind and one heart' (Acts 4:32)—many bodies but not many minds, many bodies but not many hearts—then they are rightly called *monos*, 'one alone.'"[22] Although this text is not perfectly clear, nevertheless we can make out its basic argument. The Circumcellions have taunted the Christians in North Africa because they have among them strange persons who call themselves *monachoi*. Why should anyone wish to be solitary? But, says Augustine, that is just what they are not, or should not be!

It is sometimes said that Augustine knew very little Greek, and this passage seems to prove it. For if there is anything that *monos* does mean, it is "alone"! In ancient Greek the word always meant a single unit.[23] Even now, if you call yourself *monachos* in a bar in Athens, people will understand that you are single, that is, unmarried. But Augustine has become convinced that the real meaning of *monos* is unity with another person. Even though he must have been aware that the word *monachos* first referred to hermits in the Eastern church, he insists that monks must live in close unity with others.[24]

When we recall the way Augustine read "one mind and one heart" through an individualistic lens in his early career, it is quite remarkable how he could read *monos* in a communal sense in his later days! For one thing, it shows that he was anything but a literalist in his thinking; he was quite ready to employ his creative imagination. But it also shows how far he had come in his understanding of Christianity and of monasticism. The longer he lived, the more communal he became. Throughout his later career Augustine preached community and took

---

22. *Ennar. in Ps.* 132.5, trans. Maria Boulding, OSB., in *Saint Augustine, Expositions of the Psalms* 6 (Hyde Park, NY: New City Press, 2004), 181.

23. Thus G. W. Lampe, *A Patristic Greek Lexicon* (Oxford: Clarendon Press, 1961), 863. For a full discussion of the background of the word "monk" in both the Greek and Latin speech worlds see Mark Sheridan in *RB 1980* (Collegeville, MN: Liturgical Press, 1981), 301–14.

24. In fact, Augustine rarely uses the word *monachos* in his writings, always preferring more generic terms such as "servants of God" and so forth. The reason could have been that *monachos* had acquired a bad connotation in North Africa, or it could simply indicate that Augustine did not wish to create a sharp cleavage between monks and laypersons. For Augustine's terminology in this matter see my article "Monastic Issues in Possidius' *Life of Augustine*," *American Benedictine Review* 38 (June 1987): nn. 7, 8, and 13, revised in the previous chapter of this book.

active steps to promote it. For example, in Letter 243, written shortly
after he became bishop, he addressed a man named Laetus who wished
to leave the clerical household, where he was no doubt a seminarian.
The idea did not come from Laetus, but from his mother, who demanded
he return home and take care of her. Augustine will have no part of it;
he considers that Laetus has burned his bridges:

> The very fact that a certain woman is now your mother is a sure proof
> that she is not mine. Therefore, it is a temporal and transitory thing—
> and you see that it has now passed—that she has conceived you, bore
> you in her womb, brought you forth and nourished you with her milk.
> But, inasmuch as she is a sister in Christ, she belongs to you and to me
> and to all who have been promised a heavenly inheritance with God for
> our Father and Christ for our Brother in the same kinship of love . . .
> Let each one also think this about his own life, that he may hate in it
> that private affection which is undoubtedly transitory and may love in
> it that union and sense of sharing of which it was said: "They had one
> soul and heart toward God."[25]

Someone who has been a monk for a long time might not find this
passage too strange, since we used to be taught to think this way about
our parents. A younger monk or nun could find it rather frightening,
since it seems to lead to some questionable conclusions. But it becomes
even more remarkable when we note that Augustine is addressing a
diocesan seminarian. The reasoning is clear enough: If we are now one
soul and heart, how can we have special affections for anyone? He does
not even hesitate to apply this to Laetus's mother. But for Augustine she
is no longer his mother, but the mother of everyone who is one heart
and one soul with Laetus. Was the point that Laetus now belonged to
the bishop's household, or simply that he was a Christian? Probably the
former, if we are to judge from another incident.

About the year 425, after Augustine had been bishop of Hippo for a
long time, something happened that shook him profoundly. A priest by
the name of Januarius, who lived in the bishop's house, died, leaving
a will in which he disposed of his estate to his son and daughter. Both
were religious (monk/nun), and they were fighting over it! This quarrel
was bad enough, but what drove Augustine to distraction was the sheer
fact that Januarius left a will at all, since he was supposed to be living a

25. Letter 243, in Augustine, *Letters*, trans. Sr. Wilfrid Parsons, SSND, FC
32 (New York: Fathers of the Church, 1956), 220–21.

life of common goods with the other clergy in that house. So outraged was the bishop that he preached two long sermons in the cathedral of Hippo on the subject (Sermons 355–356).

Augustine based the second sermon precisely on the text we are studying here, namely, Acts 4:32-35. First, he had the deacon read it to the congregation; then he himself took the book and read it again. Next, he told the people that he had to admit that his community—that is, the clergy—had really not lived up to its ideals, for at least one of them had cheated the system: he left a will! This remarkable episode shows us at least two things: first, Augustine expected the clergy to live out the ideal of Acts to the letter; second, he considered it important for the congregation to know how the clergy lived and also to be aware that it was not easy. Moreover, he had promised in the first sermon to investigate the other members of the household and now he is pleased to report that none of them is cheating.

Aside from the fact that Augustine must have considered community of goods very important for radical Christian community, it also seems that he wanted *all* Christians to live that way to some degree. Otherwise, why would he broadcast the situation to the whole congregation? We get the impression with Augustine, as we did with Basil, that there is no sharp line at all between religious life and ordinary Christianity. At this point we will end our remarks on Augustine's use of Acts 4:32-35 and take up various questions from the *Praeceptum*.

The Strong and the Weak; the Rich and the Poor

As we remarked earlier, this is by no means a complete Rule for community life. It treats only a few issues while leaving many others unexplored. Yet it does go into considerable depth on those few matters. Already in *Pr.* 1, Augustine plunges into the question of common goods. He started with "one heart and one mind," so it is not surprising that he connects this to shared possessions as does Acts. First, he says that the superior should give each one what is needed, again following Acts (4:35). Recall that the point is not dispossession but the elimination of want in the community.[26]

---

26. In that regard Augustine differs from RB 33.7, where Benedict interprets the text of Acts to preclude private property. But in order to do that, Benedict has to remodel the text of Acts: "Let all things be common to all, as Scripture says, so that no one may presume to call anything his own." But Acts never says that asceticism was the purpose of community of goods. Its only goal is the elimination of suffering among the members of the community. See my article,

This then brings to his mind the fact that there are very different needs in his community, and that requires more comment. *Pr.* 1.5 speaks to "those who had nothing" before they entered the community. Apparently his community included people from the lowest social order, namely, peasants and urban poor. For them community life was in fact a step *up* the social ladder, so they are warned not to abuse this new situation by a life of luxury or pride. Above all, they should not envy the treatment given to those who were formerly affluent:

> If food, clothes, a mattress, or blankets are given to those who come to the monastery from a more comfortable manner of life, the more robust individuals, to whom such things are not given and who are on this account more fortunate, ought to recall how much affluent people have altered their lifestyle in order to embrace the present one, even though the frugality practised by the stronger brothers continues to elude them. No one should desire the extras given to a few, more out of tolerance than out of deference. Deplorable disorder would occur if the monastery provided a setting, to the extent that it is possible, where the wealthy become workers while the poor become pampered. (*Pr.* 3.4)

From this statement it is obvious that there were some people from the wealthiest class in Augustine's monastery. They were not able to manage the whole ascetical program, so some concessions were made for them. The rest should not be resentful at that as long as all are given what they *need*.

To a Benedictine, of course, this is not a new idea. Indeed, RB 34 presents this very same teaching, though in a much less wordy form. Benedict fully accepts Augustine's teaching that the strongest person is the one who needs the least. If the pampered rich need more, then they should take no glory in that. As for the strong, they should not stoop to envy. It would seem, though, that the problem was much more difficult for Augustine than for Benedict. This is indicated by the sheer quantity of space Augustine gives to the discussion in the *Praeceptum*. I would estimate that about a fifth of the whole document is given over to this discussion. In contrast, Benedict has but one tiny chapter out of 73.[27]

"Poverty in the Rule of St. Benedict, Chapters 33 and 34," *Cistercian Studies* 20 (1985): 184–201; see also *Benedict's Rule*, 273–88.

27. RB 34; *Pr.* 1.3-7; 3.3-5. Other discussions, such as those on the common wardrobe (*Pr.* 5.1) and the sick (5.5-8), are probably also colored by the greatly

No doubt the context was the great social and economic gulf that separated the rich from the poor (almost everybody) in the Roman Empire. We know that it was possible to amass enormous fortunes in that society. A few people owned whole counties, whole battalions of slaves. And although most of the early Christians were urban poor, in the fourth century some of the very, very rich became Christians and also monks.[28]

Acts 4:32-35 never claims that there were rich and poor in the Jerusalem community. But some of them must have owned property or they could not have sold it to contribute to the common fund. The fact that the early Christians met in house churches suggests that some of them were property owners. Not all were dirt poor. At any rate, Augustine's purpose is not to reduce everyone to a single common denominator of consumption,[29] nor is it even to produce ascetic saints who need almost nothing. Rather, it is to create peace in the community. Surely this is the meaning that must be drawn from *Pr.* 1.8, where the admonitions to rich and poor end with the words: "Live then all of you in harmony and concord, honor God mutually in each other."

Celibacy

In his commentary on *Praeceptum* 4, Luc Verheijen remarks that the material on chastity or celibacy is not very attractive.[30] Because it constitutes about one-fourth of the entire rule, *Pr.* 4 is important, but that does not make it easy. The gist of the teaching is simple: When the brothers have to go out into the city they must not be ogling the women they see. If they do so they should be first warned and then punished:

---

differing backgrounds of the members of the community. The formerly rich were used to fine clothes and the best health care possible.

28. In *De Op. Mon.* 33, Augustine admits that most of the monks in Africa came from the poor classes. See Vogüé, *Histoire littéraire*, 3: 181. Some rich Christians who became monks were Melania, Paula, and Eustochium. These were all from Rome, but it is probable that a few rich persons in Africa became monks as well. In the *Praeceptum* it does seem that Augustine lectures the poor harder than the rich. He himself came from the impoverished nobility, so it could be that he had greater sympathy for the problems of the upper class.

29. It is possible to read Pachomius, *Pr.* 81 that way, but a wider reading of the Pachomian literature, especially the *Life*, indicates that this eminently successful cenobitic legislator understood that people have differing needs.

30. "Le très difficile quatrième chapitre: le célibat monastique et la sollicitude pour les pécheurs," *Nouvelle approche*, 107.

"The man who directs his attention towards a woman and enjoys her similar token of affection should not think others fail to notice this mutual exchange. He is certainly observed even by persons he thinks do not see him. But if his actions escape the notice of men and women, what will he do about the One who keeps watch on high, from whom nothing can be hidden?" (*Pr.* 4.5).

For someone who is looking for substantial or even inspirational teaching on celibacy this is rather disappointing. It says nothing about the meaning of monastic virginity; it is simply a disciplinary warning and probably aimed at a concrete situation to which Augustine is reacting. The *Praeceptum* was written for a very particular, limited situation. As on many questions, we have to look at the whole of Augustine's written works to flesh out his full position. We should remember that *Praeceptum* was addressed to an urban community, namely, that in the medium-sized city of Hippo in Roman Africa. The monks of the Garden Monastery had to go out into the town for various purposes, and when they did they encountered the general population. And no doubt the citizens of Hippo were like Mediterranean people in every age: they lived on the street.

In later times monasteries were usually sited out in the country, where temptation was not close at hand. Furthermore, monastic legislators like Benedict tried to keep their monks inside the walls (RB 66). Cities were dangerous for monks. But still it does seem a bit strange that Augustine should be so worried that his monks might abuse their vow of chastity. Perhaps they were mostly rude peasants who did not know how to behave in the city.[31] The insistence on surveillance and on the all-seeing eye of God may also reflect a situation from the time before the later development of the sacrament of Penance as we know it. At that time before frequent private confession people had to worry that "medium" sins did not become "major" ones. At least, that is Verheijen's opinion.[32]

Someone might be tempted to say, though, that Augustine's anxiety that a monk might see a beautiful woman simply reflects his own sexual anxieties. Certainly the modern age has often found his teachings on sexuality objectionable, not to say Manichean. Granted, Augustine *had* been a Manichean, but he had explicitly repudiated their radical dualism. Therefore he was always aware of the danger in that direction.

---

31. This is the opinion of Vogüé, *Histoire littéraire*, 3: 190.
32. *Nouvelle approche*, 114–16.

Contemporary feminist critics often state that Augustine was simply a misogynist: he hated women. As a proof of that charge they point to his treatment of his longtime common-law wife, by whom he had a son. In his autobiographical *Confessions* he never names her. And when he goes to be baptized at Milan he abandons her in ruthless fashion.

This does look awful, but we should beware of imposing anachronistic judgments on a very different age.[33] For one thing, there never was a possibility of Augustine marrying his concubine because they were of differing social status. Second, he probably did not name her out of respect for her privacy. His remark in the *Confessions* (6.15.25) that she returned to Africa and vowed a celibate life could well mean that he felt she was in fact the better of the two, for chastity was certainly a serious problem for the young Augustine.

Augustine makes it clear that unchastity did block his spiritual progress before he became a Christian. In fact, he and his friends all were living active sexual lives that did not meet Christian standards. Furthermore, all their plans for an ideal commune of contemplation were undermined by the same problem: they could not do without their girlfriends. By God's grace Augustine obtained the gift of chastity at the same time that he took the plunge of baptism. For him, to become a Christian was the same as becoming a celibate monk, and there is no sign he ever went back on that vow. But his earlier experience did mark him. Clearly he regarded chastity as a very crucial issue for monks, if not *the* main issue. Just after baptism, and writing versus the Manicheans, Augustine says this about the religious men and women in Rome: "O Mother Church, you have given birth to . . . people who burn with such love for God, that in their absolute continence and unbelievable disdain for the world, they go so far as to find their delight in solitude" (*De Mor. Chr.* 30).

Augustine taunts the Manicheans that they preach celibacy for their members, but the Christians keep it. In fact, he lists their celibacy as the first characteristic of monks after the persecutions.[34] It would not be right to claim that Augustine had a full-blown theory of monastic celibacy right from the beginning. He does not say why celibacy is so important for these religious, nor does he say how it was linked with

33. These remarks on Augustine's "marriage" are taken from George Lawless, *Augustine of Hippo*, 16–21. They may be too positive, but they do indicate that these are not simple questions and should not be handled as such.

34. *De Vera Rel.* Prologue. In his list of the renunciations of monks he names marriage first, but he does not say why.

contemplation (solitude). Writing about his own conversion shortly after it happened, he says that two things had always blocked his route to wisdom, namely, love of women and love of honor. He chose another path: celibacy and monastic contemplation.[35] He does not say that marriage and honor are evil, just that for him the other path was better.

A few years later, after ordination and now leading a much more active life, he still says that for him pursuing a wife and fame was not "light." It is, of course, the ordinary way for most people and so it cannot be objectively condemned.[36] He admits that his sacerdotal life is hectic, yet it is not without light. But he still does not, perhaps cannot, say why marriage is a block to wisdom. It should be pointed out that these are early writings, and their author later recognized that they were quite inadequate. Shortly before his death Augustine wrote his *Retractiones*, in which he carefully went back through a lot of his earlier treatises, clarifying and also taking back some of his earlier opinions. For example, he regrets that he once said that family and love were only results of sin, and that Adam and Eve would have had no children if not for sin.[37] And he waters down an early claim that one must hate one's spouse *as a spouse*, and only love him or her as a child of God. No, one should only hate one's spouse as an obstacle to God.[38]

The aged Augustine had lived long enough to see that one must make one's way very carefully through the minefield of harmful conclusions in comparing Christian celibacy with marriage. Even St. Paul did not completely avoid these traps in discussing his own celibacy.[39] How can one develop a positive theology of celibacy without disparaging the vocation of other people? Did Augustine ever succeed at this? It would seem that he did. In his treatise "On Virginity," written in 401 when he was a bishop, he seems to arrive at a satisfactory solution to the problem

---

35. *De Beata Vita* I.4 (PL 32.961; CC 29.61).

36. *De Utilitate Credendi* I.3 (PL 42.67; CSEL 25.6). This was written for a Manichean friend, so he is especially careful to insist that marriage is objectively good. The Manicheans did not think so, since marriage produces children and that is what they did not want. They think the increase of flesh in the world increases the level of suffering.

37. *Retract.* I.10, 2.

38. *Retract.* I.13, 8.

39. 1 Corinthians 7:1-15. Paul's approach is that human marriage "divides" the attention of the Christian from love of the Lord. But a positive theology of marriage might not admit such a thing. Christian spouses believe they can grow in the love of God precisely *through* their love for one another.

of how consecrated celibacy fits into the general pattern of church life. Many church fathers wrote these treatises for the consecrated virgins of their dioceses, so Augustine was not doing something new.

What is it that makes "On Virginity" more adequate than some of his other writings on celibacy? For one thing, it certainly is not critical of marriage. In fact, it was written as a complement to a treatise on marriage, and was in no way meant to undercut that earlier essay. He is at great pains to avoid odious comparisons. Still, he cannot help repeating a view that was standard Catholic teaching right up to Vatican II, namely, that religious life is a greater good than marriage. Indeed, some would contend that the present dearth of vocations to convents and monasteries is largely due to our abandonment of this hierarchical language.

Nevertheless, Augustine mostly skirts this problem in "On Virginity" by concentrating on the positive element. He ceases to harp on marriage as an impediment to wisdom and union with God and sticks to the way Christian celibacy is essentially driven by love. Some do not feel called to married love, but only to special love with Christ. This can be expressed in many symbolic forms, such as following the Lamb:

> You shall offer, at the nuptials of the Lamb, a new canticle, which you shall accompany on your harps; by no means such as the whole earth sings, to which it is said: "Sing ye to the Lord a new canticle, sing to the Lord all the earth," but such as no one shall be able to sing except yourselves . . . Where do you think the Lamb goes, where no one either dares or is able to follow, except yourselves? Where do we think he goes; to what heights and what meadows? I think where the delights of rich pastures—not the empty delights of the world, which are deceitful follies; nor such delights as belong to the others, not virgins, in the kingdom of God itself—distinct from the portion of delights of all others, the delight of the virgins of Christ, from Christ, in Christ, with Christ, after Christ, through Christ, because of Christ.[40]

Augustine is here promising Christian virgins a special reward, and it is not in this world but in the next. The reward is Christ; the whole issue is personal attachment to Christ, which need not, and must not, wait until the next world but must start right now. Sometimes we hear that

---

40. *De Virg.* 27, in *Treatises on marriage and other subjects* . . . ed. Roy J. Deferrari. "Holy Virginity," trans. John McQuade, FC 27 (Washington, DC: Catholic University of America Press, 1969).

consecrated celibacy enables a religious to work more effectively in pastoral ministry, as if married life would be an impediment. Such thoughts are irrelevant to Augustine. Let these words of John McQuade sum up this section: "Augustine's concept is full and rich in its implications. Without overlooking the element of suppression of self entailed in the surrender of natural rights and inclinations, he goes straight to the heart of the mystery of divine grace which raises the soul to angelic heights. He places the essence of virginal consecration in the positive element, the throwing of one's whole being into intimate loving union with God, so that He becomes the center of thought and action."[41]

The Correction of Faults

Regarding flirtations, Augustine urges the monks to keep an eye on each other. When someone notices another slipping into this fault, he should privately warn him. If this act of fraternal correction has no effect, a few others should be called in as witnesses. Finally, the case should be reported to the superior for official action. Should the person still refuse to amend his ways, he should be expelled from the community. A modern Benedictine who hears this passage (*Pr.* 4.8-9) would not find it innovative, for the same basic approach to correction is found in RB 23–28.[42] In fact, many early Rules used the same procedure outlined in Matthew 18:15-18 for correction. Such an approach moves from private counsel to a few witnesses to the whole community.[43] But unlike Matthew and most of the other monastic Rules, Augustine is quite explicit in providing a spirituality for his rules of correction: "Do not consider yourselves unkind when you point out such faults. Quite the contrary, you are not without fault yourselves when you permit your brother to perish because of your silence. Were you to point out their misdeeds, correction would at least be possible. If your brother had a bodily wound which he wished to conceal for fear of surgery, would not your silence be

41. Introduction to his translation of "Holy Virginity" in ibid., 141.

42. The concordance of patristic citations in *RB 1980* does not list any quotation or allusion from Augustine for RB 23–28. It does, however, cite several allusions to early monastic Rules that are heavily based on Augustine, e.g., Caesarius.

43. As with many monastic Rules, Augustine does not follow Matthew 18 in literal fashion. Perhaps the reason for this is that Matthew does not envisage the presence of a religious superior at the top of the chain of authority. It seems as if Augustine repeats the procedure in *Pr.* 4.8-9, the difference being that the superior is only brought into the picture in the second unit.

cruel and your disclosure merciful? Your obligation to reveal the matter is, therefore, all the greater in order to stem the more harmful infection in the heart" (*Pr.* 4.8).

We notice here a strongly therapeutic approach to human community and to spiritual life. Augustine is an enlightened man. He knows enough about medicine to see that the concealment of wounds is a form of suicide, and an unwillingness to point them out is the opposite of charity. He considers the duty of mutual correction to be a matter of spiritual life and death. There is nothing sentimental about him. There is also nothing vindictive about him. He is not out to punish for punishment's sake, or to avenge some abstract principle. He is only intent on improvement. A key word is "salutary punishment" (*Pr.* 4.9). Luc Verheijen has pointed out that Augustine has coined a special word (*emendatorium*) to make this point strongly.[44] Of course, the idea of correction and improvement is not particularly Christian, but characteristic of all high-minded persons. Yet for Augustine improvement has an ulterior motive that goes beyond the individual, and even the salvation of the individual. For him the whole issue here is the health and unity of the community: "If he refuses to submit to punishment even if he is determined not to leave, expel him from your society. Even this is not an act of cruelty but of mercy: to prevent the contagion of his life from infecting more people" (*Pr.* 4.9).

Again, the imagery is medical. There is more at stake here than just the life of the diseased individual. Such a person could corrupt the community; evil is not something neutral or inert: it can be contagious. Thus a confused sense of compassion that refuses to expel an incorrigible person from the community could result in the destruction of the community itself.

Someone who is versed in the history and theology of Augustine and his times might experience some surprise at this conclusion. After all, Augustine by and large took the opposite view in the Donatist controversy that wracked the African church for a century after the last great persecution (ca. 310–410 AD). The bone of contention was what to do with those Christians who had capitulated to the Roman authorities and paid worship to the emperor. The orthodox were willing to admit

---

44. In his essay "Pour le rendre meilleur," in *Nouvelle approche*, 315–21, Verheijen is able to follow *emendatorium* throughout the writings of Augustine. He shows that the word was definitely one of Augustine's strong teaching tools to inculcate the idea that God does not wish the death of the sinner, but that he be converted and live.

them back into the fold; the Donatists were not. And the theology of the latter was pretty much what Augustine puts forth in *Pr.* 4.9: tainted members will corrupt the whole church.[45]

Eventually, though, Augustine came to understand that the unity of a community may require that a troubled and troubling person be expelled. The main issue, however, is not to expel or to expel: it is to love. There is never a justification for vindictive punishment. The spiritual health of both the individual and the community must be built up and maintained by love. Sometimes that love may have to take the form of "tough love," namely, correction. Do we love each other enough to take that risk?[46]

Spiritual Beauty

Because it is a spiritual document rather than a mere rule book, it is fitting that the *Praeceptum* end with a prayer: "The Lord grant you the grace to observe these precepts with love as lovers of spiritual beauty, exuding the fragrance of Christ in the goodness of your lives; you are no longer slaves under the law, but a people living in freedom under grace." Even though Augustine has just set down some rules for his monks, he wants to make sure that the last word is not law but grace. This is in fact the central teaching of this man who is perhaps the greatest theologian in Christian history. Even though the Rule was written long before the Pelagian controversy, Augustine spent the last twenty-five or so years of his life hammering away at this point: we do not save ourselves by good works; grace alone saves us.

But the words that jump out at us in this final prayer are "lovers of spiritual beauty." Suddenly, at the end of a monastic Rule that has not been much concerned with contemplation or even prayer, the monks

---

45. Verheijen has written a fine monograph on this subject: "Expulsion, degradation, excommunication," in *Nouvelle approche*, 322–45. He points out that Augustine was once opposed to the teaching of Parmenias, the Donatist bishop of Carthage, who advocated the expulsion of heretics and schismatics (*Contra Epistulam Parmeniam*). But later he saw that the unity of a community may require such expulsion.

46. There are many more things that could be said about this complex subject. For example, the person who refuses to amend virtually excommunicates himself, even if he does not leave the community (*Pr.* 6.2). I discuss many of these considerations in my article "People Storage: Mabillon's Diatribe against Monastic Prisons," in my *Commentaries on Benedict's Rule II* (Richardton, ND: Assumption Abbey, 1995), 53–72.

are addressed in this highly evocative, poetic fashion: lovers of spiritual beauty. This is not traditional Christian language, so it needs some explanation. It seems that it was an expression Augustine brought with him into Christianity from his past. Just before Augustine became a Christian he wrote an essay called "On Order," in which he laid out a program of philosophical and religious growth. First, one must search for unity through study, and then one must live according to this morality. Virtue will then produce a beautiful soul that will see God as beauty.[47]

This essay is a sort of summary of Pythagorean theory and lifestyle, which was called by Iamblichus "love of beauty."[48] It is a reminiscence of the Pythagorean philosophical communities, which may or may not have existed. Like most ancient Greeks they regarded philosophy as not merely a matter of right thinking, but of right acting. When Augustine looked back on this essay at the end of his life he found some things to criticize. By then he no longer talked of Beauty, but of God, the living God. But the Greeks certainly were thinking of God as well. Moreover, Augustine no longer believes that study as such is necessary to spiritual progress. If it were, then many simple Christians would be excluded.[49] They must become holy without knowledge. But even morality is not the final point. If it were, that would mean we could win heaven by our good lives and deeds. Perhaps the philosophers believed in that possibility, but Augustine no longer does. Rather, heaven must be given to us; Beauty must reveal itself to us. In plain, catechetical language, God must unite us to himself.

Here at the end of the Rule, Augustine is not afraid to use a phrase that ties his teaching to that of the philosophers. He has not repudiated his past; he is willing to take the best wherever he finds it. He is a humane man, not a hater of the world. Yet he is now primarily a Christian, so we are not surprised to find Christ here at the end: "exuding the fragrance of Christ." That is a biblical phrase (2 Cor 2:15), but what does it mean? According to Verheijen,[50] Augustine means that the Christian should be like the smoke coming from the incense bowl that is Christ.

47. *De Ordine* II.8-9; PL 32; CC 29. Verheijen discusses this question in "Vers la Beauté Spirituelle," in *Nouvelle approche* 201–42. On *De Ordine* see especially 203ff.
48. *Nouvelle approche*, 231.
49. *Retract*. I.3,4 (PL 32.588; CSEL 36.19–20).
50. *Nouvelle approche*, 239–40.

Perhaps it would be better to say that our lives should be a reflection of the Risen Christ. Augustine is always fully aware that Christ attained to his Resurrection through his kenotic suffering and death; we too need to follow that path. But our goal is to be united with the Glorified Christ, to gaze on his spiritual beauty forever.

We have spent most of our time in this chapter emphasizing Augustine's teaching on community. *Pr.* 1.2 says that is why we come together, to be of one mind and one heart. Nevertheless, we should remember that the quality of each mind and each heart is crucial to monasticism and to all religion. You cannot make a community out of ciphers, and you cannot make a monastic community out of anything but monastic individuals. According to Augustine, a monk is someone who is going "toward God," a "lover of spiritual beauty."

Conclusion

This quick trip through Augustine's *Praeceptum* is over, but the reader should not see it as anything but a taste of the subject. As with anything he touched, Augustine had profound things to say about religious life. That is proven by the immense influence his rule has had on succeeding generations of religious men and women. We monks have not paid much attention to this early monastic legislator, but modern studies of Augustine show this has been a mistake. We have much to learn about our special vocation within the church from this theological genius and master of the consecrated life.

Chapter
Ten

The Rule of the Four Fathers

Introduction

Date and Place

The Rule of the Four Fathers (R4P) is a short monastic Rule written in the Latin West sometime in the fifth century. Since Benedict of Aniane included it in his collection of previous monastic Rules called *Codex Regularum* (c. 810 CE),[1] we have been aware of this Rule for a long time. Nevertheless, no one has been able to place or date the document with any assurance until quite recently.

In his magisterial critical edition and commentary on R4P,[2] Adalbert de Vogüé has succeeded in locating this document more precisely in space and time than had previous scholars.[3] He thinks the Rule was

---

1. PL 73.701–1380. The material for this chapter first appeared in *American Benedictine Review* 54 (2003): 142–80.

2. *Les Règles des Saints Pères*, SC 297–298 (Paris: Cerf, 1982). As the title indicates, this study includes several Rules, all of which were written in Gaul in the 5th–6th centuries.

3. The principal studies on this question are not numerous. Three of them are taken seriously by Vogüé in his introduction (*Les Règles* 1, 91–155): Anscari M. Mundó: "Les anciennes synodes abbatiaux et les *Regulae SS. Patrum*," in Basilius Steidle, *Regula Magistri—Regula Benedicti*, Studia Anselmiana philosophica theologica 44 (Rome: "Orbis Catholicus," Herder, 1959), 107–25; Jean Neufville, "Règle des IV Pères et Seconde Règle des Pères: texte critique," *Revue*

written by Honoratus,[4] the founder of the monastery of Lérins, one of the most famous abbeys in the West. Moreover, he believes R4P was written within a few years of the founding of that island monastery[5] in about 405 CE.[6] Therefore R4P is one of the foundational documents of monasticism in the Latin church.

Not only has Vogüé established that R4P lies at the base of the history of Lérins, he has also managed to reconstruct a plausible history of that monastery during its first century of existence on the basis of the other Little French Rules.[7] Although there were some negative reac-

---

Bénédictine 77 (1967): 47–106; François Masai, "Recherches sur les Règles de S. Oyend et de S. Benoît," *Regulae Benedicti Studia* 5 (1976): 43–73.

4. We have a hagiographical account of this saint's life in a sermon by Hilary, his successor as Bishop of Arles and also a monk of Lérins: *Vita Honorati*, PL 1.1249–72; Samuel Cavallin, *Vitae sanctorum Honorati et Hilarii, episcoporum Arelatensium* (Lund: Gleerup, 1952); English, in *The Western Fathers*, trans. Frederick R. Hoare (New York: Sheed and Ward, 1954), 247–82. This account is extremely vague as to dates, but it is still a precious record.

5. Lérins is located on the Côte d'Azur of the French Riviera, a few miles from Cannes and Antibes. After 1,400 years of almost unbroken history, the monastery was finally closed by the French Revolution, but in 1859 the bishop of Fréjus, the successor of another bishop long ago who probably brought the monks to the island, bought the island back and gave it to the Cistercians, who live there to this day.

6. Anscari Mundó, "Les anciennes synodes," thought there were only scattered hermits on Lérins until about 465 CE, but Vogüé shows the cenobium goes back almost to the beginnings, ca. 400. Jean Neufville, "Règle des IV Pères," conjectured that R4P was probably written somewhere in Italy, but Vogüé is convinced it comes from Lérins, as do most of the Little French Rules he published in *Les Règles des Saints Pères*.

7. In Vogüé's scenario, The Second Rule of the Fathers (2RP) was written when Maximus succeeded Honoratus after the latter became bishop of Arles (427–428). In 434, Maximus was made bishop of Riez, to be succeeded at Lérins by Abbot Faustus. We have many of Faustus's sermons, apparently preached to the monks during his long reign as abbot (434–460) but perhaps later (*Opera*, CSEL 21 [1891]). It might be noted that Faustus was one of the most influential theologians in Gaul, and a determined opponent of Augustine's doctrine that human effort can achieve nothing toward salvation. After a blank spot in our knowledge of Lérins for the years 460–490, Vogüé thinks that the Rule of Macarius (RMac) was written by Abbot Porcarius about 500 CE. A bit later, perhaps in 515 CE, Abbot Marinus of Lérins had the Oriental Rule (ROr) drawn up for the monks of Agaune (St. Maurice in Switzerland). One of the last Lérinian documents, The Third Rule of the Fathers, was probably drawn up by a synod

tions to this theory soon after it was published, it seems to be generally accepted today.[8]

Form and Content

The Rule of the Four Fathers presents itself as a product of a synod of abbots who have met to enact joint legislation for their monasteries. Synods as such were not unusual in Gaul at that time; in fact, we have the *Acta* from many such meetings of bishops[9] before and after the founding of Lérins. Yet as far as we know, there *were* no monasteries in southern Gaul when R4P was written, so it cannot be a product of a monastic synod.[10]

Besides taking the form of a fictitious general chapter, R4P also uses pseudonyms for its "abbots." The title, which seems to be original, gives four "Fathers" as the authors: Serapion, Macarius, Paphnutius, and a second Macarius. Yet anyone with a cursory knowledge of early monasticism knows that these names are not Gallic but Egyptian; indeed, they are names of some of the best-known monastic fathers of the Egyptian desert.

---

of bishops at Clermont in 534. It might also be mentioned that one of the most famous monks of Lérins was Caesarius. After he became Bishop of Arles in 502 he spent much of his energy legislating for religious, writing a Rule for Nuns in 534 and one for monks in 542. So it can be seen that we have a considerable body of literature from Lérins.

8. The following negative reviews are mentioned by William E. Klingshirn, *Caesarius of Arles* (Cambridge: Cambridge University Press, 1994), 25, n. 63: M. Carrias, "Vie monastique et règle à Lérins au temps d'Honorat," *Revue d'histoire de l'église de la France* 74 (1988): 191–211; Jean Gribomont, review of *Règle des Saints Pères* by Adalbert de Vogüé, *Revue d'histoire ecclésiastique* 78 (1983): 849–51. In his recent article "Un problème de datation: *La Règle des Quatre Pères*," *Studia Monastica* 44 (2002): 7–12, Vogüé answers the objections of J. P. Weiss, "Une communauté religieuse aux Iles de Lérins," *Connaissance des Pères de l'Église* 79 (2000): 21–32; "La fondation de la communauté des moines de Lérins," *Bulletin de l'Association Guillaume Budé* 47 (1988): 338–49 (see p. 345). I became aware of these articles after I finished my work on this chapter, and I have not had an opportunity to consult them.

9. Found in Karl Joseph von Hefele, *Histoire des conciles d'après les documents originaux*, trans. Henri Leclercq et al. (Paris: Letouzey et Ané, 1907–52).

10. The only monastery in Gaul in 400 CE was Marmoutier, the foundation of St. Martin on the outskirts of Tours, hundreds of miles west of Lérins.

For his part, Vogüé does not believe that these names are anything but a pious fiction. The Gallic monks were very fond of Egyptian monasticism, so there is nothing unusual about the co-optation of these names. But the writing style is homogeneous, suggesting one single author and not four. Strictly speaking, it is possible that a recording secretary homogenized the verbal accounts of a synod, but that is highly unlikely.[11] Another reason why Vogüé doubts that these are four real speakers or authors is that the material attributed to the second Macarius merely extends the discussion of the abbot found under the name of the first Macarius.[12]

Nevertheless, Vogüé does not completely discount the history underlying the literary form of four monks in council. He thinks that Lérins may well have begun as a loose grouping of hermits, but that Honoratus quickly organized them into the cenobium that became the permanent form of the community.[13] This conclusion seems well fitted to the content of R4P.

R4P is not a long Rule and does not cover every aspect of monastic life. It begins with a call to community in the same style as do the Rules of Augustine and Basil.[14] But R4P quickly parts company with those earlier champions of community life by focusing on the superior. Discourse 1 (Serapion) stresses how necessary it is to have one superior if there is to be one community. Thus are the hermits united under one head, who is simply called "he who presides."

Discourse 2 (Macarius) continues the discussion of the role of the superior, dealing with both theoretical and practical elements. Macarius knows that the superior must love the brethren, but he emphasizes that love must sometimes be disciplinary (5.5-6). R4P then instructs the superior on how to deal with both the rich and the poor, much in the same fashion as does Augustine.[15] Then there is a discussion of the relation between the superior and the cellarer.

11. *Les Règles*, 1, 63–65.

12. Ibid., 1, 74.

13. Ibid., 1, 21–26.

14. R4P 1.1-9; RAug 1.2 and RBas 3. Like these famous earlier Rules, R4P quotes Pss 132:1 and 67:7, both of which extol the advantages of living together.

15. RAug 3.3-5; 5.1. The Lérins community resembled that of Augustine in Hippo in that each had monks from both the rich and the poor classes of society. Many of the monks of Lérins came from the Gallo-Roman nobility, which is one reason why they were sought after as bishops.

Discourse 3 (Paphnutius) goes into many particulars of monastic life, but especially work. This may have been an especially sensitive issue for Gallic monks, for the monks of St. Martin at Marmoutier completely eschewed manual labor.[16] No matter what aspect of monastic life is discussed, R4P makes the superior the center of attention. In this way the Rule is quite unlike its predecessors and more like its successors.[17] Since authority is so heavily stressed in R4P it is no surprise to find that obedience is also made paramount. Discourse 4 tacks on a few ideas about the transfer of a monk, and the Addendum talks about correction.

This Translation

Since I visited the isle of Lérins in 1976 I have always had a soft spot for the place. Over the years I was keen to find out about its history, but nothing much was available. When Vogüé published his study of all the Little French Rules, I studied it out of general interest and I was pleasantly surprised to find that these Rules are probably about as close as we will come to a history of Lérins.

After laboring through the two formidable volumes of Vogüé, I thought I would report on them to the Anglophone world. In doing so I compared them to a contemporary English-language study and translation, but much to my dismay it turned out to be less than helpful.[18] And so I decided to produce a new English translation and commentary. As

16. In his preface to Conference 11, Cassian asserts that Lérins flourished and Marmoutier shrank precisely because the former practiced manual labor and the latter did not.

17. RAug and RBas only mention the superior toward the end of the document, and then do not give him much prominence. RM and RB, however, discuss the abbot near the very beginning and place him center stage in virtually every chapter. The very fact that RM and RB give the superior a distinctive name—abbot—shows how they mean to spotlight this role. Neither Augustine nor Basil has a technical name for the superior, and neither does R4P: for them he is just "he who presides." In refuting Mundó, Vogüé notes that the use of *is qui praeest* in R4P is a good sign that it precedes Cassian (fl. 425–430), who uses *abbas*. According to Vogüé (*Les Règles*, 1, 92–95), *is qui praeest* is never found in Gaul after 450 CE.

18. *Early Monastic Rules (EMR)*, trans. Carmela Vircillo Franklin, Ivan Havener, and J. Alcuin Francis (Collegeville, MN: Liturgical Press, 1982). In fairness it should be noted that these scholars did not have Vogüé's work to compare. They did have the excellent translation and study of Vincent Desprez in *Règles monastiques d'occident* (Maine-et-Loire: Abbaye de Bellefontaine, 1980), plus Vogüé's "Cenobitic Rules of the West," *Cistercian Studies* 12 (1977): 175–83.

one *ABR* referee notes, my emphasis is more on readability than literal accuracy. Still, my copious notes try to account for the exegetical decisions I have made.

The Rule of the Four Fathers

Here begins the Rule of the Holy Fathers Serapion, Macarius, Paphnutius and another Macarius.

Prologue

[1]While we were sitting in discussion, [2] we arrived at a very salutary plan: we asked Our Lord to send us the Holy Spirit [3] to teach us how to arrange the lifestyle or Rule of life of the brothers.

1. Serapion

Serapion said: [1] "The earth is full of the mercy of the Lord" (Ps 33:5) [2] and whole crowds are climbing toward the heights (of perfection). The emptiness of the wilderness and the fear of various monsters do not allow the brothers to live singly. [3] It seems best to obey the commands of the Holy Spirit, [4] for our own words cannot remain firm unless the firmness of the Scripture confirms our arrangement. [5] Scripture says: "How good and pleasant it is for brothers to live together" (Ps 133:1) and [6] again: "He makes people live harmoniously in a house" (Ps 68:7). [7] Since the Holy Spirit makes this clear teaching of piety very firm, let us get on with the task of laying down a Rule for the brothers. [8] Therefore, brothers, we want you to live with harmony and joy in a house; [9] but let us set down with God's help how this very harmony and joy can be maintained in good order.

[10] Therefore we wish that one brother preside over all, [11] nor should anyone turn aside from his advice and command to do evil. [12] But they should obey in all joy as if it were the command of the Lord, [13] as the Apostle says to the Hebrews: "Obey your leaders, for they watch over you." [14] And the Lord said: "I do not wish sacrifice but obedience." [15] Those who wish to be in harmony through such conduct should reflect that by obedience "Abraham" pleased "God and was called a friend of God" (Jas 2:23). [16] By reason of their obedience, the apostles themselves were deemed worthy of witnessing to the Lord among tribes and peoples.

An anonymous referee rejoins that *EMR* is still a useful book, with "some very interesting insights."

[17] Moreover, when the Lord himself descended from heaven to earth, he said: "I have not come to do my own will but the will of the one who sent me" (John 6:38). [18] Therefore, strengthened by such examples, let obedience be greatly maintained with much care.

2. Macarius

Macarius said: [1] The distinguishing virtues of the brothers, namely, living together and obedience, have been written down above. [2] Now with the help of God we will show the spiritual discipline that should be maintained by the superiors. [3] The superior must live up to Paul's dictum: "Be a model for the believers" (1 Thess 1:7). [4] That means to lead the souls of the brothers from earthly to heavenly things in accord with the state of holy affection and strictness. [5] Paul teaches that when he says: "Convince, reprimand, encourage with all patience" (2 Tim 4:2). [6] In another passage he says: "What do you wish? Shall I come to you with a rod, or in a spirit of mildness?" (1 Cor 4:21). [7] The superior ought to discern how best to show marks of affection toward each person. [8] One must maintain fairness, [9] remembering the Lord, who says: "The measure with which you measure will be measured out to you" (Matt 7:2).

[10] So when you assemble for prayer, no one should presume to intone a psalm without the order of the superior. [11] Let this order be held to: no one in the monastery should presume to stand before his senior or intone a psalm before him. [12] For as Solomon says: "Son, do not seek the first place; [13] and do not take the first couch at a banquet, lest one of your betters arrive and you be told: 'Get up!' Then you will be covered with shame" (Sir 7:4; Luke 14:8-9). [14] And again he says: "Do not be haughty, but stand in awe" (Rom 11:20). [15] But if the superior comes late, one must first bring it to his attention and then do what he commands.

[16] Now we will show what kind of test should be applied to those who leave the world (to join the monastery). [17] First they must be stripped of their worldly riches. [18] If a poor man leaves the world, even he has riches to strip away. [19] The Holy Spirit shows this by the words of Solomon: "I hate the proud poor person" (Sir 25:3-4). [20] Elsewhere he says: "The proud one is like a cancer" (Ps 89:11). [21] Therefore the superior should hold strictly to this principle: If a poor person wants to join the monastery, first he must jettison his baggage of pride [22] and then, having passed this test, he may be received. [23] Above all, he must be formed in humility. For it is a great thing and a sacrifice pleasing to God to not do one's own will but to be ready for anything. [24] Whatever happens he should remember the saying: "Be patient under trials" (Rom 12:12). [25] When such a person wishes to escape from the confusion of the world,

at his first approach to the monastery he should lie prostrate outside the door for a week. [26] None of the brothers should visit with him except to drive home to him what a hard and burdensome life (he is undertaking). [27] Now if he keeps on knocking, the petitioner should not be denied entry. [28] The superior should instruct such a man how to lead the life of the brothers and according to the Rule.

[29] But if a rich person who has much worldly wealth wishes to join the monastery, he must first fulfill the will of God [30] and carry out that paramount command addressed to the rich young man: [31] "Sell all you own and give it to the poor; then take up your cross and follow me" (Matt 19:21; 16:24). [32] Then the superior must teach him to leave aside everything but the cross that he carries, and to follow the Lord. [33] Now the extent of the cross is this: in all obedience to do not one's own will but that of another. [34] But if he wishes to bestow some portion (of his wealth) on the monastery, he should know on what terms either he or his offering are being received. [35] On the other hand, if he wishes to have one of his slaves with him, he should know that he no longer has him as a slave but as a brother (Phlm 16). Then he will be found perfect in all things.

[36] How wayfarers should be received as guests. [37] When such people show up, no one except the one assigned to do so should go out to meet them. [38] He is not permitted to pray (with the guest) nor offer him the kiss of peace unless the superior permits it. [39] Once the prayer is finished, the kiss of peace should follow in its order. [40] No one is permitted to converse with a new arrival except the superior alone, and those he wishes. [41] When they come to the refectory, the wayfaring brother is not permitted to eat with the brothers. He should eat with the superior so as to be edified. [42] No one is permitted to speak, nor should any word be heard except that of God drawn from the text of Scripture, and that of the superior or those he commands to speak. And thus the talk will be of God.

3. Paphnutius

Paphnutius said: [1] Everything said so far is great and useful to the soul's salvation (see 1 Pet 1:9). [2] But we must not remain silent about the order of fasting to be kept. [3] The only sure testimony appropriate to the matter is this one: [4] "Peter and John were going up to the temple to pray at about the ninth hour" (Acts 3:1). [5] Therefore this is the order to be kept: Except for Sunday, one must not eat before None in the monastery. [6] Sunday, however, is to be kept free for God alone. [7] No work should take place on that day; it should be spent solely in hymns, psalms and spiritual canticles (see Eph 5:19).

⁸ We now decree how the brothers ought to work. ⁹ This is the order that should be followed: ¹⁰ The period from the first to the third hours should be free for God. ¹¹ From the third to the ninth hour, they should take up whatever work they are told to do without any grumbling. ¹² Those who are told to do some task should remember this saying of the Apostle: "Whatever you do, do it without grumbling" (Phil 2:14). ¹³ They ought to fear that terrible saying: "Do not grumble, for some of them grumbled and died at the hand of the Destroyer" (1 Cor 10:10). ¹⁴ Further, the superior should tell one of the brothers what is to be done, and the others should obey the orders of this foreman.

¹⁵ How the superior should acknowledge the strength or weakness of the members. ¹⁶ If one of the brothers, because of his fasting or manual labor—¹⁷ which the Apostle orders when he says: "We work with our hands so as not to be a burden to any of you" (1 Cor 4:12; 1 Thess 2:9; 2 Thess 3:8)—¹⁸ if such a one is greatly weakened, the superior should make provision for his condition. ¹⁹ But if the brother's malady is a spiritual one, he should work all the harder, mindful of the Apostle, who "made his body serve him" (1 Cor 9:27). ²⁰ In no case, however, should he be allowed to act as he pleases.

²¹ How the brothers should precede one another in communal offices. ²² If the community of brothers is large, the superior should decide the order of weekly servers and the offices which they succeed one another in fulfilling.

²³ What kind of person should have charge of the storehouse of the brothers. ²⁴ Choose someone who can resist all the temptations of gluttony, ²⁵ and who fears the punishment of Judas, "who was a thief from the beginning" (John 12:6; 8:44). ²⁶ Anyone named to this office should strive to merit this promise: ²⁷ "Whoever serves well gains a high rank" (1 Tim 3:13).

²⁸ The brothers also should be aware that whatever they handle in the monastery, be it jars or tools or anything else, is consecrated. ²⁹ If anyone treats anything carelessly, ³⁰ he should know he is like that king who drank with his concubines from the vessels of God's house. And he will merit the same punishment (see Dan 5:1-30).

³¹ These precepts are to be kept and read every day for the brothers to hear.

4. Macarius

Macarius said: ¹ Truth declares: "Two or three witnesses verify a claim" (2 Cor 13:1; see Deut 19:15; Matt 18:16). ² Thus the rule of piety (Scripture) is to be confirmed.

[3] We must not remain silent as to how monasteries secure lasting peace among themselves. [4] It will not be permissible to receive a brother from another monastery without the consent of his superior. [5] Not only should one not receive him, one should not even see him, [6] for the Apostle says that "one who denies his first faith is worse than an unbeliever" (1 Tim 5:8, 12). [7] But if someone petitions his superior for leave to enter another monastery, he should recommend him to the superior where he wishes to live. [8] And the latter should only receive him on condition [9] that he consider all the brothers he finds in the monastery to be his seniors. [10] Take no account of his past achievements, but pay close attention to how he begins his new life. [11] But once received, if he is seen to possess any goods or books, he must not keep them any longer. [12] That way he can now live a life of perfection that he could not attain elsewhere. [13] When the brothers have sat down together for a conference on Scripture, even though the newcomer is the most learned one among them, he is not to speak unless the superior bids him to do so.

[14] How should clerical guests be received? [15] With all reverence as ministers at the altar. [16] No one but them may conclude the oration, for even a doorkeeper is a minister of the temple. [17] But if he has fallen into some fault and is convicted of what he is accused, he may not complete (the prayer) before the superior or the second in command. [18] No cleric should be allowed to live in the monastery [19] except those whom a moral collapse has led to humility and vulnerability. Thus they can be cured in the monastery by the medicine of humility. [20] This is enough for you to observe and guard. Do so and you will be blameless.

5. Appendix

[1] Nor should we be silent about how the faults of various persons are to be corrected. Excommunication will correspond to the nature of the fault. This is the order to be followed: [2] If one of the brothers engages in idle chatter, [3] we order him to abstain for three days from associating or conversing with the brothers; otherwise, he will be subject to the council (see Matt 5.22). No one should visit with him.

[4] If anyone is caught laughing or telling off-color jokes—[5] as the Apostle says, that is simply out of place (Eph 5:4)—[6] we decree that such a one be afflicted with every sort of humiliating punishment for two weeks in the name of the Lord. [7] The Apostle says: "If anyone called brother among you is wrathful or proud or slanderous (1 Cor 5:11), [8] take note of him, but do not consider him as an enemy; correct him as a brother" (2 Thess 3:14-15). [9] Elsewhere he says: "If a brother is caught in some fault, you who are spiritual should instruct such a one

and correct the brother" (Gal 6:1). [10] Thus each one should act, with the result that tested but not condemned by frequent lessons of humility, he may persevere in the monastery.

[11] Above all else, we order you who occupy this office to avoid favoritism (Rom 2:11 + Eph 6:9; Jas 2:1). [12] All should be loved with equal affection and all should be healed by correction. [13] For equality is pleasing to God, [14] as the Prophet says: "If you want to talk about justice, then judge justly, you sons of men" (Ps 58:2).

[15] We do not want to hide from you that the person who does not correct the erring brother should know that "he will have to answer for him" (Heb 13:11). [16] Be faithful and good cultivators (of souls). [17] Correct the restless, support the weak, be patient with everyone (1 Thess 5:14). [18] And you will be rewarded for as many persons as you gain (Matt 18:15). [19] "In the name of the Father and Son and Holy Spirit. Amen" (Matt 28:19).

Commentary

Prologue title: Vogüé, *Les Règles* (n. 2 above), 1, 180, believes this title is not original, but was concocted by someone who assumed the Macarius who speaks in 3.31 is a second person of that name. But the text says nothing of that, and since the content of part 4 seems to merely continue that of part 2, also by Macarius, it probably refers to the same person. Vogüé also thinks that all these Egyptian names are a literary fiction.

Prol. 1. "While we were sitting in discussion" (*sedentibus nobis in unum*); literally, "sitting together." The word "discussion" is inferred from "sitting," and is not a translation of *consilium* in the next verse, which I take to mean "plan" or "decision" and not "discussion."

In his critical edition of R4P (n. 3 above), Jean Neufville suggests that the document was written in Rome in the second half of the fifth century. He bases this opinion on the fact that Roman synods of that period often begin their decrees with an ablative absolute like *sedentibus nobis*, but the episcopal synods of south Gaul begin theirs with a *cum-*clause. Vogüé (*Les Règles*, 1, 112–15), however, points out that many episcopal synods of the period 380–400 AD, from Aquileia to Saragossa to Carthage, begin with the same formula, that is, *sedentibus nobis*, so it cannot be used as an indication of location.

While R4P mimics the language of episcopal synods, it is not a decree by bishops. Bishops in the early church often legislated for monks, but no known decree is *exclusively* about monks. Furthermore, synodal decrees always bear signatures and a specific reference to date and place, but R4P has none of these (Vogüé, *Les Règles*, 1, 59–60). Anscari Mundó (n. 3 above) thinks R4P represents a historical general chapter of south Gallic abbots, told by the bishops to put their houses in order. He points to a variant form of 4.20 (manuscript *a*) that reads: "Here ends the synod of thirty-eight abbots." No subsequent scholar has taken this variant seriously.

Both Mundó and Neufville avoid placing R4P at Lérins because (1) they believe it had only one house, and R4P seems to present a meeting of the heads of several houses; (2) the cenobium at Lérins was only formed in the second half of the fifth century. Vogüé has no problem placing R4P at Lérins ca. 400 AD. He considers the "conciliar" form of the Rule to be a literary artifice. Or it could represent a gathering of early hermits on the island, at which they decide to form a community. But to judge from the uniform style (except perhaps for the appendix), R4P is the work of one author, and that is probably Honoratus (Vogüé, *Les Règles*, 1, 22–26).

Prol. 2. "we arrived at a very salutary plan" (*consilium saluberrimum conperti*). *Early Monastic Rules* (*EMR*) (Collegeville, MN: Liturgical Press, 1982) has "seeking knowledge from a most beneficial deliberation," but that seems to be a mere repetition of v. 1. The Latin carefully distinguishes the two participles: "while sitting in discussion" (*sedentibus*: present); "we arrived" (*conperti*: perfect).

"plan" (*consilium*) refers to the writing of the Rule, not the prayer for grace.

Prol. 3. "to teach us" (*qui nos instrueret*). As the next part (1.4) shows, R4P is determined to search the Bible, that is, the written record of the Spirit's teaching, for monastic guidance. Vogüé (*Les Règles*, 1, 181, nn. 2-3) also refers to *Latin Basil* (RBas 12), which demands that all teaching be biblically warranted. In fact, R4P is laced with biblical proof-texts, some of which are better chosen than others.

"lifestyle or Rule of life" (*conversationem vel regulam vitae*). Vogüé has "le comportement religieux" for *conversationem*, but strictly speaking the word means *any* recognized lifestyle: clerical, married, military, monastic, etc. *EMR* has "manner and rule of life," which is adequate, but it also has a puzzling note declaring that *regulam* here does not mean a monastic Rule in the technical sense. I think it does, and that is why I capitalize it.

I. Serapion

1.1. "whole crowds" (*multorum agmina*). The image is of a great mass of people on the move, perhaps climbing a mountain. Probably it refers to the fact that more and more people were seeking admittance to the monastery of Lérins. Given the infantile state of monasticism in Gaul in 415–20 when R4P was written, "crowds" seems like an exaggeration, but Honoratus is comparing them to a few hermits. Jerome uses *agmina* to refer to three monastic groups in Bethlehem (*Ep.* 108.20, 3), but Vogüé (*Les Règles*, 1, 111, n. 61) does not think the plural number of *agmina* proves that the superiors of several monasteries wrote this Rule.

"toward the heights (of perfection)" (*ad vitae fastigium*). Probably a reference to the monastic life itself. The Lérinian writer Eucher of Lyons (*Laude* 33) uses the phrase *ad perfectionem tendibus*. Vogüé has "la vie parfaite," which is an abstract version of "heights." *EMR* has "summit of life," which is too vague. One is reminded of RB 73, which twice uses similar language: *ad celsitudinem perfectionis* (73.2); *doctrinae virtutumque culmina* (73.9). Benedict, however, is urging the monks to move beyond ordinary monastic observance, whereas R4P is not.

1.2. "emptiness of the wilderness" (*heremi vastitas*). If one takes the Egyptian names of the four speakers literally, this could be a reference to Sketis, which is indeed a vast desert. But Lérins is on a small and rather lush island on the French Riviera, so this should be taken as a literary trope. In his *Vita Honorati* (PL 1.1249–72), Hilary of Arles often calls Lérins a "desert" (15.1; 20.2, etc.).

"fear of various monsters" (*diversorum monstrorum terror*). Hilary claims that Lérins was snake-infested when Honoratus arrived, but the founder refused to be intimidated and the snakes all left (*VHon* 15.2-4). Vogüé notes (*Les Règles*, 1, 109) that this may be a clue to the early date of R4P: even before the snakes vacated the island Honoratus was gathering the hermits into community.

1.4. "firm" (*firma*). This elaborate rhetorical flourish features three uses of *firma*, but the purpose is probably more than aesthetic. Vogüé (*Les Règles*, 1, 61, n. 15) notes that *firmare* was a favorite term of Gallic episcopal synods when they wanted to lend legal weight to their decrees. Here, of course, the weight is not legal but biblical. *EMR* ignores this wordplay completely.

1.5-6. Psalms 133:1 and 68:7 are quoted at the beginning of two of the mother Rules of cenobitic monachism, the RAug (1.2, quoting Ps 68:7) and Rufinus's Latin version of the RBas (3, quoting Ps 133:1). Honoratus could have seen both Rules by the time he wrote, yet he still goes his own way. Both Basil and Augustine emphasize the community from start to finish. Honoratus begins by declaring that the Scripture wants us to live together but then quickly turns to the question of the superior. Vogüé (*Les Règles*, 1, 80–81) contends that authority is the basic theme of R4P from beginning to end.

1.7. "Since . . . clear" (*firmam . . . praeclaram*). The grammar of this clause is accusative absolute, which is often corrected to ablative absolute in the manuscripts. The keyword *firma* surfaces again, proving that it refers to the divine, not the legal foundation.

"rule of piety" (*regulam pietatis*) is probably a reminiscence of RBas 202. In fact, R4P uses it twice, here and at 4.2. Although Rufinus only uses it once in RBas, it is one of his favorite expressions in other writings (Vogüé, *Les Règles*, 1, 140). As for Basil, he speaks of "pious judgment" (*eusebous kriseos*: SR 275) and not a rule.

"get on with" (*prosequamur*). The Latin word can mean to begin or to continue. I would agree with *EMR* ("to proceed") and not Vogüé (*continuons*) that the Rule as such begins at this point.

1.8. "harmony and joy" (*unianimitas . . . jocunditas*). The references are to Ps 68:7 (*unianimes*) and 133:1 (*jocundum*). "Harmony" does not account for the Latin roots of *unianimitas*: one + soul, but the English word has its own strength.

"good order" (*recto ordine*). Since this is the fourth time Honoratus has spoken of order (Prol. 3; 1.4; 1.7; 1.9), one must suspect it is a high priority with him.

"with God's help" (*Deo juvante*) is a Basilian phrase (RBas 2), but it is also a commonplace.

1.10. At this point the emphasis on the superior commences, and not at 2.1 as the heading in *EMR* would indicate. Although R4P is like RBas and RAug in beginning with a discussion of community (1.1-9), those earlier Rules do not mention the superior until much later, whereas R4P will refer to him in almost every sentence (Vogüé, *Les Règles*, 1, 80–81).

"one brother preside over all" (*unum praeesse super omnes*). While R4P emphasizes the superior, it never gives him the usual formal title *abbas*, but rather the quasi-title *is qui praeest* ("he who presides"). Vogüé (*Les Règles*, 1, 106–8) uses this as a means of dating R4P; RBas (ca. 370 AD), a Rule well known to R4P, never speaks of the *abbas*, only of *is qui praeest*.

This usage occurs thirty-three times in RBas. By 425–430, however, John Cassian, writing at Marseilles near Lérins, uses only *abbas* and never *is qui praeest*. Indeed, *abbas*, and not the circumlocution, was to be the standard term for the superior in the West, including Lérins. Faustus, who was superior of Lérins 434–462, uses *abbas* twice to designate the superior (*Hom* 35,12 and 38,2). So Vogüé dates R4P between Basil and Cassian, and perhaps even before the *Dialogues* of Sulpicius Severus. Writing in 405 AD, Sulpicius uses *abbas* nineteen times in *Dialogues* 1 alone.

1.12. "obey" (*oboedire*). Obedience is, of course, the necessary concomitant of authority. It does no good to vest someone with authority if no one is willing to follow her. In the preceding verse R4P virtually equates with evil (*sinistrum*) any deviation from the will and wishes of the superior.

"as if it were the command of the Lord" (*sicut imperio Domini*). R4P makes it abundantly clear that it considers obedience an action of faith and not just social compliance. Yet the little word *sicut* keeps the equation between the will of God and that of the monastic superior from being absolute. Cassian uses the same nuanced language in *Inst.* 4.10 and 4.27, 4.

"in all joy" (*omni laetitia*). Cheerful obedience is greatly emphasized by RB 5, although the word *laetitia* is not used.

1.13. "obey your leaders, for they watch over you" (*Oboedite praepositis vestris, quia ipsi vigilant pro vobis*). The point here is not surveillance but spiritual responsibility. The remainder of Hebrews 13:17 shows this: "and [they] will have to give an account." Thus our obedience ought to be *compassionate* toward the superior, for he or she has taken on a heavy responsibility for our sake. St. Augustine cites Hebrews 13:17 in RAug 7.1 but does not dwell on the eschatological responsibility of the superior. Hebrews 13:17 is also cited in the *Lib. Hors.* 19, where it is quoted in full. RB 2.38 also stresses the accountability of the abbot before God.

1.14. A sort of summary of many biblical passages, e.g., 1 Samuel 15:22; Hosea 6:6; and Matthew 9:13. In his *Sermon* 156.6, Caesarius of Arles, a Lérinian monk, writing as archbishop of Arles about a hundred years after R4P, joins these two Scripture passages (Heb 13:17 and *Nolo sacrificium*).

1.15. "in harmony through such conduct" (*tali opere unianimes*). EMR has "in accord with such a work," which does not make much sense.

Unianimes in verses 8-9 referred to harmony in the community, and that is the meaning here too as understood by Vogüé and also Vincent Desprez (n. 18 above). Yet the question remains as to how obedience to God creates human communion. Apparently the answer implied here is that obedience makes one a friend of God, and the obedient friends of God become friends of each other. The citation is from James 2:23, but the author has truncated it, substituting "pleased" for "believed God and it was reckoned to him as righteousness." James would not be upset with this summary of his text, but I suspect St. Paul would!

1.16. There are verbal echoes of Acts 1:8 and Revelation 11:3, 9 here. Perhaps the obedience of the apostles lay in their ready response to Jesus' initial call, as in Matthew 4:18-22. Yet their ultimate rehabilitation and mission were the result of grace, not merit. The immediate response demanded of the obedient monk in RM 7.7-8 and RB 5.7-8 is not exactly germane here because the demand is that *teachers* (or missionaries) first be obedient so they will be heard.

1.17. "descended from heaven to earth" (*de superna ad inferiora discendens*) is not a historical but a theological statement. It is equivalent to Philippians 2:6: "(Jesus), who, though he was in the form of God, did not regard equality with God something to be grasped."

Vogüé, who has made a thorough study of the use of John 6:38 by early monastic legislators (*The Community and the Abbot* [Kalamazoo: Cistercian Publications, 1978], 1, 224–51), notes that the use of this text by R4P connects it to the Rule of Basil, which uses it often (80.1; 84.4; 181.1; 184.2). This serves to balance his treatment of obedience by emphasizing the individual, ascetical aspects of obedience over against the social. This is because Jesus talks about obedience as putting aside his own will. Further, self-will becomes one of the worst enemies of monastic obedience in those Rules that follow John 6:38, especially Basil, the Rule of the Master, and the Rule of Benedict. Earlier, R4P had quoted Hebrews 13:17, which is an obedience text employed by Augustine and Horsiesi. Those writers never use John 6:38 and they emphasize social obedience. See Vogüé, *Les Règles*, 1, 85–86.

1.18. "examples" (*virtutes*). Vogüé and Desprez give this translation, which is demanded by the context although it is not within the linguistic range of *virtutes*. EMR dutifully gives us "virtues," but it has little meaning here. What R4P probably means are examples of the virtue of obedience.

2. Macarius

2.1. "distinguishing virtues of the brothers" (*fratrum insignia virtutum*), literally "the marks of the brothers' virtues," as *EMR* has it. The formula *insignia virtutum* or an equivalent was typical of Gallic Latin: Reverentius of Marseilles, *VHil* 2.21; 3.30; 10.14; 20.4; *VPJ* 167.2-3; 179.8.

"living together" (*habitationis*). The literal meaning is simply "dwelling place," as *EMR* again renders it, but that is hardly "distinguishing." Everyone has to live someplace. As Desprez sees it, the point is that the brothers live *together* (R4P 1.1-9). Faustus of Riez, third abbot, liked to refer to Lérins as *habitatio*: *Hom* 39.2, 30, 32; 39.3,48 = 44.1-5; 40.3, 11. All references are from Vogüé, *Les Règles*, 1, 185, n. 2.

"written down" (*conscripta praevenerunt*), not "prescribed" as in *EMR*. The use of *praevenire* as an auxiliary verb is odd, but comprehensible: "now that we have finished describing in writing." In 3.31, Paphnutius concludes by saying that "the prescriptions are to be observed and repeated in the ears of the brothers," which implies that they are written down.

2.2. "spiritual discipline" (*spiritale exercitium*) probably refers to the whole tenor of a healthy monastic life for the community. The term is common in early monastic literature, ranging from general use as in *Hist. Mon.* 29.453d to specific meanings such as *lectio divina* for Pelagius, *Ep. ad Dem.* 2.3.

"superiors" (*his qui praesunt*). The author reverts back to a topic begun in 1.10. Desprez (*Règles monastiques*, 97, n. 2.2) says that *is qui praeest* is a translation of Basil's *proestos*. The "most evolved" manuscript of R4P (P: BN 12205) already changed *is qui praeest* to *praepositus*; 2RP (ca. 427) uses *prepositus* and RMac (ca.500) uses *abbas*. Thus the term *abbas* comes into general usage in the monastic West.

2.4. "that means to" (*hoc est*) seems to link verses 3-4 in a logical sequence, but the points are different: v. 3: be a model; v. 4: adapt your approach to the case.

"by means of holy affection and severity" (*pro qualitate misticae pietatis et severitatis*). Although he admits both the text and the meaning are obscure, I think Vogüé has it right when he reads "severity." The subsequent biblical warrants have to do with flexible use of authority depending on the mentality of the subject, whether sensitive or obtuse. *EMR* and Desprez prefer the reading *veritas* (truth) for *severitas*, but that is not what the Scripture texts are talking about. Moreover, *pietas* and *severitas* are found yoked in Faustus, *Hom.* 72.7, and Salvian of Marseilles, *Gub.* 1.48, 58.

2.5. 1 Thessalonians 1:7 is also quoted by RM 2.23 = RB 2.23, where the abbot is urged to know the individual monks well so as to know best how to guide each one to spiritual progress.

2.7. "marks of affection" (*pietatis affectum*). Because severity is not mentioned, this verse tends to undercut the preceding discussion. Yet probably the author means that a superior may have to be firm with a monk "for his own good," no matter what tenderness he feels for him.

2.8. "Maintain fairness" (*aequalitatem tenere*). "Equality" here (all the translators simply transliterate it) cannot mean absolutely equal treatment. Since each individual is different, stereotyped treatment would be *experienced* (received) variously. Granted the need for differentiated treatment, there is still danger of favoritism. There must be a basic atmosphere of fairness for any authority to function well. RB 2.22 struggles with the same issues: "Therefore let the abbot have equal (*equalis*) charity for all, and let him maintain the same discipline in all cases, depending on their merits."

2.10. "when you assemble" (*astantibus*). No doubt some word like *fratribus* or *vobis* is understood. The reference is to the public choir office.
   "intone a psalm" (*psalmi laudem emittere*). Although vague, this must have to do with *leading* the office in some official way as an acolyte or cantor. No doubt everyone present sang the psalms, but *EMR* does not reflect this. It does, however, refer to RB 47.3, which is about psalm-leading.

2.11. "stand before his senior" (*priorem . . . ad standum . . . praecedere*). The very fact that one monk is "before" (*priorem*) another means that R4P assumes a hierarchical system. Probably it was based on date of entry, as in RB 63.1-9, which speaks explicitly of standing and intoning in rank (v. 4). Such a system was rigidly adhered to throughout monastic history (RPach, *praef* 3; RPaul St 12.2, etc.) but is often downplayed in present-day Benedictine life.

2.12. "Solomon" (*Salomone*). The text that follows is a loose paraphrase of 3 John 9 and Luke 14:7-14, neither of which is by Solomon. Nevertheless, there are overtones of Sirach 7:4 and Proverbs 25:6-7, which *were* attributed to Solomon.

2.13. "first couch" (*adcubueris prior*), literally "lie down first." *EMR* has "recline . . . too early," but time is not the problem; place is. The context here is the monastic *statio*, where each has a "place." To usurp the place of a senior is unacceptable in a hierarchical society.

"shame" (*confusionem*). In a culture where rank is the constant emphasis (see RB 63), to be *displaced*, and especially in public, constitutes a severe social setback. Like the Rule of Benedict, R4P was written in the Mediterranean culture, where shame and honor were (and are) exceedingly powerful social motivations.

2.14. Now the author quotes Scripture precisely, but there is still some question as to what he means. *EMR* has "Do not wish to be extremely wise," probably reading *sapere* as "to know." The Revised NAB, which is quoted here, along with Vogüé and Desprez, seems to take *sapere* as "have a taste for."

2.15. Vogüé, *Les Règles*, 1, 72, n. 67, suggests that verses 11-14 are an interpolation that interrupts the flow of 10-15. Verses 10 and 15 concern obedience to the superior regarding the liturgy, while the middle verses (11-14) discuss fraternal relations.

"bring it to his attention" (*in notitiam eius deferre*). All translators agree on this meaning, which refers to liturgical initiatives taken in the superior's absence. But *deferre* can also mean "draw back," and it could mean to suspend the order now operating in view of new orders given by the superior. This alternative, however, does not jibe well with *notitiam*.

2.16. "test" (*examinatio*) does not mean a verbal scrutiny here, though that was no doubt also involved, but rather a challenge to the *impedimenta* the postulant might bring. Cassian, *Inst.* 4.3, uses the same word. Virtually all the early monastic Rules require that a newcomer be thoroughly tested before entry (see RPach Prec. 49 and RBas 6-7).

2.17. "stripped" (*amputandae*). This violent language also turns up in Cassian, *Inst.* 7.21, and RB 33.1, both of which inveigh against avarice. Cassian makes it plain that avarice is the sort of vice that entrenches itself so thoroughly that every last bit of the root must be extirpated. It is not clear whether R4P wants the despoliation of the newcomer merely to be complete, or whether it is to be deliberately harsh so as to disabuse the candidate of any notion that he is God's gift to the monastery.

2.18. "comes to the monastic life" (*converti videatur*), literally "seems to be converted," as *EMR* has it. Although the implication is that one has turned from the world, as we saw in 2.16 the term quickly becomes a technical one for the person who comes to the monastery as an adult. Thus in RM 87.1, a private monk who petitions for entry into the monastery is called *frater jam conversus*. In RB 58.1, 17, *conversatio morum suorum* simply refers to the monastic life.

"riches to strip away" (*divitias quas amputare debeat*). This verse suggests that "riches (*divitias*) are understood somewhat loosely in the preceding verse and here metaphorically. "Strip away" is definitely not punitive here, since one does it to oneself. St. Augustine often discusses the problem of poor peasants who become proud monks. How ironic that the rich can learn humility in the monastic life much easier than the poor! See RAug 1.6; *Op. Mon.* 33; *Serm.* 14.4.

2.20. "The proud one is like a cancer" (*sicut vulneratum superbum*). The intention of the psalmist was not quite the same as that of R4P. *Superbum* is accusative case because it is the object of *humiliasti* ("you have crushed"). *Vulneratum* shows that the proud enemy is weak, but R4P wants to show pride as a vice. Hence my risky translation: "cancer."

2.21. "jettison his baggage of pride" (*exponat sarcinam superbiae*). EMR has the vivid "heavy sack of pride," but "expose" is not what is meant. The way to dispose of a heavy sack is to *put it down*. RM *Thema* 22 has a comparable image in a scene in which the people are jettisoning heavy burdens of sin (*sarcina peccatorum*) at baptism. Unfortunately, the Master continues the figure: monks are those who refuse to take up the baggage of sin once more; layfolk gladly resume this burden. See *The Rule of the Master*, trans. Luke Eberle (Kalamazoo: Cistercian Publications, 1977).

2.23. "formed in humility" (*humilitate imbui*). Vogüé translates "on doit lui inculquer l'*humilité*," implying that the candidate must *be* taught this fundamental monastic virtue by the community or its delegate. "Inculquer" means to impress a value deeply on another person.

"not to do one's own will" (*ut . . . suam . . . voluntatem non faciat*). The grammar of the Latin has this *ut*-clause dependent on "formed in humility," which it explains.

"a sacrifice pleasing to God" (*Deo sacrificium acceptum est*). Obedience as *the* most pleasing sacrifice to God is a biblical commonplace.

"ready for anything" (*ad omnia paratus sit*), that is, anything called for by obedience. See 2 Timothy 2:21.

2.25. "confusion" (*latebris*). The usual meaning is "secret place" (*EMR*) or "darkness" (Vogüé, *Les Règles*; Desprez, *Règles monastiques*), but I have opted for a more psychological word.

"for a week" (*ebdomada*). Vogüé, *Les Règles*, 1, 142-43, nn. 173, 176-78, makes much of the trajectory formed by the ancient Rules on the question of keeping a postulant waiting at the gate. Pachomius, RPach, Pr. 49, has him wait only "some days," while Cassian, *Inst.* 4.3, 1, stipulates a wait of ten days. Since R4P has a wait of seven days, it seems to lie between those two benchmarks, as to date of composition. Although it does not share much vocabulary, R4P 2.24 contains the same ideas as RPach Pr. 49. One problem for this theory is that Palladius, *Hist, Laus*, 18.13, says Pachomius kept Macarius waiting for a week at the door. Another break in the trajectory is that Benedict (RB 58.3) has them wait "four or five days." Thus Pachomius (ca. 350 AD): a few days; R4P (ca. 400): seven days; Cassian (ca. 425): ten days; RB (ca. 540): four or five days.

"such a person" (*is qui talis*) refers to whoever wishes to join the community, not just a poor person. The same holds true for *huiuscemodi* in v. 28. If we take these words as references to the poor only (2.18), it means that the rich are spared the harsh test at the gate, a remote possibility.

2.26. "visit with him" (*cum eo . . . jungatur*). As with an excommunicated brother, the newcomer is kept in a kind of quarantine. See RB 25 and 26.

"hard and burdensome" (*dura et laboriosa*). Cassian, *Inst.* 4.38, uses the same two words; RB 58.8 has *dura*; RBas 6 has *laboriosa*. All of them insist that the monastic prospect not be enticed with sweet words, but told plainly the harsh truth: monastic life is aimed at one thing alone: to die with Christ so as to rise with him. Only this lofty goal could justify the apparent lack of hospitality to a newcomer.

2.27. "keeps on knocking" (*perseveraverit pulsans*), vocabulary reminiscent of Cassian, *Inst..* 4.3, 1; 4.30, 3; 4.46, 2.

2.28. "instruct" (*instruere*), as in RPach Pr. 49. Since the superior does the training of the newcomer we seem to be in a primitive state of the monastic institution, before various tasks have been delegated due to increase of numbers. Cassian, *Inst.* 4.7, and RM 88.7-10 depute this work to the porter or guestmaster. Benedict, however, reserves it to a "senior . . . who is gifted in spiritual guidance" (RB 58.6). If he cannot find a suitable delegate, the abbot must carry out this crucial rule himself.

2.29. "But if a rich person" (*quod si dives*). To judge from the language here, the author is starting a new section. 2.18ff. discusses the need for the poor postulant to put aside the "riches" of pride, but it segues into the practice of detaining the candidate for a week at the door. Surely, though, that treatment was not reserved only for the poor. On the other hand, 2.29-35 is devoted solely to the rich.

2.30. "paramount command" (*praeceptum . . . praecipuum*). Desprez has "the precept *first* addressed to the young man." Another possibility would be "addressed *specifically* to the young man." The latter is the first meaning given in the *Oxford Latin Dictionary* for *praecipuum*, but that is probably not what is meant here; *EMR* and Vogüé do not think so either.

2.31. "take up your cross" (*tolle crucem tuam*). Matthew 19:21 is joined to Matthew 16:24, making it considerably harsher than the original. In Matthew 19:21 the rich man is promised heavenly riches as a reward for putting aside earthly wealth; here, there is no such promise. As a matter of fact, many of the first members of Lérins were Gallo-Roman aristocrats who had much wealth to lose. *VHon.* 11.4 shows the founder divesting himself, and *VHil.* 6 shows his disciple doing likewise.

2.32. *EMR* has "seen to preside," which is a literal rendition of *praeesse videatur*. Desprez and Vogüé ignore *videtur*, as seems reasonable.
   "the cross he carries" (*crucem quam teneat*). Although Matthew 16:24 has *tollat* ("take up"), Vogüé, *Les Règles*, 1, 63, nn. 19-23, shows that *tenere* is a "verbal tic" of R4P. Vogüé cites Matthew 19:21, but he must mean Matthew 16:24.

2.33. "essence of the cross" (*crucis . . . fastigia*). *Fastigium* means the extreme point, so *fastigia* could mean "extremities," as Desprez has it. Vogüé has a more plausible reading in "the great cross." R4P has already indicated in 1.11-17 that obedience is the primary monastic virtue. It is also the inner meaning of the *dura et laboriosa* propounded to the newcomer in 2.26.
   I have omitted any English word for *primum* (after the colon). Vogüé, *Les Règles*, 1, 65, n. 34, considers *primum* a verbal tic; if that is so, then one can ignore it. If one does translate it, the reader is waiting for a second "extremity of the cross," but I do not think what follows merits that description. In fact, 2.29-35 is a rather disorderly composition that begins with dispossession, moves to obedience, and then returns to dispossession.

2.34. "But if" (*quod si*). The adversative here suggests a break in the logical sequence, for the bestowal of part of one's assets on the monastery is not contrary to obedience (vv. 32-33). The real reference would be v. 31, with its biblical injunction to "sell what you have and give to the poor."

"on what terms" (*quo ordine*). Implied here is the monastic ideal of dispossession: no one retains ownership after admittance to the community, especially of that which one previously donated to the monastery.

2.35. "If, on the other hand" (*si autem*) introduces an exception, but it will turn out to be only apparent. The very fact that some of the Lérins postulants had personal slaves shows they were from the richest class of nobility. The biblical background is Paul's letter to Philemon, a slave-holder. The difference is that Paul merely suggests that Onesimus be freed, but R4P demands liberation. It is not clear if the slave is subject to the same scrutiny at entrance as the master, but he must have been. The idea of slaves entering the monastery with their owners is seen in Jerome, *Ep.* 108.20; *Hist. Laus.* 61.6; Caesarius, RVirg 7; RTarn 1.14-15. In medieval times rich monks and nuns simply kept servants, who were not equals in any sense.

"perfect" (*perfectus*). Probably the reference is to Matthew 19:21 (R4P 2.31): "If you wish to be perfect, go, sell what you have. . . . Then come, follow me."

2.36. "guests" (*hospites*). *EMR* manages to ignore this keyword entirely. Desprez does not do it justice with "How stranger-guests are to be received." The point is that the stranger is hospitably received; he becomes a guest, but in a special monastic way.

"How" (*qualiter*). This verse functions as a title for 2.36-42, on hospitality. Vogüé, *Les Règles*, 1, 65–66, comments that this subtitle begins a series of five (3.15, 21, 23; 4.14) that do not correspond to the main divisions of the treatise, that is, the four speakers. Before and after this series the subtitles take the form of dependent clauses, as in 2.16: "We will now show how . . ." In Vogüé's view, which is surely correct, this shows that we are dealing with the thought and style of one author, Honoratus, and not a transcript of the speeches of four abbots.

2.37. "meet them" (*venienti*) appears for the second time in the same verse, the first being plural. It seems the translator must choose. The

notion of assigning one brother to meet and care for guests is very ancient in cenobitism, going back to the mother Rules: RPach, Pr. 50 and
59; see RBas 98–99. The alternative would be to allow spontaneous care
of guests by all members. This is what is envisaged in RB 53.1-15, based
on *Hist. Mon.* 7 and Genesis 18. But Benedict changes his tune in RB
53.16-24 when he appoints a guestmaster and rigidly restricts contact
between guests and monks.

2.38. "He will not pray (with the guest)" (*non licebit ei orare*). *EMR* and
Desprez think the guest is the subject, but I agree with Vogüé that it is
the guestmaster.

   "the superior permits it" (*videatur ab eo qui praeest*). All the other
translators take *videatur* to mean "(the guest) is seen," but I think the
extended sense is meant: "It seems good = it is permitted." See *Oxford
Latin Dictionary*, s.v. *videre*, 12.

2.39. "in its order" (*ordinem suum*). All the ancient Christian monastic
Rules prescribe prayer before the *pax*. Perhaps heretics would give themselves away by praying a little differently.

2.40. "No one is permitted to converse with a new arrival" (*nec licebit
alicui cum supervenienti sermocinari*). Since the construction (*licebit
+ dative*) is the same as in v. 38, this suggests the subject in v. 38 is not
the guest but the guestmaster. The prohibition against monks casually
chatting with wayfarers is seen in many monastic texts: Basil, LR 2 and
45.1-2; ROr 26.4; *VPJ* 172; RB 53.23-24.

2.41. "the traveling brother" (*peregrino fratri*). As *EMR* points out, *frater*
always refers to a monk in R4P. However, it does seem strange that a
monk would not eat with the monks. Here the word is the subject of
the *licebit* construction.

   "edified" (*aedificari*). Probably one eats with the superior, not to
avoid being scandalized by the brothers but because the superior would
be expected to engage in uplifting conversation.

2.42. "No one is permitted to speak" (*nulli licebit loqui*). The subject
has now shifted from the guest table to the general table. All the ancient Rules have silence at table; most have table reading of Scripture;
RM 24.9 and RB 38.9 have the superior speak; only RM 24.34-37 and
this text have him ask another brother to speak, no doubt about the
biblical text.

3. Paphnutius

3.1. *EMR* has "All things great and useful for the welfare of the soul have been spoken of." That is a possible translation of the Latin, but it makes little sense here. Vogüé, *Les Règles*, 1, 193, note, thinks the emphasis may be on the spiritual nature of discourse two (Macarius), whereas discourse three will be more material: fasting and work. I doubt that this distinction holds up to much scrutiny; Paphnutius is merely engaging in *captatio benevolentiae*.

3.2. "order of fasting" (*jejuniorum ordo*). The monastic method of fasting, unlike that of the great church, did not refer to quantity as much as timing. The monks ate a normal amount of food, but they ate only once a day, and that late in the afternoon. See Jerome, *Ep.* 22.35; *OM* 3; RM 28.1-7.

3.4. *EMR* has "the ninth hour of prayer," which renders the Latin woodenly and is quite misleading in English. The Revised NAB has "three o'clock hour of prayer." Vogüé says: "the argument seems to suppose an office of None before the meal." I wonder if there *is* an argument to be made here, since there are no biblical texts that prove that one should not eat before 3 p.m.

3.5. "before None" (*nisi Nona*). Desprez has the literal "except None," but in fact during Lent they ate even later. The "order" was to not eat before None. The Latin here is extremely verbose, and by following it literally *EMR* has produced an unreadable English sentence.

3.6. "God alone" (*nisi Deo*). The word *nisi* is used over and over in this section of R4P, occurring in verses 3, 5, 6, and 7. The section 3.1-7 is marked by an abundance of negatives that are awkward to render into graceful English. They also give the text an unpleasant, legalistic tone. Jerome, *Ep.* 22.35, 7, also has Sunday as a day of rest and prayer for monks. Desprez, *Règles monastiques*, 102, nn. 6-7, says it was not yet so for the Christian laity at the end of the fourth century.

3.9. "order" (*ordo*) here really means "horarium" rather than just "rule." Yet the following few verses do not provide a complete schedule for the whole monastic day, but merely the hours of *lectio* and work. Indeed, the main topic is "murmuring" (3.11-14).

3.10. "free for God" (*Deo vacetur*). Desprez takes this as a reference to *lectio divina*, which was often done during the early morning hours.

Two early mentions of this are found in Pelagius, *Ep. ad Dem.* 23 and *OM* 3, both of which may have been influenced by the public *lectio* of the Jerusalem church during Lent. See Vogüé, *Les Règles*, 1, 131, nn. 123ff. RB 48.4, 10, 13, 14, 17 uses the same verb for *lectio divina*: "free for *lectio*." This does not imply that *lectio*, which means biblical prayer, is easy or some kind of vacation. It does indicate, however, that it is not in the same category as work.

3.11. "without any grumbling" (*sine aliqua murmuratione*). Counting the biblical quotations given in vv. 12-13, *murmuratio* is mentioned three times in this section. Indeed, it seems to be the answer to the rhetorical question posed in the subtitle (v. 8): how are the brothers to work? Cheerfully! The injunction against grumbling is found in virtually every early Rule of the Latin West: *OM* 5; R4P 3.11-13; 2RP 26–27; RMac 4.2; 12.1; 3RP 5.4; Caesarius RVirg 17.2; 28.3; 32.4; Aurelius, RMon 54.3; RTarn 12.8; RF 7; 30.4; R Paul St 18.2-3; 22.1, 25.3.

3.13. "some of them grumbled" (*quidam eorum murmuraverunt*). In 1 Corinthians 10:10 Paul warns his readers against falling into the pattern of the Hebrews in the long sojourn in the desert. They were punished by God for all their sins, but especially for "grumbling." This vice is more serious than mere random complaining, for it implies disregard for the grace of God that set them free from Egyptian slavery.

3.14. "this foreman" (*cui injunctum fuerit*). This reference may imply that the community was large enough that there were several work gangs; the superior could not be present to all of them. Or it may suggest that the superior, as in RAug 7.2, did not actually live with the monks.

3.15. According to his biographer (Hilary, *VHon* 18.1-4), Honoratus was careful not to burden anyone with too much work, and that no one languish from too much leisure. RBas 131 insists that the superior observe closely the strength and energy of every member, no doubt precisely to avoid the pitfalls thus avoided by Honoratus. RB 48.8-9 speaks to the same point.

3.16. "manual labor" (*operam manuum*). Although the previous section discusses work (*operare*), it is not necessarily physical work but "whatever is commanded." Vogüé, *Les Règles*, 1, 197, n. 16, remarks that it is mentioned here because the Pauline text (1 Cor 4:12) has it, but I suspect the case is the reverse: Honoratus chooses the Pauline text because it mentions manual labor. Since the discussion is about physical fatigue, heavy manual labor comes to mind. It is worth remembering that before the time of R4P the only monastic movement in Gaul, that of Martin at Marmoutier, performed no manual labor at all.

3.18. "weakened" (*infirmitate*). This word could be translated as "sickness," but R4P does not have a comprehensive teaching on sickness as do, for example, RAug 3.5 and RB 36. It only treats of physical problems caused by excessive fasting or heavy work.

"make provision for his condition" (*providendum est . . . qualiter ipsa infirmitas sustentetur*), literally "make provision as to how this condition may be borne." This awkward, prolix statement still remains unclear. My own, shorter version is deliberately vague. No doubt the superior must first put an end to the monk's excessive fasting or labor, but he must also deal compassionately with the weakened condition resulting therefrom. For an extreme case see *VPJ* 71–78.

3.19. "work all the harder" (*frequentius operari*), literally "work more frequently." Perhaps the idea is that the person should be assigned more often to manual labor. One of the favorite remedies of the desert monks for *acedia* was manual labor. At any rate, the problem of spiritual weakness is quite different from its physical counterpart, so a different therapy is called for.

3.20. "as he pleases" (*voluntatem suam*) rather than "his own will." The problem is not the will as such but *self-will*. R4P makes frequent, almost constant, reference to the need to consult the superior in all things rather than simply steering one's own course. Once the superior has shown the way, then one applies one's will to that way of acting.

3.21. "precede one another" (*se . . . praeveniant*). Unlike all the other translators, I take this as a statement of fact, not exhortation. The idea of Christians vying to serve one another is an attractive one and reminiscent of Romans 12:10. But it seems quite different from what follows, namely, that the superior determines an orderly round of weekly service, less dependent on enthusiasm than obedience. If v. 21 is a subtitle it should not present an exception to the rule proposed in v. 22.

3.22. "weekly servers" (*ebdomadarum*). A weekly round of household chores, usually unskilled, is almost endemic to community life and it goes back to the earliest cenobitic reports, viz., Jerome, *Ep.* 22.35 (Egyptians) and Cassian, *Inst.* 4.19, 1 (Palestinians).

"if the community of brothers is large" (*si fratrum congregatio multa est*). Vogüé, *Les Règles*, 1, 79–80, muses that either the Rule was destined for several houses or the author envisaged extensive growth at Lérins. I would vote for the latter on historical grounds since we do not know of any other house whose superior could have been present at a synod in Lérins at the time this Rule was written.

3.23. The title for this official, who was called *cellararius* throughout most of Latin monastic history, took a long time to crystallize. Some used paraphrases such as we find here in R4P; RBas 111; *Lib. Hors.* 26; Gregory, *Dial.* 2,28.1. Some called him *oeconomus*: Jerome, *Ep.* 22.35, 6; Cassian, *Inst.* 4.6, 18, 20. And he is called *dispensator* by RPach Pr. 77–78 and Cassian, *Inst.* 4.19, 2.

3.24. "gluttony" (*guilae*). Early cellarers actually dealt directly with the contents of the cellar, namely, food. Therefore the warning against gluttony was frequent in monastic legislation: ROr 25.1; RM 16.62-63; RB 31.1.

3.26. "strive to merit" (*studere . . . ut audiat*), literally "to hear." The implication, of course, is that the cellarer *has* served well, so he will receive a (heavenly) reward. *EMR* does not connect *studere* with *audiat*, so the verse is left hanging in the air.

3.28. This seems to be the inspiration for the famous verse of St. Benedict: "He should consider all the receptacles of the monastery and all its goods as if they were the sacred vessels of the altar" (RB 31.10). RB 32 speaks of the iron tools (*ferramenta*) of the monastery. Vogüé thinks this verse of R4P could draw on RBas 103–104. Cassian, *Inst.* 4.19-20 also knows these chapters of Basil.

3.30. The reference to Daniel 5 seems far-fetched. It is quite a stretch from a monk carelessly dropping a jar or leaving a scythe out to rust in the rain to a pagan king purposely profaning the Jewish Temple vessels by using them at a drunken orgy!

3.31. Vogüé, *Les Règles*, 1, 199, n. 31, says that RAug 8.2 ends with an injunction that the text be read aloud in public every week. He suspects that R4P also ended at this point in an early recension. RB 66.7-8 also calls for frequent reading of the Rule, and as in R4P, this early ending is also camouflaged by additional material (RB 67–73).

4. Macarius

4.2. "rule of piety" (*regula pietatis*) refers to the preceding biblical text (see Vogüé, *Les Règles*, 1, 74, n. 71). It is "confirmed" by the fact that three abbots have spoken. Vogüé, *Les Règles*, 1, 58, also remarks that "Macarius the Second" is all the more fictitious in that he carries on the discussion of the reception of guests where Macarius the First left off (Part 2).

4.4. This fraternal rule was very common in South Gaul: Synod of Agde I (506) can. 27; 3RP 14.1; Orleans I (511) can. 19; RF 6. It is also echoed in RB 61.13-14.

4.5. "receive" (*recipere*) means to accept someone as a new member of the community. "See" (*videre*) probably means to entertain such a possibility by means of an interview or visit.

4.6. "denies his faith" (*primam fidem inritam fecit*) seems like an excessively severe biblical text to use for a person merely wishing to transfer monasteries!—especially since the biblical proof text has been artificially spliced together.

4.7. Letters of recommendation for transferring clergy are demanded by several Gallic provincial synods: Angers (453), can. 8; Vannes (461–491), can. 5–6; Agde (506), can. 388. Honoratus is not telling the superior he *must* agree to the transfer of one of his men, but that if he agrees to do so he should send a dimissorial letter (modern canonical term) to the new superior.

4.9. In fact, the Latin is more elaborate: "as many brothers as he finds in the (new) monastery, that is how many seniors he knows he has." This simply means that he takes the lowest place. RB 63.8 proposes a similar rule, but RB 61.11-12 allows the abbot to adjust the rank of a transferring monk, taking into account his "merit," that is, experience and stature. It is not clear if Benedict wants the monk judged on the basis of the past or the present.

4.12. It is hard to avoid the feeling that the author is being sarcastic here. He wants to transfer to a better monastery? Very well, we will help him become more perfect!

4.13. Among the Pachomian monks the same attitude was no doubt present, for even when Pachomius asked young Theodore to give a talk on Scripture there was grumbling among the seniors. See Pachomius, *Sbo* 69.

4.14-15. "ministers of the altar" (*ministri altaris*). Among the ancient monks the priesthood was often a source of tension. On the one hand the monks reverenced the clergy as God's representatives; on the other hand they usually avoided ordination as a danger to monastic humility and stability. Although R4P here implies that even the superiors were not ordained clergy at Lérins, Hilary tells a different story in *VHon* 16, where he claims Honoratus was ordained soon after he founded the monastery on Lérins.

4.16. "conclude the oration" (*orationem complete*), that is, the closing prayer at the end of an hour of the Divine Office. RB 60.4 has the cleric standing next to the abbot, presumably at the Office, but not permitted to offer the final prayer (*missa*) except by the abbot's leave. See Vogüé, *Community and the Abbot* (1979), 1, 300–2.
    "doorkeeper" (*ostiarius*) is the lowest clerical rank.

4.17. "conclude" (*complere*). The spoken oration was given at the end of a short period when all prayed in silence. The superior normally concluded all prayer sessions. See RM 15.26; 21.7; 50.67; 52.1, 2-4.
    "some fault" (*aliquo casu*). Clerics who fell into serious trouble were committed to monasteries by many early Gallic councils: Epaone (517), can. 22; Marseilles (533), p. 85,14; Orleans III (538), can. 8; Narbonne (589), can. 5–6, 11. In fact, this was the common practice in the Latin church until Vatican II—and may still be used in some countries.

4.18-19. "humility and vulnerability" (*ad humilitatem . . . et est vulneratus*). It seems that not just any misbehaving cleric was acceptable to the monks, but only one who had "hit bottom" and was ready to change his ways. This is expressed awkwardly, for why does one have to learn humility (v. 19) if one has already reached it (v. 18)?

4.20. This verse sounds like another ending, and in fact some manuscripts have the following: "Thus ends the Rule of the Holy Fathers Serapion, Macarius, Paphnutius and another Macarius." A literal translation is given in *EMR*: "Let these things suffice for what ought to be followed by you, fitting for what needs to be kept, and you will be blameless

(1 Tim 5:7)." Rather than stay with something so clumsy and ungrammatical, I attempted a coherent English sentence.

5. Appendix

Jean Neufville, who did the first critical edition (n. 3 above), believed this appendix was by a different author than the first four chapters. He based his opinion on the fact that this chapter, on penalties, is addressed to several superiors: *vobis, qui huic officio praesto estis* (5.11), whereas chapters 1–4 are addressed to only one: *is qui praeest*. Vogüé (*Les Règles*, 1, 106–62), however, thinks that as numbers at Lérins grew, authority was delegated to more officials, at least for correction. He also denies any real difference in vocabulary between chapters 1–4 and 5. In short, Vogüé thinks the author of 1–4 (probably Honoratus) also added chapter 5, and that it was done before 426–27, the putative date of The Second Rule of the Fathers.

5.1. "excommunication" (*excommunicatio*). This is not an ecclesial prohibition from the Eucharist, but in-house punishment for lesser faults. Vogüé, *Les Règles*, 1, 203, n. 5.1, claims that the practice does not appear in any earlier monastic Rule. Yet R4P seems to take it for granted. When we recall that there was hardly any earlier cenobitic life in Gaul, R4P looks all the more innovative.

"corresponds to the nature of the fault" (*pro qualitate culpae erit*). *EMR* and Desprez have the "gravity of the fault," but Vogüé is more accurate with "the nature of the fault." He points to the following texts as corroboration: 2RP 28; Caesarius RVirg 13; RM 12.4; RB 24.1. None of these actually stipulates that the punishment ought to match the *nature* of the fault, but R4P 5.2-3 attempts to do that. Although St. Benedict rarely fits punishment to fault, RB 43.19 is a case in which he does: if the brother is offered some special food but refuses it, let it be refused him when he decides he wants it!

5.3. "subject to the council" (*reus sit concilii*). In Matthew 5:22 one is "subject to the Sanhedrin" for calling someone a "fool." Here, though, the offense seems much less—unless *sermonem otiosum* means more than idle chatter. Honoratus himself is reported to have especially disliked *sermo otiosus* (Faustus of Riez, *Hom.* 72.10).

5.4. "laughing or telling off-color jokes" (*in risu vel scurrilitate*). Probably laughing *at* off-color jokes is the point. Benedict is also hard on those who engage in rough talk: RB 4.54; 6.8; 7.59, 60; 43.2; 49.7. Although *scurrilitas* does not have to be obscene, the author quotes Ephesians 5:4, which is a comment on obscenity among Christians, in the next verse: "out of place."

5.6. "every sort of humiliating punishment" (*omni flagello humilitatis*), literally "every whip of humility." Here there is no talk of excommunication, but rather of humiliation, which usually implies an audience. Perhaps the punishment is fitted to the crime, for scurrility breaks the taboo barrier of shame; hence it is only fitting that such a one be shamed in return.

"in the name of the Lord" (*in nomine Domini*). If this is a citation of 1 Corinthians 5:4, is it a coincidence that that text is also aimed at sexual impropriety among Christians?

5.7. "called brother among you" (*frater nominatur inter vos*). All the other translators connect "called" with the adjectives "wrathful, proud, or slanderous," but the Revised NAB for 1 Corinthians 5:11 connects it with "brother." The point then is: if he is called "brother," treat him as a brother—with fraternal correction.

5.8. The Latin text given by Vogüé for this verse makes no sense, and he calls it "uncertain." *EMR* gives a better text, based on the Vulgate 1 Thessalonians 3:15, but then gives us the howler: "do not consider him as a brother."

5.9. "is caught in a fault" (*fuerit praeventus in aliquo delicto*). The term *praeventus* can either mean to be literally discovered or to be overtaken by surprise. In the latter case the person is surprised by his own fall.

5.10. "Thus each one should act" (*sic debet unusquisque*). Desprez, *Règles monastiques*, 107, n. 10, thinks this verse teaches that everybody in the community should participate in fraternal correction, as is taught by RAug 4.6-10. Perhaps the rest of the verse means this: If one is tempered by regular, measured correction, one is equipped for a lifetime in community.

5.11. "you who occupy this office" (*qui huic officio praesto estis*). The material on corrections is addressed to several superiors, no doubt subordinate. The odd phrase *praesto estis* seems to be an attempt to pluralize *is qui praeest*. The *Oxford Latin Dictionary* lists *praesto* as an adjective meaning "ready," but here the meaning is clearly "occupy." The person is in the office, not just "fit for it," as Desprez has it (*Règles monastiques*, 107). See RM 2.16-19; RB 34.2.

5.12. "equal affection" (*aequali affectu*). Vogüé has an interesting variation on this verse: "Use equally affection toward all when they need love, and correction when they need a cure." (My rendition of his French.) This enables him to avoid the idea of "equal affection," which is humanly impossible. R4P 2.7-9 repeats the same dubious idea. One can try to *treat* everyone the same, but one cannot *feel* the same about everyone. Perhaps "equal charity" would be a better expression. One of the most significant changes made by Benedict in the Rule of the Master occurs in chapter 2 on the abbot, where he insists that different persons need to be treated differently by the abbot (2.23-29).

5.13. The Latin has a conditional clause for Psalm 58:2, but to judge from the RSV, the Hebrew original does not; it simply twice accuses the judges of favoritism in Hebrew parallelism.

5.15. The duty of correction is made clear by RBas 17 and RAug 4.8.

5.16. "cultivators" (*cultores*). Perhaps this was a traditional Lérinian term for spiritual leadership, for it appears in *VHon* 18.5; Faustus of Riez, *Hom.* 51.9; and Caesarius, *Serm.* 1.4. The *EMR* translation "caretakers" is less dynamic than the image of promoting growth in plants. Correction can be painful, but so can pruning. Manuscript P reads *doctores* (teachers) for *cultores*.

5.18. "as you gain" (*fueritis lucrati*) is taken from Matthew 18:15, where it refers to mutual correction. Yet the point is not whether the other *accepts* the correction; the dutiful corrector will be rewarded (by God) in any event.

Chapter
Eleven

The Second Rule of the Fathers

Introduction

The Second Rule of the Fathers is another one of the Little French Rules that have been known since the ninth-century appearance of Benedict of Aniane's *Codex Regularum* (PL 103.442–43). Following, as I do in my study of the Rule of the Four Fathers, the theory of Adalbert de Vogüé, I assume here that this little Rule was written for the monastery of Lérins on the island of St. Honorat about the year 428.[1]

At that time, a couple of decades after the founding of the monastery by St. Honoratus, the latter was appointed archbishop of Arles. Apparently his successor, Maximus, and probably some other church officials including Honoratus and the local bishops, felt it was time to update the original Rule, that is, the Rule of the Four Fathers. The result is a short but substantial document that is worth our scrutiny.[2]

---

1. Vogüé, along with his confrère, Jean Neufville, presents The Second Rule of the Fathers in *Les Règles des saints Pères*, SC 297, 298 (Paris: Cerf, 1982), 1, 209–83; see also Jean Neufville, "Règle des IV Pères et Seconde Règle des Pères: texte critique," *Revue Bénédictine* 77 (1967): 47–106. My article on R4P was found in *ABR* 54 (June 2003): 142–80. As in my work on R4P, the present chapter, which appeared in *ABR* 57 (September 2006): 235–48, is heavily dependent on Vogüé's work.

2. 2RP runs to just three pages (46 verses) in a modern English version such as *Early Monastic Rules*, trans. Carmela Vircillo Franklin, Ivan Havener, and J. Alcuin Francis (Collegeville, MN: Liturgical Press, 1982).

Since 2RP is quoted by two of the Little French Rules that appeared toward the end of the fifth century and beginning of the sixth, it must be earlier in the fifth century.[3] It is also quoted by the Gallic writer Gennadius of Marseilles about 480[4]; he ascribes it to a deacon named Vigilius. This man was probably the secretary of a synod of church officials of the same type as wrote the original Rule of the community. 2RP always follows R4P in the manuscript.

As concerns the content of 2RP, the main emphasis seems to be on horizontal relations between the members rather than the importance of the superior. Since the occasion of the departure of the founder was and is a momentous occasion for any community, it is not surprising that this supplementary document attempts to lay down a broader foundation of authority. The Rule itself, and not the superior, is now the focus.[5]

Apart from its stress on fraternal love, 2RP suggests that two aspects of life at Lérins had become problematic and needed adjustment. First, it seems that the Divine Office had become a burden due to its length. Second, the cells of the hermits, which had been abolished by Honoratus in his effort to strengthen cenobitic life, now reappear. Vogüé thinks that Honoratus himself probably had done this shortly before he left for Arles. Apparently once cenobitism was solidly established it was felt that hermitages would be no threat.

The Second Rule of the Fathers

[Preface] 1. While we were sitting in discussion in the name of our Lord Jesus Christ according to the tradition of the Fathers, those holy men, 2. it seemed good to us to compose and set out a Rule to be followed in the monastery for the progress of the brothers. 3. We did this lest we be troubled, and the holy superior whom we have installed in this place suffer any doubt. 4. And we did it so that "they all might be united in mind," as it is written, "and of one heart, honoring one another" (Acts

---

3. 2RP is quoted by the Rule of Macarius (ca. 500 AD) and the Oriental Rule (RO) in the early sixth century.

4. *De Viris Illustribus* 51. Gennadius calls the document *Regula Monachorum* and quotes 2RP 1–2.

5. This process has been labeled the "routinization of charisma" by Max Weber, *The Theory of Social and Economic Organization* (part 1 of *Wirtschaft und Gesellschaft*, 1922), trans. A. M. Henderson and Talcott Parsons (New York: Oxford University Press, 1947).

4:32), and so they would guard those things decreed by the Lord with - a faithful observance.

[I] 5. Before all, let them have charity, humility, patience, gentleness, and the other things the Apostle teaches, 6. with the result that no one calls anything his own, as it is written in the Acts of the Apostles: "Let them hold all things in common" (Acts 4:32). 7. As for this man who is superior because of God's judgment and episcopal installation, you must fear, love, and obey him in all things. 8. For if anyone thinks he is rejecting him, he is really rejecting God, 9. as it is written: "The person who hears you, hears me, and the person who rejects me, rejects the one who sent me" (Luke 10:16). 10. Therefore, let no brother do anything without his permission, nor accept or give anything, nor ever separate himself at all without a verbal order.

[II] 11. Make sure also that you do not ruin one another by useless gossip; each one should see to his own work and *lectio divina*, and keep his thoughts focused on God. 12. At public meetings, no junior monk should speak unless he is asked. 13. On the other hand, if anyone needs encouragement or wishes to have a private conversation, he should look for a suitable time.

III. 14. When pilgrims arrive, give them no more than a humble and peaceful greeting. 15. Beyond that, do not inquire where they came from, why they came, or when they will be leaving. 16. And do not swap stories with them.

[IV] 17. This too shall be observed: If any senior is present, or some-one who has precedence in the order of psalmody, a junior has no leave to speak or presume anything. 18. This is reserved, as we said, to one who has precedence in the order. 19. This must be followed down to the last brother, especially in prayer, in work or in giving an answer. 20. But if the senior is a bit simple or less skilled in speaking, and therefore steps aside, only then may the junior speak. 21. Yet all things should be done in love, not with quarreling and aggression.

[V] 22. You shall keep the order of the prayers and psalms already long established, and that also goes for the schedule of *lectio* and work. 23. So the brothers should do their *lectio* up to the third hour 24. unless there is some necessary common work that preempts *lectio*. 25. After the third hour, each one should be ready to work till the ninth. 26. Let them do what they are ordered "without murmuring or reluctance" (Phil 2:14), as the Apostle teaches.

27. If anyone murmurs or is quarrelsome or takes a contrary stand against official orders, 28. after being duly admonished, at the discretion of the superior he should be excommunicated as long as the gravity of

the fault demands and until he humbles himself through penance and changes for the better. 29. When he is admonished, he is not to withdraw in any way. 30. If any brother, whether in the monastery or in the outlying cells, joins his erroneous cause, he should be considered very worthy of excommunication.

[VI] 31. When the signal has been given for the hour for the Office, if someone is not ready to put aside at once whatever he is doing—for nothing may be put ahead of the Office—he should be kept outside so as to embarrass him. 32. If it is necessary to stand for a long time at the Divine Office, whether during the day or night, each brother will be sure not to give up or to go outside without a good reason. 33. For it is written: "We must pray always and not give up" (Luke 18:1), and in another place: "Do not let anything stop you from praying" (Sir 18:22). 35. If anyone gets the idea to go out, not out of necessity but for some vice, let him know he will be judged guilty when he is found out. 36. For he leads others into wrong by his negligence. 37. When they all come together for Vigils, if someone is weighed down with sleep and goes outside, he should not engage in gossip. 38. He should return to the work for which they have gathered. 39. When there is reading in the Liturgy, they should always listen to the Scriptures, and everyone should keep silence.

[VII] 40. This must be added: If a brother is confronted and scolded for some fault, he should be patient and not argue back at his accuser. But let him be humble in all regards, 41. according to the Lord's precept that says: "God resists the proud but favors the humble" (1 Pet 5:5) 42. and "Whoever humbles himself will be exalted" (Luke 14:11). 43. If someone will not change even after frequent correction, he should stand last in the ranks. 44. But if he will not change even then, he should be considered as a stranger. 45. For the Lord said: "He should be like a Gentile or a tax-collector to you" (18:17).

46. Especially at meals no one should speak, except the superior or someone who is asked to do so.

Commentary

Title: Literally *Incipit Statuta Patrum* ("Here begin the rules of the Fathers"). Adalbert de Vogüé, *Les Règles des Saints Pères I–II*, SC 297–298 (Paris: Cerf, 1982), 259–60, thinks this title was added by a later hand, so the paraphrase "Second Rule of the Fathers" is justified. It is a helpful label because (1) it distinguishes the document from its predecessor, The Rule of the Four Fathers, and (2) it describes the position of this Rule in the series of Little French Rules.

Preface: This subtitle, and the Roman numerals that follow, are found in the edition of 2RP in Benedict of Aniane's *Codex Regularum* as printed in Migne, PL 103.441–44. The versification is from the critical edition of Jean Neufville, *Les Règles* (SC 297), 209–83.

1. "While we were sitting in discussion." This beginning is almost identical with the beginning of R4P, except that the participle is now re*sidentibus*. This is due not to any lack of imagination of the author, but to his desire to associate his Rule with that earlier document. Vogüé, *Les Règles* 2, 213–14, thinks 2RP was written in 428 on the occasion of the installation of the second abbot of Lérins, Maximus.

"in the name of our Lord Jesus Christ." In R4P the authors beg the Lord to send the Holy Spirit to assist them, but here they do not, nor do they formally invoke Scripture ("precepts of the Holy Spirit": R4P 1.7), which makes them seem more self-assured in 2RP. Vogüé, *Les Règles*, 2, 212–13.

2. "compose and set out." *Conscribere vel ordinare* are more or less synonymous. If *ordinare* had not appeared in R4P 1.3, it might look as if 2RP was trying to better organize the earlier Rule. Instead, it means to update and modify it.

"progress of the brothers." Whereas R4P was largely concerned with establishing the very necessity of having a superior, 2RP takes this for granted. The latter Rule will be much devoted to strengthening fraternal relations.

3. "the holy superior we have installed." The use of *praepositus* (not *abbas*) for the superior suggests that this document was written before 450. The superior is probably Maximus of Riez, who ruled Lérins in 428–434. The installers were no doubt the local ordinary, the bishop of Fréjus, plus other bishops or abbots (see RB 64.3-6). They seem to assume that this installation is their duty. The willingness of the bishops of Fréjus to intervene in monastic affairs intensified in the period 449–461. Finally, Abbot Faustus appealed to a provincial council at Arles and was vindicated. Vogüé, *Les Règles*, 1, 213–15.

"united in mind . . . and of one heart, honoring one another." Serapion also urged the monks to unite (*unanimes*) in R4P 1.6, 8-9, 15, but he quoted Psalm 67:7. Here the biblical sources are Philippians 2:2

and Romans 12:10. The same sequence is found in Augustine, *Praec.* 1.8, a Rule that stresses mutual obedience more than that owed to the superior.

5. *Ordo Monasterii* (*OM*) 1 (school of Augustine, ca. 400) begins similarly: "Dear Brothers, you should especially love (*diligatur*) God and then your neighbor." This African monastic document forms a kind of liturgical code with the Rule of Augustine (*Praec.*), which also begins with mutual charity.

"humility, patience, gentleness." These Pauline (1 Tim 6:11 and Eph 4:2) virtues might seem to dilute the focus on love, but they probably are meant to reinforce it. This is suggested by the result clause (v. 6) that implements the love ethic with shared goods. Vogüé, *Les Règles*, 1, 217.

6. "no one calls anything his own." Almost verbatim with *OM* 4.

"they hold all things in common." Augustine, *Praec.* 1.3, cites the same text from Acts 2:44 with slightly different words. The combination of (1) disappropriation, (2) sharing of goods, (3) love, and (4) unanimity give 2RP a strongly Augustinian flavor.

Compared to R4P, 2RP centers on charity, not obedience, and when R4P *does* mention divestment of personal property (2.29-31 and 4.11-12), it is to promote asceticism, not mutual love. Vogüé, *Les Règles*, 1, 218–19.

7. In treating the superior early in the document, 2RP follows R4P and not Augustine. Obedience comes up already in R4P 1.10-17, but only at the end of Augustine's Rule (*Praec.* 7.1-4, 8-9).

"fear, love, and obey" is perhaps a reference to Jerome's *Letter* 125.15 to Rusticus. Jerome says R. should "fear the superior like a lord, but love him like a parent," a saying that is quoted verbatim in RMac 7.1. The latter is another Rule from Lérins, probably written about 500.

"God's judgment and episcopal installation." Probably the brothers elected him and the local ordinary (bishop) ratified the proceedings (Vogüé, *Les Règles*, 1, 220). "Episcopal installation" is a free rendering of *ordinatione sacerdotali*; it can hardly mean that the superior was ordained a priest. *Sacerdotali* refers to the local bishop, and *ordinatione* must mean the blessing/installation of the new superior. See Vogüé, *Community and Abbot in the Rule of Saint Benedict* (Kalamazoo: Cistercian Publications, 1979), 1, 7. Although 2RP does not subordinate the religious superior to a priest as does Augustine in *Praec.* 4.9,11; 7.1-2, it clearly gives the local bishop a good deal of oversight.

8. "rejecting God." While the verse wishes to bolster the authority of the monastic superior, Luke 10:16 originally referred to the apostles. Coming just after the demand for episcopal sanction, this weighty biblical injunction tends to give the monastic superior a quasi-episcopal authority.

9. "rejects the one who sent me." In Luke 10:16, Jesus establishes a clear chain of authority: to obey him is to obey God, and vice versa. 2RP applies this without hesitation to monastic authority, replacing Jesus with the superior. Although R4P 1.13-17 uses five biblical *testimonia* to make the same point, none of them does so as forcefully as this text. Vogüé, *Les Règles*, 1, 222.

10. "do anything without his permission." 2RP does not spend a lot of time on authority, but it is by no means wishy-washy on the subject. This verse gives the superior total control of every aspect of community life.

"nor accept or give anything." The words follow up on the theme of personal dispossession and community of goods discussed in vv. 5-6.

"separate himself at all." Although all the modern translations (Vogüé, Desprez, and *EMR*) give a more general sense of "go anywhere" to *recedat*, in 2RP 2.29 it refers to a withdrawal from some aspect of common life after suffering correction.

11. "Make sure also that." The participle *observantes* is used here with imperative force. The subject is probably the brothers, since they and not the superior are addressed in what precedes and what follows.

"work and *lectio divina*." These activities are not to be disrupted by useless conversations. *Meditem* (accusative) is an unusual word, probably based on Greek *meletē*. *Meditem habere* occurs again in 2RP 23. The translation "study" as used here is not adequate, but neither is "meditation" (Desprez, *EMR*). What the author has in mind is *lectio divina*, the ancient practice of committing biblical texts to memory for later rumination. The practice of constant rumination of biblical texts throughout the day is seen in Pachomius, *Prec.* 59–60, and Cassian, *Inst.* 15, 1.

12. "speak unless he is asked." This prohibition is also found in R4P 2.40-42; 4.13. The idea of not speaking until asked is not found elsewhere in primitive cenobitism. It is, however, found in the *Apophthegmata* (*VP* 5.10, 58 and 7.32, 3), and especially in the *Rule of the Master* (9.42, etc.). Vogüé, *Les Règles*, 1, 224. Although this ruling reflects the hierarchical bent of 2RP, the equally hierarchical Rule of Benedict (3.3) insists that the opinion of junior monks be not merely tolerated but solicited.

14-16. "no more than a humble and peaceful greeting." Obviously guests need a lot more than a kiss of peace. As R4P 2.36-42 makes clear, the visitor is cared for largely by an appointed guest director and the superior. This passage, however, is addressed strictly to the rest of the monks, who are not to mix freely with guests. As in RB 53.23-24, they are warned not to pester guests. Someone in authority may have to ask the guest certain questions. These verses show that unless 2RP is seen as a complement to R4P it could be misinterpreted. The point is obviously not to snub guests, but to spare them inconvenience or even scandal.

17. "any senior is present." *Senior* is an ambiguous word in ancient cenobitism. It can refer to chronological age or date of entry into the community (RB 63). Since the next phrase, "someone who has precedence in the order of psalmody," is equivalent to date of entry, I take *senior* here to be chronological.

"to speak or presume anything." As with the previous two sections (11-12; 14-16), these verses are specifically about proper speech. There is also a general prohibition against "presumption," which here refers to stepping out of one's proper place in the community order. "Speaking" (*loquendi*) in the psalmody probably refers to intonation or solo performance. But this section, unlike R4P 2.11-15, which is its analogue, refers to all speech in the cenobium. 2RP 12 forbids juniors to speak freely in community meetings; vv. 17-21 extend this restriction to all aspects of community life. Vogüé, *Les Règles*, 1, 227, points out that the emphasis on hierarchy is probably interpolated in R4P; without question, 2RP puts great stress on hierarchy.

"a junior." Literally *sequens*, "the one who follows." This seems to correlate with "the one who has precedence," but not the senior. For lack of an equivalent English term I have used "junior," which does not appear in the Latin at all.

19. "down to the last brother." *Ad imum*, "to the lowest," could also mean "to the least detail," as Vogüé has it.

21. "all things should be done in love, not with quarreling." The author sums up the major section 2RP 11-21 on a main theme, love. "Not with quarreling" (*non per contentionem*) is taken from Philippians 2:3, which also was cited in 2RP 4-5.

22. "the order of prayers and psalms already long established." No doubt the reference is to the arrangements of Honoratus twenty years earlier, although R4P does not legislate the details of the Divine Office. Sometimes *orationes* (prayers) alternate with psalms, but here it seems more general: prayers + psalms = Divine Office.

23. "*lectio* and work." *Meditandi operandique* could give the impression that *lectio* and work are done simultaneously, as may have been the case in v. 11 (Vogüé, *Les Règles*, 1, 230). But the next verse says clearly that the two things are to be kept separate. *Meditare* refers to reading and memorizing Scripture rather than the modern meaning of abstract cogitation.

"do their *lectio*." Literally "have their meditation" and "read," which are both descriptive and misleading.

"up to the third hour." Normally *lectio* would begin about the first hour (ca. 6 a.m.) and continue through the third hour complete (ca. 9 a.m.). This three-hour block was first claimed for *lectio* by R4P 3.11-12 (see Michaela Puzicha, *Kommentar zur Benediktusregel* [St. Ottilien: EOS Verlag, 2002], 404). Since this is "quality" time in most cultures it always is under pressure from work needs. Manuscript T of 2RP and RMac 10 reduce *lectio* to two hours.

24. "necessary common work." Vogüé, *Les Règles*, 1, 231, thinks this means the common good and that charity must trump private *lectio*. He feels the Lérinian monks may have been too attached to their *lectio*, but I would add that Benedict's monks found it quite difficult (RB 48.17-21).

25. "ready to work." This could be an oblique reference to the restriction on manual labor at the only earlier Gallic monastery, that of St.

Martin at Marmoutier. That the Lérins monks were sometimes reluctant to leave their cells and their *lectio* for work is obvious from the verses that follow. Vogüé, *Les Règles*, 1, 232, suggests that the root cause for too little time for work *or lectio* in Gaul was the excessive number of psalms in the Office. See Cassian, *Inst.* 3.3,1.

27. "If anyone murmurs or is quarrelsome." Compared to R4P, 2RP represents a more developed approach to community sanctions. Whereas R4P relegates discussion of punishment to an appendix, and applies it only to loose talk and ribaldry, 2RP places it in the main body of the Rule and applies it to all kinds of contrariness.

"takes a contrary stand against." Literally "opposing a contrary will to." The root monastic fault here is self-will and not any particular overt act. The same holds true for RB 23, the introduction to Benedict's penal code.

Vogüé, *Les Règles*, 1, 234, cites many Pachomian texts as possible sources of 2RP 27-30: *Iud.* 6: "If anyone is disobedient or quarrelsome or a contradictor or a liar"; *Inst.* 9-10 and *Iud.* 13 and 16: gravity of fault; *Inst.* 4-5: humble penance and amendment.

28. "excommunicated." Literally, "set apart" (*abstineatur*), but it is clear from v. 30 that this means excommunication. Of course this is not ecclesiastical excommunication from the Holy Eucharist, but internal monastic separation from the community. The person is not expelled but is barred from common table and liturgy.

29. "he is not to withdraw in any way." Withdrawal (*recedere*) occurs in a more general context in 2RP 10. It seems to indicate physical retreat and not just pouting. Since Lérins is a small island one could not "withdraw" very far from the monastery, but there were cells, as is noted in the next verse. Apparently there were hermits on Lérins in 427–428; the community began twenty years earlier as a grouping of hermits.

30. "or in the outlying cells." Contrary to R4P 1.2-8, which bans life in "remote" cells, this lifestyle is again permitted. In 428 Eucher, *De Laude* 42, also noted that "there are old men who have, with their separate cells, introduced the Fathers of Egypt" to Lérins. Vogüé, *Les Règles*, 1, 236.

"joins his erroneous cause." It is not too hard to imagine cenobites who have been rebuked by the abbot fleeing to the hermits for solace. Vogüé once came across this very situation in an obscure ancient manuscript: "L'anecdote pachômienne du *Vaticanus graecus* 2091. Son origine et ses sources," *Revue d'Histoire de Spiritualité* 49 (1973) 401–19.

31. "ready to put aside at once." While other early monastic legislators such as Pachomius (*Praec.* 9–10) and Cassian (*Inst.* 3.7, 1-2) allow late-comers to the Office a certain amount of leeway before they are punished, 2RP makes no exceptions. This could be because the emphasis here is on instant, spontaneous response rather than on fanatical devotion to promptitude. RB 43, which much resembles 2RP, includes both alacrity (43.1) and merciful concessions (RB 43.4, 10). For my interpretation of RB 43 as promoting responsiveness more than promptness see my *Benedict's Rule: A Translation and Commentary* (Collegeville, MN: Liturgical Press, 1996), 372–73.

"kept outside." Is this excommunication or merely locking the door (*foris excludatur*) as they do in theaters during the acts? Vogüé, *Les Règles*, 1, 237, notes that the author remains rather vague on this point, as if he had little experience or previous teaching to guide him.

"so as to embarrass him." RB 43.4-9 uses the same motive to argue *against* excluding latecomers. Benedict has them sit on a special "sinners' bench" as a cautionary lesson for both others and themselves.

"for nothing may be put ahead of the Office." Similar sentiments, without sanctions, are found in Pachomius, *Praec.* 3 and Cassian, *Inst.* 4.12, but the ultimate source of the formulation may be located in much earlier documents: Cyprian, *Or Dom* 15, and Athanasius, *V Ant* 13, who say that nothing is to be preferred to *Christ*.

"hour of the Office." The general term "prayer" (*oratio*) is used here to designate the Divine Office. The reason for this may lie in the author's wish to base some of his regulations on biblical texts that only refer to prayer in general, as is seen in v. 33 with Luke 18:1 and Sirach 18:22. But 2RP uses other generic terms for the Office as well: in v. 32 it refers to *missae*; v. 38 speaks of the *opus*; v. 39 talks of the *congregatio*, which admittedly could refer to any gathering of the community.

32. "stand for a long time." *Stare* can mean either to remain or to stand erect. Since the ancient monks probably stood for all or most of the liturgy, this translation may be a bit misleading. The problem here is

duration, not posture. We know from various sources that the Gallic Office tended to be long—longer than Cassian thought it should be (*Inst.* 2.2-6). Caesarius had to urge the nuns at Arles not to flag during the long night vigils (RVirg 15).

"be sure not to give up." *EMR* and Desprez address this verse to the superiors, telling them to keep an eye on the brothers, but the grammar makes the brothers alone the subject. "Not to give up" is my rendition of *non deficient*. Vogüé has "not get discouraged" and Desprez has "not grow weak." *Deficere* will recur in the next verse. It looks to me as if the author may have converted a general Scripture saying, "Pray and don't give up" into a practical maxim for the Office: "Don't stop singing!"

35. "get the idea to go out." Since this whole section is about the Office, apparently this is simply an injunction against monks leaving the liturgy without good reason. The reference to "necessity" seems to follow up on *superfluo* ("without necessity") in v. 32.

"but rather for vice." Although the reader is a bit taken aback by the term "vice," this may be too strong a translation for *vitium*. According to the Oxford Latin Dictionary most of the meanings given for that word are considerably milder than our "vice." Vogüé has the innocuous "by his own fault" and Desprez has "for mischief" (*par malice*). Still, it is not unheard of for monks to get themselves in big trouble when they should be participating in the Divine Office.

37. "goes outside." Presumably to walk around to wake up. Vogüé, *Les Règles*, 1, 238, points to the *Vita Patrum Jurensium* 130, a Gallic monastic document of the fifth century, which praises St. Oyend (Eugene) for never leaving the Divine Office.

"engage in gossip." RB 43.8 says the same.

39. "and everyone should keep silence." This chattering during the readings of the Office resembles the gossip (*fabulis*) condemned in v. 37. For some reason Mediterraneans find it hard to keep quiet in church.

40. "This must be added." This is not a casual expression. but the introduction to a supplement and adjustment to the main body of 2RP. Vogüé, *Les Règles*, 1, 240–41, thinks that vv. 40-45 were added later to bolster vv. 27-30, which is also a "penal code" of sorts. But whereas vv. 27-30

are addressed to a specific fault (murmuring about work assignments) to which a single penalty (in-house excommunication) is applied, vv. 40-45 provide a graduated approach to all faults. That is probably why it is quoted by Caesarius, RVirg 13, RTarn 5.2, and RMac 16–17.

Vogüé feels that 40-45 are an obvious interpolation since both the verses that precede and follow it pertain to silence. In addition, 2RP introduces biblical quotations with "says," whereas the main body of 2RP does so with "writes."

If 2RP is considered as teaching systematic principles for community discipline, it is not the first or the last Christian document to do so. Matthew 18 sets a precedent by arranging three levels of confrontation: (1) privately by an individual, (2) semiprivately by a small committee, (3) publicly by the whole community. St. Benedict repeats this in modified form in his penal code (RB 23–30), and he also provides three gradations of punishment: (1) exclusion from common table for minor faults, (2) exclusion from both common table and liturgy for major faults, (3) expulsion from the community for the incorrigible. For its part, 2RP 40-45 addresses three possible responses to correction: (1) patient acceptance and conversion, (2) amendment after punishment, (3) refusal to amend.

"be patient and not argue back at his accuser." One is not forbidden to defend herself from unjust reproofs, but she should first listen calmly and not lash back in a reflexive manner. The assumption in this verse is that one is in fact guilty as charged. There is no mention of the superior; this is a matter of mutual correction, an indispensable duty in a cenobitic monastery. That these were not abstract considerations at Lérins comes out clearly in a remark made by Faustus, who was abbot from 434 to 460. He speaks of a monk who bragged that he had spoken with authority when he was confronted by an accuser (*Hom* 38.6).

42. "Whoever humbles himself will be exalted." Besides serving fraternal relations well, humility was regarded as one of the primary monastic virtues. St. Benedict produced a major treatise on the subject (RB 7) and he headed it with this verse of Luke (14:11).

43. "If someone will not change, even after frequent correction." After presenting the ideal case in vv. 40-42, namely, the person who is corrigible and profits from correction, 2RP moves on to the harder case of someone who is impervious to words but needs to experience punishment to change his ways. Still, he *does* change.

"stand last in the ranks." R4P and 2RP 27-30 have nothing to match this, but Benedict (RB 2.19) allows the abbot to adjust the rank of the monks according to merit, and in RB 43.5, 7, 10 he instructs latecomers to the Divine Office to stand in the last place for the duration of the liturgy. The wording here is almost the same as in OM 10, but the African Rule gives no specific penalty.

44. "But if he will not change even then, he should be considered a stranger." We now come to the third and worst possibility, that is, the person who proves to be truly incorrigible. Even after he has been punished he returns to his wayward behavior. What is to be done with such a recidivist? "Consider him a stranger!" say the authors of 2RP. But what does *extraneus* mean exactly? Matthew 18:17 is quoted here: "Treat him as a Gentile and a tax-collector." But how did the first (Jewish) Christians actually treat those who had to be disciplined? They were not members of a closed community, so they could not exactly expel them. Nor would ostracization be quite so harsh as it would in a closed community.

The Gallic provincial council of Orleans (511; *Concilia Galliae*, CC 148) used *extraneus* to mean ecclesiastical excommunication. RO 38, from the early sixth century, certainly read 2RP 44 to mean expulsion: "let him be expelled from the monastery and considered as an outsider." Perhaps R4P 5.8 can help us here: "Do not consider him an enemy, but correct him as a brother." This makes it clear that fraternal correction is owed to a brother, but when someone persistently ignores correction he ceases to deserve it as a brother. Now he is a "Gentile and a tax-collector." The question still remains whether the Lérinian monks actually expelled members from the island. If they did not, how was it possible to not treat them as brothers, even for a short time?

46. Although it is not surprising for the Rule to end with such an important monastic subject, this is rather an abrupt, curt verse on silence at table. Vogüé says that the authors may have closed 2RP with this verse in order *not* to end it with the harsh subject of punishment.

R4P 2.42 also asks for silence at table, but there it is in the service of the reading of Scripture. This is done for the edification of guests. Here, however, there is no mention of table-reading, although we may assume it. Again, 2RP prefers to present a general principle: there should be silence during monastic meals. The superior or his designee may offer some words.

Sigla

After the acronym is given (1) the usual English title; (2) the place in the traditional collections [usually Migne, PL or PG]; (3) the critical edition if one
exists; (4) the English translation if one has been done.

2RP: Second Rule of the Fathers; PL 103.441; Jean Neufville, "Règle de IV Pères
et Seconde Règle des Pères: Texte critique," *RBén* 77 (1967): 47–106, esp.
92–95; "The Rule of the Four Fathers. The Second Rule of the Fathers,"
Monastic Studies (1976): 260–63.

3RP: Third Rule of the Fathers; PL 103.443; *Les Règles des saints Pères*, ed.
Adalbert de Vogüé (Paris: Cerf, 1982), 2, 532–43; *Early Monastic Rules (EMR)*,
trans. Carmela Franklin, Ivan Havener, and J. Alcuin Francis (Collegeville,
MN: Liturgical Press, 1982), 52–59.

Augustine, *Op Mon: The Work of Monks*; PL 40.547; *Sancti Aurelii Augustini
Opera*, sec. 7, ed. Michael Petschenig, CSEL 51 (Vienna: Gerold, 1908);
Augustine, *Treatises on Various Subjects*, FC 16 (New York: Fathers of the
Church, 1952).

Augustine, *Serm.*: *Sermons* of Augustine; PL 38.

Aurelian, RMon: Aurelian of Arles, Rule for Monks; PL 68.385.

Basil, LR: Long Rules; PG 31.889; no critical edition; *St. Basil, Ascetical Works*,
trans. Monica Wagner, FC 9 (New York: Fathers of the Church, 1950).

Basil, SR: Short Rules; PG 31.889; no critical edition; English trans. W. Lowther
Clarke, *The Ascetic Works of St. Basil* (London: S.P.C.K.; New York: Mac-
millan, 1925).

Caesarius, RVirg: Caesarius of Arles, Rule for Virgins; PL 67.1105; *Regula
sanctarum virginum*, ed. Germain Morin (Bonn: Hanstein, 1933); *The
Rule for Nuns of St. Caesarius of Arles*, trans. Maria Caritas McCarthy
(Washington, DC: Catholic University of America Press, 1960).

Caesarius, *Serm*: Caesarius of Arles, *Sermons*; PL 39 and 47; *S. Caesarii
Omnia Opera*, Part 1, ed. Germain Morin (Turnhout: Brepols, 1953); no
English.

Cassian, *Inst.*: John Cassian, *Institutes*; PL 49.53; CSEL 17; *John Cassian, The
Institutes*, trans. Boniface Ramsey, ACW 58 (New York: Newman Press,
2000).

EMR: Early Monastic Rules, trans. Carmela Franklin, Ivan Havener, and J. Alcuin
Francis (Collegeville, MN: Liturgical Press, 1982).

Eucher, *Laude*: Eucher of Lyons, *In Praise of the Desert* (Lérins); PL 50.70; *S.
Eucherii Lugdunensis Opera omnia. 1, Formulae spiritalis intellegentiae
[u.a.]*, CSEL 31 (Prague: Tempsky, 1894).

Faustus, *Hom.*: Faustus of Riez, *Homilies*; PL 58.783; *Fausti Reiensis Praeter
sermones pseudo-eusebianos opera: Accedunt Ruricii Epistulae*, CSEL 21
(Vienna et al.: F. Tempsky, G. Freytag, 1891); no English.

Gregory, *Dial.*: *The Dialogues of St. Gregory*; PL 77.149; Umberto Moricca,
Gregorii Magni Dialogi Libri IV (Rome: Tip. del Senato, 1924); *Dialogues of*

St. Gregory the Great, ed. Odo John Zimmerman, FC 39 (New York: Fathers of the Church, 1959).

Hist Mon: *The History of the Monks in Egypt*; PL 21.387; *Historia monachorum in Aegypto*, ed. André Jean Festugière (Brussels: Société des Bollandistes, 1961); *Lives of the Desert Fathers*, trans. Norman Russell (Kalamazoo: Cistercian Publications, 1981).

Jerome, *Ep.*: *Letters of Jerome*; PL 22.325; *Sancti Eusebii Hieronymi Epistulae, LXXI–CXX*, ed. Isidorus Hilberg, CSEL 55 (Vienna et al.: Tempsky et al., 1912).

Liber Hors: *Testament of Horsiesi*; PL 103.453–76; Amand Boon, *Pachomiana Latina* (Louvain: Bureaux de la Revue, 1932), 109–47; Armand Veilleux, *Pachomian Koinonia* 3 (Kalamazoo: Cistercian Publications, 1982).

OM: Ordo Monasterii (probably by Alypius, one of Augustine's friends); PL 32.1449; Luc Verheijen, *La Règle de Saint Augustin* (Paris: Études Augustiennes, 1967), 1, 148–52; George Lawless, *Augustine of Hippo and His Monastic Rule* (Oxford: Clarendon Press, 1987), 74–79.

Pachomius, *Sbo*: *The Life of Pachomius*, Sahidic and Bohairic Version; Armand Veilleux, *Pachomian Koinonia* 1 (Kalamazoo: Cistercian Publications, 1982).

Palladius, *Hist Laus*: *Lausiac History*; PG 34.995; Cuthbert Butler, *The Lausiac History of Palladius* (Cambridge: The University Press, 1898–1904); *Palladius: The Lausiac History*, ed. Robert T. Meyer, ACW 34 (Westminster, MD: Newman Press, 1965).

Pelagius, *Ep ad Dem*: Pelagius, *Letter to Demetriades*; PL 30.15-45.

RAug: Augustine, *Praeceptum* (monastic Rule for men); PL 32.1377–84; Luc Verheijen, *La Règle de Saint Augustin* (Paris: Études Augustiennes, 1967); George Lawless, *Augustine of Hippo and His Monastic Rule* (Oxford: Clarendon Press, 1987), 80–103.

RBas: St. Basil, The Latin Rule; PL 103.485–554; Klaus Zelzer, *Basili Regula a Rufino latine versa*, CSEL 86 (Vienna: Hoelder-Pichler-Tempsky, 1986); no English translation.

RMac: The Rule of Macarius; PL 103.447–52; Adalbert de Vogüé, *Les Règles des saints Pères* (Paris: Cerf, 1982), 1, 372–88; *Early Monastic Rules* (Collegeville, MN: Liturgical Press, 1982).

ROr: The Oriental Rule; PL 50.373–80; Adalbert de Vogüé, *Les Règles des saints Pères* (Paris: Cerf, 1982), 2, 462–95; *Early Monastic Rules* (Collegeville, MN: Liturgical Press, 1982).

RPach Pr.: The Rule of Pachomius Precepta; PL 23.65; no critical edition; Armand Veilleux, *Pachomian Koinonia* 2 (Kalamazoo: Cistercian Publications, 1982).

R Paul St: The Rule of Paul and Stephen; PL 66.949-58; *Regula Pauli et Stephani*, ed. J. Evangelista M. Vilanova (Montserrat: Abadia de Montserrat, 1959); no English.

RTarn: The Rule of Tarn; PL 66.977–86; F. Villegas, "La *Regula monasterii Tarnantensis*. Texte, sources et datation," *RBén* 84 (1974) 7.65; A. W. Godfrey, "The Rule of Tarn," *Monastic Studies* 17 (1986): 219–40.

R4P: The Rule of Four Fathers; PL 103.435–42; Adalbert de Vogüé, *Les Règles des IV Pères et Seconde Règle des Pères* (Paris: Cerf, 1982), 1, 180–205; "The Rule of the Four Fathers. The Second Rule of the Fathers," *Monastic Studies* 12 (1976): 249–59.

RF: The Rule of Ferriolus; PL 66.959–76; Vincent Desprez, "La *Regula Ferrioli. Texte critique*," *Revue Mabillon* 60 (1982), 117–48; no English.

Salvian, *Gub.*; Salvian of Marseilles, *De Gubernatione Dei*; PL 53.25–238; critical text in *Salviani Presbyteri Massilinensis Opera omnia*, trans. Franciscus Pauly, CSEL 8 (Vienna: C. Geroldi, 1883); English, *On the Government of God*, trans. Eva Matthews Sandford (New York: Columbia University Press, 1930).

VHil: *The Life of Hilary of Arles* by Reverentius; PL 1.1213–79; critical text in *Vita Sanctorum Honorati et Hilarii, episcoporum Arelatensium*, ed. Samuel Cavallin (Lund: Gleerup, 1952); no English.

VHon: *The Life of Honoratus* by Hilary of Arles; PL 1.1249–72; critical text in *Vita Sanctorum Honorati et Hilarii, episcoporum Arelatensium*, ed. Samuel Cavallin (Lund: Gleerup, 1952); English in *The Western Fathers*, trans. Frederick R. Hoare (New York: Sheed and Ward, 1954), 247–82.

VPJ: *Vie des pères du Jura*, critical ed. by François Martin, SC 142 (Paris: Cerf, 1968); *The Life of the Jura Fathers*, trans. Jeffrey Burton Russell, Kim Vivian, and Tim Vivian (Kalamazoo: Cistercian Publications, 1999).

Select Bibliography

Basil of Caesarea

Primary Sources

Basil. *The Asketikon of Saint Basil the Great* [Long and Short Rules]. Translated by Anna M. Silvas. Oxford: Oxford University Press, 2005. PG 31.889ff.

————. *Letters*. 2 vols. Translated by Agnes Clare Way. FC 13, 28. New York: Fathers of the Church, 1951–1955. PG 32.220ff.

————. *Moralia*. In Basil, *Ascetical Works*. Translated by M. Monica Wagner. FC 9. New York: Fathers of the Church, 1950.

Gregory of Nazianz. *Funeral Orations*. Translated by Leo P. McCauley. FC 22. New York: Fathers of the Church, 1953. PG 35–36.

Gregory of Nyssa. *De Anima et Resurrectione*. Translated by Anna M. Silvas in *Macrina the Younger, Philosopher of God*. Turnhout: Brepols, 2007. PG 44–46.

————. *Life of Saint Macrina*. Translated by Kevin Corrigan. Toronto: Peregrina, 1997. PG 44–46.

Secondary Sources

Amand de Mendieta, Emmanuel. *L'Ascèse monastique de saint Basile*. (Maredsous: Éditions de Maredsous, 1948).

Bamberger, John Eudes. "MNEME-DIATHESIS: The Psychic Dynamisms in the Ascetical Theology of St. Basil," *Orientalia Christiana Periodica* 34 (1968): 233–51.

Baudry, Étienne. "A propos du rigorisme de saint Basile: gravité du péché, libération du pécheur," *Studia Anselmiana* 70 (1977): 139–73.

————. "Il 'Radicalismo Evangelico' e la Questione del 'Rigorismo' de Basilio il Grande," in *Basilio tra Oriente e Occidente: convegno internazionale "Basilio il Grande e il monachesimo orientale,"* Cappadocia, 5–7 ottobre

1999. Edited by Étienne Baudry, 67–91. Magnano: Qiqajon/Community of Bose, 2001.

Clarke, W. Lowther. *St. Basil the Great, a Study in Monasticism*. Cambridge: Cambridge University Press, 1913.

Cremaschi, Lisa. *Le Regole. Regulae fusius tractate. Regulae brevius tractate*. [Magnano]: Qiqajon/Community of Bose, 1993.

Gribomont, Jean. *Saint Basile, évangile et église: mélanges*. 2 vols. Begrolles-en-Mauges: Abbaye de Bellefontaine, 1984.

———. "Basilio." *Dizionario degli Istituti di Perfezione*. 10 vols. Edited by Guerrino Pellicia and Giancarlo Rocca. 1, 1107, number 17, "cenobitismo." Rome: Paoline, 1974–2003.

———. "Le Monachisme au IV. s. in Asie Mineure: de Gangres au Messalianisme," *Studia Patristica* 2 (1957): 400–15.

———. "Eustathe." *Dictionaire de Spiritualité, ascétique et mystique, doctrine et histoire*. 17 vols. General editor Marcel Viller. Vol. 4, col. 1709. Paris: Beauchesne, 1937–1995.

———. "The Commentaries of Adalbert De Vogüé and the Great Monastic Tradition," *American Benedictine Review* 36 (1985): 229–62.

Holmes, Augustine. *A Life Pleasing to God*. Kalamazoo: Cistercian Publications, 2000.

Rippinger, Joel. "The Concept of Obedience in the Monastic Writings of Basil and Cassian," *Studia Monastica* 19 (1977): 7–18.

Rousseau, Philip. *Basil of Caesarea*. Berkeley: University of California Press, 1994.

Vogüé, Adalbert de. "The Great Rules of St. Basil: A Survey," *Word and Spirit* 1 (1979).

———. "L'Influenza de Basilio sul Monachesimo Occidentale," in *Basilio tra Oriente e Occidente*. Edited by Étienne Baudry, 209–24. Magnano: Qiqajon/Community of Bose, 2001.

Pachomius

Primary Sources

Anonymous. *The Life of Pachomius* [First Greek Life]. Translated by Apostolos N. Athanassakis. Missoula, MT: Scholars Press, 1975.

Pachomius. *Pachomian Koinonia*. 3 vols. Translated by Armand Veilleux. Kalamazoo: Cistercian Publications, 1980–1982.

———. *Pachomiana Latina. Règle et épîtres de St. Pachôme, épître de St. Théodore et Liber de St. Orsiesius*. Edited by Amand Boon. Louvain: Bureaux de la Revue, 1932.

Palladius. *Lausiac History*. Translated by Robert T. Meyer. ACW 34. New York: Paulist Press, 1964. PG 34.991–1262.

Schenute of Atripe. *De Vita Monachorum* 25, CSCO Script Copt II.5. (1903–13).

Secondary Sources

Amand de Mendieta, Emmanuel. "Le système cénobitique basilien comparé au système cénobitique pachômien." *Revue de l'Histoire des Religions* 152 (1957): 31–80.

Bacht, Heinrich J. "Antonius und Pachomius." *Studia Anselmiana* 38 (1956): 66–107.

———. *Das Vermächtnis des Ursprungs: Studien zum frühen Mönchtum 2: Pachomius: Der Mann und sein Werk*. Würzburg: Echter, 1983.

Chitty, Derwas. *The Desert a City*. Oxford: Blackwell, 1966.

Cremaschi, Lisa. *Pacomio e I Suoi Discepoli: Regole e Scritti*. Magnano: Qiqajon/Community of Bose, 1988.

Delhougne, Henri. "Autorité et Participation chez les Pères du cénobitisme," *Revue Ascétique et Mystique* 45 (1969): 369–94; 46 (1970): 3–32.

Deseilles, Placide. *L'esprit du monachisme Pachômien, suivi de la traduction française des Pachomiana Latina par les moines de Solesmes*. Bégrolle-en-Mauge: Abbaye de Bellefontaine, 1968.

Goehring, James. "Monastic Diversity and Ideological Boundaries in Fourth-Century Christian Egypt." *Journal of Early Christian Studies* (1997): 61–84.

———. "New Frontiers in Pachomian Studies." In *The Roots of Egyptian Christianity*. Edited by Birger Pearson and James Goehring. Philadelphia: Fortress Press, 1986.

Gribomont, Jean. "Pacomio." *Dizionario degli Istituti di Perfezione* 6, 1067–73.

Harmless, William. *Desert Christians*. New York: Oxford University Press, 2004.

Lehmann, Konstantin. "Die Entstehung der Freiheitsstrafe in den Klöstern des hl. Pachomius." *Zeitschrift der Savigny-Stiftung für Rechtsgeschichte: Kanonistische Abteilung* 37 (1951): 1–94.

Molle, Marie-Magdeleine van. "Confrontation entre les règles et la littérature pachômienne postérieure." *La Vie Spirituelle. Supplement* 86 (1968): 394–424.

———. "Essai de classement chronologique des premières règles de vie commune connue en chrétienté." *La Vie Spirituelle. Supplement* 84 (1968): 108–27.

Rubenson, Samuel. *The Letters of St. Antony*. Lund: Lund University Press, 1990.

Ruppert, Fidelis. *Das pachomianische Mönchtum und die Anfänge klösterlichen Gehorsams*. Münsterschwarzach: Vier Türme Verlag, 1971.

Veilleux, Armand. "Monasticism and Gnosis in Egypt." In *Roots of Egyptian Christianity*. Edited by Birger Pearson and James Goehring, 271–306. Philadelphia: Fortress Press, 1986.

———. *La liturgie dans le cénobitisme pachômien au quatrième siècle*. Studia Anselmiana philosophica theologica 57. Rome: "I.B.C." Libreria Herder, 1968.

Vogüé, Adalbert de. "Deux reminiscences scripturaires non encore remarquées dans les règles de saint Pachôme et saint Benoît." *Studia Monastica* 25 (1983): 7–10.

———. "Les pièces latines du dossier pachômien. Remarques sur quelques publications récentes." *Revue Histoire Ecclesiastique* 67 (1972): 26–67.

———. *De saint Pachôme à Cassien.* Studia Anselmiana 120. Rome: "I.B.C." Libreria Herder, 1996.

Augustine

Primary Sources

Possidius. *Life of Augustine.* Critical Latin text in *Vita Cipriano, Vita di Ambrogio, Vita di Augustino.* Edited by Antoon A. R. Bastiaensen. Introduction by Christine Mohrmann. Milan: Mondadori, 1975. Translated by Sister Mary Magdeleine Mueller in *Early Christian Biographies.* FC 15. New York: Fathers of the Church, 1952.

Augustine. *De Moribus Ecclesiae Catholicae et de Moribus Manichaeorum.* PL 32.1300–76.

Augustine. *De Opere Monachorum.* In *Sancti Aureli Augustini, De fide et symbolo . . . De opere monachorum. . . .* Edited by Joseph Zycha. CSEL 41. Vienna: F. Tempsky, 1900. English in *Treatises on Various Subjects.* Edited by Roy J. Deferrari. Translated by Mary Sarah Muldowney and others. FC 16. New York: Fathers of the Church, 1952.

Alypius, "Monastic Order" [*Ordo Monasterii*]. Translated by George Lawless in *Augustine of Hippo and his Monastic Rule*, 75–79. Oxford: Clarendon Press, 1987. PL 32.1449.

Augustine. "Rule for Monks" (*Praeceptum*). Translated by George Lawless in *Augustine of Hippo and his Monastic Rule*, 81–103 (Oxford: Clarendon Press, 1987). PL 32.1377.

Secondary Sources

Berrouard, Marie-François. "Possidius." *Dictionaire de Spiritualité* 12 (1985): cols. 1997–2008.

Brown, Peter. *Augustine of Hippo.* Berkeley: University of California Press, 1967.

Courcelle, Pierre. *Les Confessions de saint Augustin dans la tradition littéraire. Antécedants et Posterité.* Paris: Études augustiniennes, 1963.

———. *Recherches sur les Confessions de saint Augustin.* Paris: E. de Boccard, 1950.

Diesner, Hans-Joachim. "Possidius und Augustinus." *Studia Patristica* 6 (1962): 350–65.

Folliet, George. "Aux origines de l'ascétisme et du cénobitisme africain." *Studia Anselmiana* 46 (1961): 25–44.

Frend, William H. C. *The Donatist Church, a Movement of Protest in Roman North Africa*. Oxford: Clarendon Press, 1952.

Lawless, George. *Augustine of Hippo and his Monastic Rule*. Oxford: Clarendon Press, 1987.

Mandouze, André. *Saint Augustine, l'aventure de la raison et de la grâce*. Paris: Études augustiniennes, 1968.

Pellegrino, Michele. *Possidio, Vita di S. Agostino. Introduzione, teso critico, versione e note*, Verba Seniorum IV. Alba: Paoline, 1955.

Verheijen, Luc. *La Règle de saint Augustin*. 2 vols. Paris: Études augustiniennes, 1967.

———. *Nouvelle approche de la Règle de saint Augustin*. Bégrolle-en-Mauges: Abbaye de Bellefontaine, 1980.

———. *St. Augustine's Monasticism in the Light of Acts 4:32-35*. Villanova, PA: Villanova University Press, 1979.

Vogüé, Adalbert de. *Histoire littéraire du mouvement monastique. 3: Jérome, Augustin, et Rufin au tournant du siècle (391–405)*. Paris: Cerf, 1996.

Rule of the Four Fathers and Second Rule of the Fathers

Primary Sources

Faustus of Riez. *Homilia*. CSEL 21.

Hilary of Arles. "Life of Honoratus." In Roy J. Deferrari, *Early Christian Biographies*. FC 15. New York: Fathers of the Church, 1952. Hilaire D'Arles, *Vie de Saint Honorat*. Translated by Marie-Denise Valentin. SC 235. Paris: Cerf, 1977. PL 50.1249–72.

Rule of the Four Fathers. Translated by Carmela Franklin, Ivan Havener, and J. Alcuin Francis. Collegeville, MN: Liturgical Press, 1982. Also in *Monastic Studies* 12 (1976): 249–59.

Second Rule of the Fathers. Translated by Carmela Franklin, Ivan Havener, and J. Alcuin Francis. Collegeville, MN: Liturgical Press, 1982. Also in *Monastic Studies* 12 (1976): 260–63.

Secondary Sources

Desprez, Vincent. *Régles monastiques d'occident*. Bégrolle-en-Mauges: Abbaye de Bellefontaine, 1980.

Masai, François. "Recherches sur les Règles de S. Oyend et de S. Benoît." *Regulae Benedicti Studia* 5 (1976): 43–73.

Mundó, Anscari. "Les anciennes synodes abbatiaux et les *Regulae SS. Patrum*." In Basil Steidle, *Regula Magistri—Regula Benedicti*, 107–25. Studia Anselmiana philosophica theologica 44. Rome: "Orbis Catholicus," Herder, 1959.

Neufville, Jean. "Règle des IV Pères et Seconde Règle des Pères. Texte critique." *Revue Bénédictine* 77 (1967): 47–106.

Vogüé, Adalbert, de. "Un problème de datation: La Règle des Quatre Pères." *Studia Monastica* 44 (2002): 7–12.

———. *Les Règles des Saints Pères*. 2 vols. SC 297, 298. Paris: Cerf, 1982.

Index of Scripture References

Gen 1:26	22	Luke 14:26	105n66
Exod 32:27-28	79	John 6:38	206
Lev 27:10	125	John 13:8	19
		John 13:34	26
Deut 32:32	27		
		Acts 4:32	41
Ps 67:7	170n11	Acts 4:32-35	155, 170–78
Ps 79:13	27		
Ps 132	175	Rom 9:3	27
Prov 1:7	30	1 Cor 7:1-15	183
Prov 13:24	40	1 Cor 7:15-16	50n10
Prov 29:18	54n15	1 Cor 10:10	216
		1 Cor 12:8	39
Dan 5	218	1 Cor 12:14-26	54
		1 Cor 14:40	53
Matt 5:29-30	53	1 Cor 15	23
Matt 5:44	28		
Matt 16:24	47	2 Cor 6:14-17	35
Matt 18	237		
Matt 18:15-18	56, 185	Eph 4:28	57
Matt 22:37-40	170n10		
Matt 25	28	Phil 2:6-7	26
		Phil 3:20	31
Mark 2:23-28	113n21		
Mark 12:28-31	20	Heb 5:12	29
Luke 12:48	24	1 John 4:8	21
Luke 14:10	52		
Luke 14:33	31	Rev 18:4	35

Index of Rule of Benedict References

RB 1.4-5	42	RB 35.13	113n23
RB 7.10-11	33	RB 43.9	140n65
RB 22	121n57	RB 43.18	114
RB 23–28	185	RB 46.1-4	137n47
RB 31.10	218	RB 55	11n34
RB 33.2	126n4	RB 57	112n20
RB 34	98, 117, 179		

Index of Names and Terms

abbas, 205
abbot, 55n17
abbot general, 114n26
acedia, 217
Adeodatus, 152
aequalitas (fairness), 208
Aerius, 7n21
affection, 223
Alexandria, 82, 115, 122, 132n28, 133, 133n35
Alypius, 148n3, 152, 154, 168
Amand de Mendieta, E., 8n27, 18n11, 62n5, 96n35, 144n80, 198n3
Amaseia, 9n30
Amelineau, A., 65n11
ameteoriston (recollection), 58
anachoresis (withdrawal), 48
anamnesis, 32
anchoritism, 71, 112, 115
angels, 89n10
animals, 130
Annisa, 3, 4, 10, 13, 14
Antony, xi, 85n35, 150n9, 164
apotaksis (renunciation), 100
Arbesmann, R., 120n51
Arianism, 50n9, 103
aristocracy, 53, 212
Arius, 83
Armenia (Roman) 2, 6

asceticism, 73, 78, 160, 167n3
Asketikon of Basil, xii
Assumption Abbey, ix
Athanasius, 88n5, 103n61
Athanassakis, A., 61n1
Athens, 2
audience of Basil, 34
Augustine, ix, 24, 42, 42n58, 99, 147–89, 194
Augustine, Rule of, 21
Aurelius, 168
authority, 56n20, 204
avarice, 209

Bacht, H., ix, 62n6, 67n14, 73n20, 88, 88n4, 89n8, 89n9, 93, 93n24, 94n26, 95n33, 96n37, 97n40, 98n42, 100n51, 101n56, 104n62, 108n4, 109n5, 111, 111n15, 111n17, 113n23, 114n27, 115, 115n29, 118n40, 118n43, 120n51, 121n57, 122n60, 126, 126n5, 129n18, 130, 133n32, 134n36, 134n37, 135n40, 136n44, 137n46, 138n55, 139n60, 140n64, 140n66, 141n69, 142n71, 142n74, 143n78, 143n79, 144n80
bakery, 131, 132
Bamberger, J.E., 31

baptism, 65, 182
Bardy, G., 90n11, 144n80
Barnabas, 175n21
Barns, J., 84n32
Basil, 1–60
Basil, Liturgy of, 1
Basil Senior, 2
Basiliade, 12, 13, 28, 57
Bastiaensen, A.A.R., ix, 149, 152, 161
bathing, 120n54
Baudry, E., 8n27, 18, 18n12, 19, 19n13, 19n15
Baumstark, A., 91
beauty, 170, 187–90
Bellah, R., 28
Benedict, 17n8, 55, 62, 73, 99, 144n82, 149, 171
Benedict, Rule of, 21n21, 33
Benedict of Aniane, xiv, 191
Bernard of Clairvaux, vii, 147n2, 148n3, 163
Bethlehem, 89n8
Bible, 55, 59, 90
Biography, xiv
Blaise, A., 142n73
boat, 117n39, 133–34
books, 126
Boon, A., 61n1, 62n2, 88n6, 125n2, 145n85
Borias, A., 104n63
boundaries, 129–31
Boyle, M., 16n4
brothers, 101
Brown, P., 150n8, 153, 153n20, 157n29, 159n35, 162, 163n45, 167n2

Caesarea, 2, 3, 12
Caesarius, 192n7, 205
Calama, 147, 159, 163
Canopus, 88n5, 133n35
cantor, 139
Cappadocia, 13

Capraria, 169
Carrias, M., 193n8
Carthage, 150n8, 168, 174n18
Cassian, John, vii, 21n21, 44, 56n20, 119n47, 195n16, 205, 209, 211
Cassiciacum, 151–52, 153
catechesis, 79, 95, 132, 142, 143n76
Cavallera, A., 90n11
Cavallin, S., 192n4
cellararius (business manager), 114n25, 218
cells, 129, 131, 234
cenobitism, 71
Chadwick, H., 84
chaplain, 145n86
chastity, 49, 117, 120, 180, 182
Chenoboskion, 84
Chitty, D., 63n7, 88n5
choice, 115
Circumcellions, 148n3, 159, 159n35, 160, 165, 176
cities, 181
Clarke, W.L., 38n53
Clement, 132n28
Clerical Monastery of Hippo, 156
clothes, 110, 125–29
Codex Regularum, xiv, 191, 225, 229
commandments, 15
common life, 38–44, 72, 115
community, 38–44, 172, 204
concentration, 30
Confessions, 150, 182
conflict, 81
confusio (shame), 209
congregatio (community), 218
Constantine, Peace of, 50
Constantinople, 2, 8
Constantinople, Council of, 1, 5, 39, 84
contagion, 186
conversatio (lifestyle), 162, 202
conversus (turned away), 210
cook (*ebdomadarius*), 98, 110

Coptic, 90n11

correction, 38, 40, 56, 140, 222, 237

Corrigan, K., 11n36

council of advisors, 56

Courcelle, P., 150n9, 164

Cremaschi, L., viii, 37n50, 46n2,
    48n5, 51n11, 53n13, 54n14,
    55n16, 56n18, 58n22, 60n25,
    92n19, 95n32, 102n57, 103n59,
    103n60, 105n64, 111n16, 125n3

criminals, 102

Crispinus, 148n3

cross, 212

Crouzel, Henri, 23n25

cultores (leaders), 223

darnel, 123

De Civitate Dei, 164

De Judicio Dei of Basil, 19n14

De Moribus Ecclesiae, 161n41

De Opera Monachorum (work of
    monks), 160, 168, 174n18

De Ordine, 188n47

De Utilitate Credendi, 183n36

De Virginitate, 183–84

Dead Sea Scrolls, 84

death, 137

Deferrari, R., 6n17

deficere (give up), 236

deificari in otio, 153

Delhougne, H., 115n30

Denis the Little, 100n53

department managers, 113

departure, 142

Deseilles, P., 62n6, 94, 94n28

desert, 203

desire, 37

Desprez, V., ix, 195n18, 207, 212,
    221

dialogue, 21

diathesis, 31, 33

Diesner, H.J., 150, 150n10, 159n35

Dillon, Richard, 41n55, 175n21

Diocletian, 2

disciple, perfect, 77

discretion, 140

discussion, 95, 142

dispensator (procurator), 142

dispossession, 101n54, 116, 177–78,
    209

distribution of goods, 98

Divine Office, 91, 92, 94, 168, 226,
    235

Donatism, xii, 154, 159, 160, 164,
    186

donkey, 130

dough, 133n33

Draguet Fragment, 75

drink, 119n48

dualism, 51, 113n24

eating, 112

ebdomadarum (weekly servers), 217

Egypt, 164, 194

eisagomenoi (catechumens), 29

embarrassment, 235

emendatorium (punishment), 186

Emmelia, 2, 3

enclosure, 108n5, 117

engkrateia (self-control), 49–50

Epiphanius, 7n21

eremitical life, 42

eros, 25

Eucharist, 95

Eucher of Lyons, 203

Eunomius, 12n41

Eusebius of Caesarea, 8, 12

Eustathians, 5, 48

Eustathius, xi, 3, 4, 5–7, 9, 10,
    11n37, 13

Eustochium, 89n9, 180n28

eutaxia (good order), 20, 52

Evagrius, vii, 21n21, 44

Evodius, 152, 158

examinatio (test), 209

excommunication, 75, 187n46, 221,
    234, 237, 238

exothen (those outside), 47

expulsion, 56, 56n18, 185, 238
eye of the community (superior),
    53–54, 54n14

fabula (chatter), 236
family, 104, 177
farmers, 129
fasting, 78, 113, 215
father (spiritual), 71
father of the *koinonia* (head abbot),
    140
faults, 185, 220, 221
Faustus, 192n7, 205, 207, 229, 237
favoritism, 16, 223
fear of God, 29–30
field work, 107–10, 108n5, 127
firmare, 203
Firmus, 157
Folliet, G., 153, 153n18
food, 51, 103
formation, 100, 100n50
Fortesque, Adrian, 6n17
Fortunatus, 158
Four Fathers, Rule of, 191–222
frater (brother), 214, 222
Fréjus, 229
Frend, W.H.C., 159n35
friendship, 162, 165, 167n2, 206
Fructuosus, 121n58, 122n59
Funeral Orations of Gregory, 2n4,
    3n5

Gallo-Roman nobility, 194n15
Gangra, Synod, 6, 16n5, 50, 53n13
Garden Monastery, 154, 168, 169,
    181
garden, 112
Gaul, 193
Gelasian Sacramentary, 142n73
Gennadius, 226
Genseric, 147
gifts, 129
Gindele, C., 93n21
Gnosticism, 84n33

Goehring, J., 77n25, 82, 85, 85n34,
    102n58, 103n61, 126n7
gossip, 118, 161
grace, 187
Great Asketikon, 9n32, 13, 14, 17,
    20, 21
Gregory the Great, 21, 42n59, 169
Gregory of Nazianz, xiv, 2, 4–5,
    4n11, 10, 10n33, 12, 32, 35, 43,
    43n61, 43n62
Gregory of Nyssa, xiv, 3n7, 4n9, 10,
    11, 11n36, 53n13
Gregory Thaumaturgus, 2
Gribomont, J., 3n6, 5, 6n17, 7n21,
    9n32, 27, 27n35, 27n36, 31, 43,
    47, 47n3, 48n4, 48n5, 50n8,
    58n2, 58n21, 64n9, 193n8
Gruber, M., 118n44
guests, 213–14, 232
Guillaumont, A., 95n31

habit, 102
habitatio (dwelling), 207
hagiography, 63, 163n46
haircuts, 122
Halkin, F., 61n1
Hallinger, K., 108, 108n3
handwork, 91
Harmless, W., 139n61
Harnack, A., 23
harvest, 114
hate, 105n66
Hausherr, I., 100n51
health care, 99
heaven, 146
Hefele, K.J., 193n9
Heraclas, 83
hesychia, 35, 43
Hexameron of Basil, 27
Hilarion, 163n46
Hilary of Arles, xii, xiv, 192n4, 216
Hippo, 153, 154, 157, 160, 167, 181
Holmes, A., viii, 23n25, 24n26, 25,
    25n28, 25n30, 26n33, 27n35,

27n36, 30n40, 31, 31n43, 32n44, 33, 34n47, 42n58, 43n62

Holstenius, L., 145n85

Holy Spirit, 39, 40

Holzherr, G., 116n33

homoiousios, 8, 12

homosexuality, 102n57, 120, 121, 122, 123, 130

honey, 65

Honoratus, xii, xiv, 192, 202, 204, 216, 219, 225

Horsiesi, xi, 81, 91n14, 96n36, 132, 132n30

hospice, 103n60

hospitality, 103

housemaster (*praepositus domus*), 109n5, 128, 141

Huber, H., 111, 112n18

humanism of Basil, 26

humiliation, 222

humility, 210, 220

Iamblichus, 188

idiorrhythmic monasticism, 115n29

Indiculum, 148

individualism, 28

infirmarians, 117n35

infirmitas (weakness), 217

inventory, 97

is qui praeest (superior), 204, 207, 221

janitor monasterii (doorkeeper), 109, 109n8

Jansenism, 18

Januarius, 177

Jerome, 4n11, 62, 88–90, 89n10, 98n45, 111, 119n50, 120n52, 125n2, 128n12, 129n19, 132n27, 134, 134n36, 135, 136, 136n42, 137, 138n52, 138n54, 139n57, 157n29, 203, 230

Jerusalem community, 41, 175, 180

Kardong, T., 30n40, 34n46, 75n23, 141n70, 171n12, 178n26, 187n46

kitchen, 112

Klingshirn, W., 193n8

Koinonia, Pachomian, 61–146

kosmos (world), 48

Laetus, 177

Lampe, G.W., 176

Latin Basil, 202

Latopolis, Synod, 77, 83

laughter, 221

Lausiac History, 119n47, 126n6

Lawless, G., 42n58, 168n5, 170n11, 182n33

leaders (*ductores*), 109n5

leadership (servant), 73

lectio divina, 216, 233

Lefort, L.T., 61n1, 65n11, 125n2

Lehmann, K., 93n23

Leipoldt, J., 121n58

Lérins, xii, xiii, xvii, 191–223, 192–222, 225–38

Levites, 79

Life of Augustine, xvi, 147–66

Life of Macrina, 11, 11n36

Life of Pachomius, xiv, xvi, 61, 61–87

literacy, 144n80

logos spermatikos, 22–26, 39

loitering, 133

Long Rules, 1, 13, 20–22

Lorie, L.T., 151n13

lost goods, 139

love, 21–29, 170

love of God, 22–26

love of neighbor, 26–29

Macarius, 193

Macarius, Rule of, 226n3

Macarius the Second, 219

Macrina the Elder, 2

Macrina Junior, 2, 3, 7, 9

Mandouze, A., 152, 152n17

Manicheism, 151, 162, 164, 181
manual labor, 216
Marinus, 192n7
Marmoutier, 169, 193n10, 195
marriage, 50, 183
Marrou, H., 144n81
Martin, xii, 169, 193n10, 195, 217
Masai, F., 191n3
mass media, 118n41
Master, Rule of, 14n48, 17n8, 21n21, 75n24, 99
Maurice, St. (Agaune), 192n7
Maurists, 158n31
Maximus, 192n7, 225, 229
McQuade, J., 185
meals, 97–98
meat, 162
meditation, 92n19, 110n10, 133, 231
Megalius, 159
Melania, 180n28
Melitius, 83, 103n61
memorization, 92, 101, 143
memory of God, 32, 36
Meredith, A., 27n36
Merton, Thomas, vii, 44
Messalianism, 33, 168, 174n18
metanies, 94, 141
Metanoia (monastery), 88, 88n5
Migne, J.P., xvi
Milan, 149
Milan, Edict of, 2
military, 64, 93, 108
milk, 65
minister, 96
miracles, 163, 165
missa (closing prayer), 220
moderation, 161
Modestus, 10
modesty, 111, 111n14
Mohrmann, C., 6n20, 150, 160, 163n46, 164
Monachos (monk), 48, 149, 160, 176n24
monastikon, 27

Monica, 151
monios, 27
monos, 175
Moralia of Basil, 7, 7n25, 15, 15n3, 59–60
Morin, Germain, 17n8
Moses, 27
mud, 141
Mueller, M.M., 147n1, 152, 156
Mundó, A., 108n3, 191n3, 192n6, 195n17, 202
murmuring, 79, 216, 234
Musurillo, H., 113n24
mutual love, 170–78

Nag Hammadi library, 84, 126n7
Naucratius, 4, 42
Nebridius, 152, 153
Neocaesarea, 2
Neoplatonism, 12, 21n21
Neufville, J., 191n3, 192n6, 201, 221
Nicaea, Council, 2, 8, 103n60
None, 215
Noonday Devil, 120
nuns, 145–46

obedience, 37, 56n20, 70, 96, 205
obscenity, 222
oikeiosis, 27
oikonomos (procurator), 114n25
oiling, 128
On the Soul and Resurrection of Gregory of Nyssa, 11, 11n38
one heart, one mind, 170–78
oratio, 91n17, 220
ordination, 157, 230
Ordo Monasterii, 154, 162n42, 168, 170n10, 230
Oriental Rule, 226n3
Origen, 4, 23, 25, 54n14, 83, 84, 85n35, 132n28
orthodoxy, Pachomian, 83
Ostia, 151

ostiarius (doorkeeper), 220

Pachomius, viii, 42, 61–146, 211, 220, 234
Palamon, 66, 68
Palestine, 157, 163, 168
Palladius, 89n10, 119n47, 126, 211
Paphnutius, 84, 193
parents, 78, 177
Parmenias, 187n45
Paul, St., 27, 183
Paul of Egypt, 163n46
Paula, 89, 89n7, 89n8, 180n28
Pauline Privilege, 50n10
Paulinus, 154, 164, 172
Pelagius, 207, 216
Pellegrino, M., 162n43
penalty, 140n65, 141–42
Peregrinus, 158
perfection, 203
Perler, O., 158n31
persecution, 186
Peter, 18
Peter of Sebaste, 3
Petronius, 81
Phbow, 74, 122, 123n63
Philagrius Arcenus, 53n13
Philo of Alexandria, 31
Philokalia, 4
philosophy, 188
piety, 204, 219
plaiting, 136
Plato, 21, 32, 151, 172
Plotinus, 172
Pontus, 3, 6
poor, 178–80
Porcarius, 192n7
possessions, 116
Possidius, xiv, 147–66
postulant, 90, 102, 209, 211
pothos, 24–26
poverty, 139, 158, 174, 175
Praecepta of Pachomius, xii–xiii, 87–146

Praeceptum of Augustine, xiii, 98n43, 155, 167–90
praepositus domus (housemaster), 109n5, 114n26, 128, 141, 229
prayer, 57, 58, 169, 174, 233
pride, 210
priesthood, 220
princeps monasterii, 140
prior (senior), 208
procurator (*dispensator*), 114n25
proestos (presider), 55
Profuturus, 158
promptness, 235
propositum, 149n7
prospatheia (attachments), 46n2
protreptic, 16
psalms, 94, 138, 208, 233
punctuality, 93
punishment, 80, 93, 140, 237
Pythagoreans, 188

rank, 139n58, 219, 238
reading, 143, 144, 218
reeds, 96
Regnault, L., 103n60
relatives, 146n87
renunciation (*apotaxia*), 45, 100
responsibility, 205
Resurrection, 189
Retractiones, 148, 183
rich, 178–80, 210
rigorism, 77, 78, 98n42, 161
Rippinger, J., 56n20
Rousseau, Philip, xv, 1n2, 2n4, 5n13, 5n16, 6, 7n22, 7n23, 7n24, 8n28, 10n34, 11, 11n37, 12n40, 12n41, 12n42, 13n43, 13n44
routinization of charisma, 82
Rubenson, S., 85n35
rudis (uninstructed), 143
Rufinus, 4n11, 9n32, 14n47, 24n26, 25n32, 33n45
Rule of the Four Fathers, 191–222

Rule of the Master, 14n48, 17n8, 75n24, 99
Rule of Touch, 121
Rules, monastic, xii–xiii
rumination, 101, 135
Ruppert, F., 65, 67, 70n16, 70n17, 71n19, 74n21, 77n26, 78n28, 97n39, 100n49, 131n26, 144n82
ruses, pious, 80

sailing, 133–34
Salvian, 207
Sartre, Jean Paul, 39
Schenute, 103n59, 119, 119n45, 120, 120n53, 121, 121n58, 122n59, 138n53, 139n57
schismatics, 103
Schmitz, A., 115n29
Scripture, 79, 95, 101, 109, 142–45
Sebaste in Armenia, 3
second (housemaster), 132
Second Rule of the Fathers, 225–26
secundus (assistant housemaster), 127
sedentibus nobis, 201
seeking God, 171
self-will, 36–38, 45, 206, 217, 234
sellula (sleeping chair), 118, 118n42
senior, 232
separation from the world, 30, 34–35
Serapion, 193
Servant of God, 150, 151
Servi Dei, 150n8, 157
servire, 149n7
severitas (severity), 207
Severus, 158
shepherd, 55
Sheridan, M., 176n23
shoes, 127, 128
Short Rules of Basil, 13, 17
sick, 98, 98n44, 128n15, 138n54
silence, 109, 110n10, 119n46, 232, 238

Silvas, Anna, viii, xv, 2n3, 3n8, 4n10, 6n18, 8n26, 9, 9n29, 9n31, 9n32, 10, 10n35, 12n39, 13n45, 14n46, 16, 16n6, 16n7, 17n9, 17n10, 20n16, 23, 24, 26n34, 35n49, 49n6, 74
Siricius, 142n73
slavery, 53, 102, 213
sleep, 118, 134
Small Ascetikon, 9, 16, 25n32
snack, 113n23, 131
snakes, 203
Sozomen, 6n17
speech, 232
spousal love of Christ, 184
standard of living, 116n31
statio, 108
Steidle, B., 99n46, 191n3
Stephen, 163
Stoicism, 15, 23, 27n36, 39, 46n2
study, 188
Suetonius, 163n46
Sulpicius Severus, 21, 205
summary, 128
Sunday work, 111
superior, 53, 204
surety, 131
sweets, 97

Tabennesi, 66, 68, 117n38, 124n66
Tagaste, 152, 153
taste, 113n22
taxes, 102
teleioi (able to be perfected), 29
Tentyra, 104
Thagaste, 168
Thebes, 64
Theodore, xi, 63, 71, 74–85, 77, 78n28, 91n14, 96n36, 103n59, 105, 117n37, 132, 137n51, 220
Theodore the Alexandrian, 73
Theodosius, 5
Theophilus, 88n5
Therapeutae, 31

therapy, 186
thorns, 117, 121
tonsure, 122n60
tou theou pothos, 22
transfer, 219
tribe, 131, 131n26
tunics, 111
Turbessi, G., 114n27
Turck, A., 132n28
Tyana, 13n43

unianimes, 205–6
unity, 173
universalism, 28
Urbanus, 158

Valens, 12
Valerius, 154
Van der Meer, F., 6n20
Van Molle, M.M., 70n17, 93n20
Vandals, 147, 168
Vatican II, 18
Veilleux, A., viii, 61, 65, 67, 67n12,
    70n16, 77n25, 78n27, 83, 85n36,
    87, 89n10, 90n12, 90n13, 91n16,
    92n18, 92n20, 94n27, 94n29,
    95n30, 97n39, 109n5, 122n61,
    123n63, 128n13, 130, 132n28,
    133n34, 135, 135n38, 137n49,
    141n68, 143n76
Verheijen, L., ix, 154, 154n23, 155,
    155n25, 162n42, 167n1, 169n9,

171, 171n13, 173n15, 174n17,
    174n19, 180n30, 187n45, 188
Vespers, 134–35, 137
villages, 127
visions, 77, 89n10
Vogue, A., vii, ix, xvi, 4n11, 20n17,
    21–22, 33n45, 41n56, 52, 63n8,
    67, 67n13, 70n18, 75, 83, 83n31,
    90n13, 91n15, 91n16, 99n48,
    109, 109n5, 109n9, 110n10,
    116n33, 118n40, 119n47, 125,
    125n3, 128n14, 129, 129n17,
    135, 135n39, 143n77, 146n89,
    168n4, 180n28, 181n31, 191n2,
    195, 201–23, 225–38
vows, 103n59

washing, 110
water-wheel, 136n44
Wathen, Ambrose, 40
Weber, Max, 226
Weiss, J.P., 193n8
will of God, 60
window (*fenestra*), 127n8
wine, 162
Winkler, G., 49n7
withdrawal, 234
women, 134, 146, 182
work, 57–60, 96–97, 107–110, 130,
    136, 168, 217, 230, 233–34
workshops, 130
world, 103, 108